"YOUR
`-DAYS OF
`-LIVING ARE
`-NUMBERED!!!~'''

PREVIOUS BOOKS:

1) The REAL PROPHET of DOOM!...(...!)
2) The REAL PROPHET of DOOM VOL.2 (...!)
3) The REAL PROPHET of DOOM VOL. 3 (...!)
4) The REAL PROPHET of DOOM (KISMET) (INTRODUCTION) PENDULUM FLOW
5) The REAL PROPHET of DOOM (KISMET) (INTRODUCTION) PENDULUM FLOW - (II)
6) The REAL PROPHET of DOOM (KISMET) (INTRODUCTION) PENDULUM FLOW - (III)
7) NEW BOOK - REAL MESSAGES of GOD I, II, & III-!!!~'
8) BOOK TITLE: GOD is The `-MATHEMATICIAN!!!~'
9) The `-GOD `-BOOK of `-NUMEROLOGY!~'
10) DEATH CIPHERS/CYPHERS for LIFE & DEATH!!!~'
11) DO `-YOU BELIEVE in `-GOD??? 'IS, `-DESTINY 'REAL???
12) "YOUR `-DAYS of ``-LIVING are `-NUMBERED!!!~'"

"YOUR `-DAYS OF `-LIVING ARE `-NUMBERED!!!~'"

DWAYNE W. ANDERSON

"YOUR `-DAYS OF `-LIVING ARE `-NUMBERED!!!~'"

iUniverse books may be ordered through booksellers or by contacting:

iUniverse
1663 Liberty Drive
Bloomington, IN 47403
www.iuniverse.com
844-349-9409

Because of the dynamic nature of the Internet, any web addresses or links contained in this book may have changed since publication and may no longer be valid. The views expressed in this work are solely those of the author and do not necessarily reflect the views of the publisher, and the publisher hereby disclaims any responsibility for them.

Any people depicted in stock imagery provided by Getty Images are models, and such images are being used for illustrative purposes only. Certain stock imagery © Getty Images.

ISBN: 978-1-6632-4597-7 (sc)
ISBN: 978-1-6632-4598-4 (hc)
ISBN: 978-1-6632-4596-0 (e)

Library of Congress Control Number: 2022917900

Print information available on the last page.

iUniverse rev. date: 01/13/2023

WITHOUT a `-DOUBT, OUR LIVES are `-ETCHED; and, `-ARTICULATED in `-TIME' to an `-EVENTUALITY; of `-GOD'S VERY OWN `-PURPOSE, to `-OUR `-VERY `-OWN PURPOSE of `-BEING; in the `-EXISTENCE/EXPANSE of `-TIME!!!~' OUR `-time OF `-LIVES (BIRTHS, DEATHS, MARRIAGES, CHILDREN, etc.); are `-EXACTLY `-SET by `-GOD!!!~' ALREADY `-PROVEN through `-**R**ECIPROCAL-**S**EQUENCING-**N**UMEROLOGY-**RSN**; and, **R**ECIPROCAL-**S**EQUENCED-**I**NVERSED-**R**EALITIES-**RSIR**!!!~' AGAIN; ENJOY the `-READS**!!!~'**

BULLET POINTS FOR: "YOUR `-DAYS of `-LIVING are `-NUMBERED!!!~'"

- *THE LIFE AND DEATH OF CELEBRITIES –*
- *THE LIFE AND DEATH OF SCIENTISTS –*
- *THE LIFE AND DEATH OF COMMON PEOPLE –*
- *INTRASPECTION of GOD, the UNIVERSE; and, the MAN/WOMAN `-INSIDE –*
- *READING; and, UNDERSTANDING the`-SCIENCE of `-NUMBERS in the FOCUS of <u>R</u>eciprocal-<u>S</u>equencing-Numerology-<u>RSN</u>-'*
- *DISCOVERER & FOUNDER of RECIPROCAL SEQUENCING INVERSED REALITIES – EQUATIONS of `-REALITY in LIFE & DEATH - AUTHOR: DWAYNE W. ANDERSON -*

1

I've `-CREATED a NEW TYPE of PHILOSOPHY (Reciprocal-Sequencing-Numerology)/ (*Reciprocal-Sequenced-Inversed-Realities*) that `-PROVES without `-QUESTION the `-PRESENCE of GOD'S EXISTENCE in our DAILY AFFAIRS!!!!!-'

TELL ME if I'M a TWITTER BOT!-' The PROPHET is TELLING the WORLD that your LIVES are ITEMIZED!-' SHINZO ABE got MARRIED in 87 = RECIP = 7/8 = DAY of DEATH!-' YOU'RE ALL like THIS!-' AGE of DEATH = 6x7 = 42 = 20+22 = YEAR of DEATH!-' This is a PATTERN for ALL of YOUR GREATEST LEADERS & COMMONERS!-'

GENNARO ANTHONY "TONY" SIRICO JR. died at the AGE of 79 ON (7/8) with the NEXT DAY being 7/9!-' BIRTHDAY = 7(2)9!-' BIRTHDAY # = 7+29+19+42 = 97! = RECIP = 79 = AGE of DEATH!-' BIRTHYEAR = 42 = 20+22 = DEATHYEAR!-' BIRTHDAY = 7x29 = 203 = FLIP 2 to 7; 3 to 8 = 7(0)8 = DEATH/DAY!!!-'

GENNARO ANTHONY "TONY" SIRICO JR. died at the AGE of 79 ON (7/8)!-' BIRTHDAY = 7+29 = 36 = RECIP = 63 = 7x9 = AGE of DEATH!-' BIRTHDAY = 7/29 = FLIP 9 to 6 = 7/26 = 7/(2+6) = 7/8 = DEATH/DAY!-' DIED 21 DAYS from BIRTH-TO-DEATH = FRAG DEATHDAY # = 7+8+2+0+2+2 = 21!-' U are ITEMIZED!!!-'

IVANA MARIE TRUMP died at the AGE of 73 TODAY on 7/14 = 7(1-4) = 73!-' DIVORCED DONALD J. TRUMP in 1992 = (19-92) = 73 = AGE of DEATH!-' DONALD J. TRUMP was BORN on 6/14 = (6+1)(4) = 74!-' SHINZO ABE got MARRIED in 87 =

RECIP = 7/8 = DAY of DEATH!~' ALL of YOUR MARRIAGES are TIED TOGETHER!!!~'

BATMAN ADAM WEST'S FIRST MARRIAGE to BILLIE LOU YEAGER = 1950 = 19+50 = 6/9 = DEATH/DAY!~' FIRST DIVORCE from BILLIE = 1956 = 19(-)56 = 37 = 20+17 = DEATH/YEAR!~' DIVORCE 19+56 = 75 = ADAM WEST'S BIRTHDAY # = 9+19+19+28 = 75 = that HE had HIS ENTIRE LIFE = ADAM WEST ANDERSON!!!~'

WILLIAM M. "SONNY" LANDHAM "BILLY BEAR" / "BILLY SOLE" was MARRIED to BELITA ADAMS in 1995 = 19(-)95 = 76 = AGE of DEATH for "SONNY" LANDHAM!~' DIVORCE from BELITA = 19(-)98 = 79 = FLIP 9 to 6 = 76 = AGE of DEATH!~' 19+98 = 117 = DAY of BIRTH & DAY of DEATH in 1 #!~' ALL MARRIAGES!!!~'

WILLIAM M. "SONNY" LANDHAM "BILLY BEAR" / "BILLY SOLE" BIRTHDAY # = 2+11+19+41 = 73 = RECIP = 37 = 20+17 = DEATH/YEAR!~' DEATH/DAY # `-NUMBER = 8+17+20+17 = 62 = FLIP 2 to 7 = 67 = RECIP = 76 = AGE of DEATH~ for "SONNY" LANDHAM!~' HEIGHT = 6'3" = FLIP 6 to 9; FLIP 3 to 8 = 98 = DIVORCE!!!~'

ACTOR ARTHUR CHRISTOPHER ORME PLUMMER CC was BORN on 12/13 = 12+13 = (25) = HIS VERY OWN DEATH/DAY!!!~' FIRST LADY MARY TODD LINCOLN had a BIRTH/DAY as WELL of 12/13 = 12x13 = 156 = 1x56 = 56 = AGE of DEATH of HUSBAND PRESIDENT ABRAHAM LINCOLN in the YEAR = RECIP = 65!~' STAMP!~'

AMERICAN ACTRESS PATRICIA ANN CARROLL died at the AGE of 95!~' BIRTH/DAY = 5/5; and, MARRIED in (55)!!!~' DIVORCED in 1976 = 19+76 = 95 = AGE of DEATH!!!~' TOO

3

DWAYNE W. ANDERSON

MANY EXAMPLES of THIS CALIBER to NUMBER!!!~'
BIRTHDAY # = 5+5+19+27 = 56 = 7x8 = FLIP 8 to 3 = 7x3 =
DEATH/DAY = 7/3(0)!!!~' DEATH/DAY # = 7+30+20+22 = 79
= FLIP 9 to 6 = 76 = DIVORCE/YEAR!!!~' MARRIED from
1955 TO 1976 = 21 YEARS = 7x3 = DEATH/DAY = 7/3(0)!!!~'
BIRTH/YEAR = 1927 = (1x9)(2-7) = 95 = AGE of DEATH!!!~'
DEATH/DAY # `-NUMBER = 79 = 7x9 = 63 = RECIP = 36 =
(19-55) MARRIAGE/YEAR!~' DIVORCE/YEAR = 76 = 7x6 =
42 = (20+22) = DEATH/YEAR!!!~' DEATH/DAY = 7/30 = 7(-)30
= 23 = FLIP 2 to 7; FLIP 3 to 8 = 78 = 7x8 = 56 = BIRTH/DAY #
`-NUMBER!!!~' WAS `-MARRIED to LEE KARSIAN (55-76)!!!~'
(19-76) = 57 = WAS BORN in the MONTH of (5) & DIED in the
MONTH of (7)!!!~'

AMERICAN ACTOR JAMES EDMUND CAAN "The
GODFATHER" was MARRIED to SHEILA CAAN in 76; AND,
DIED on 7/6!!!~' MARRIED in 1976 = 19+76 = 95 = RECIP = 59
= BIRTH/YEAR = 19+40 = 59!!!~' BIRTH/DAY # `-NUMBER =
3+26+19+40 = 88 = 2(8's) = 28 = RECIP = 82 = AGE of DEATH!!!~'
DIVORCE from SHEILA CAAN in 1977 = (1-9)(7+7) = (8)(14)
= (84 x 1) = 84 = BIRTH/DAY = 3/26 = FLIP 3 to 8 = 8/2-6 =
(84)!!!~' DEATH/DAY # `-NUMBER = 7+6+20+22 = 55!!!~' Was
MARRIED to DEE JAY MATHIS in 61 = BIRTH/DAY = 3/26 =
RECIP = 62/3 = 6(2-3) = 61!!!~' MARRIAGE in 1961 = (19-61) = 42
= (20+22) = DEATH/YEAR!!!~' DIVORCED DEE JAY MATHIS
in 1966 = (1-9)(6+6) = (8)(12) = (82 x 1) = (82) = AGE of DEATH!!!~'
BIRTH = 3/26 = RECIP = 62/3 = (62(-)3) = 59 = BIRTH/YEAR =
19+40 = 59!!!~' DEATH/DAY = 7/6 = 7x6 = 42 = 20+22 = DEATH/
YEAR!!!~' DAY of BIRTH = 26 = 2(6's) = 66 = DIVORCE from
DEE JAY MATHIS!!!~'

AMERICAN ACTRESS NICHELLE NICHOLS "NYOTA UHURA from STAR TREK" died at the AGE of 89!!!~' BIRTH/ YEAR = 32 = RECIP = 23 = FLIP 2 to 7 = 7/3 = DEATH/DAY = 7/3(0)!!!~'

BIRTH/DAY # `-NUMBER = 12+28+19+32 = 91!!!~'

91 = RECIPROCAL = 19 /|\ 91(-)19 = 72 = 8x9 = (89) = AGE of DEATH for AMERICAN ACTRESS NICHELLE NICHOLS "NYOTA UHURA from STAR TREK"!!!~'

DEATH/DAY # `-NUMBER = 7+30+20+22 = 79 = 7x9 = 63 = FLIP 6 to 9; FLIP 3 to 8 = 98 = RECIP = 89 = AGE of DEATH for AMERICAN ACTRESS NICHELLE NICHOLS "NYOTA UHURA from STAR TREK"!!!~'

DEATH/DAY = 7/30 = 7+30 = 37 = FLIP 7 to 2 = 32 = BIRTH/ YEAR!!!~'

23 = RECIPROCAL = 32

23 + 32 = (`-55)!!!~'

HEIGHT = 5' 5"!!!~'

(365 (-) 214) = 151 = 1x51 = (`-51) = BIRTH/YEAR of `-SON!!!~'

FROM BIRTH-to-DEATH there are (`-214) DAYS = (2 x 14) = 28 = RECIP = 82!!!~'

(21 x 4) = (`-84) = WAS `-BORN in (`-12); and, `-DIED in (`-7) = (12 x 7) = (`-84)!!!~'

BIRTH of `-SON (AMERICAN ACTOR KYLE JOHNSON) = 8/14 = 84x1 = (`-84)!!!~'

84 + 84 = 168 = RECIP = 861 = 86x1 = 86 = FLIP 6 to 9 = 89 = AGE of DEATH for AMERICAN ACTRESS NICHELLE NICHOLS "NYOTA UHURA from STAR TREK"!!!~'

NICHELLE'S `-BIRTH/DAY = 12/28 = RECIP = 82/21 = (82) (2+1) = 82+3 = (`-85)

SON KYLE'S `-BIRTH/DAY = 8/14 = 8(1+4) = (`-85)

85 + 85 = 170 = 1x70 = 70 = KYLE'S `-BIRTH/YEAR = 19+51 = 70; and, `-AGE at `-TIME of `-MOTHER'S DEATH AMERICAN ACTRESS NICHELLE NICHOLS "NYOTA UHURA from STAR TREK"!!!~'

FRAGMENTED BIRTH/DAY # `-NUMBER = 1+2+2+8+1+9+3+2 = 28 = "SEE `-ABOVE"!!!~'

28 = RECIP = 82 = (82(-)28) = (`-54)!!!~'

FRAGMENTED DEATH/DAY # `-NUMBER = 7+3+0+2+0+2+2 = 16!!!~'

16 = RECIP = 61 = (16(-)61) = (`-45)!!!~'

(`-54) = RECIP = (`-45)

54 + 45 = (`-99) = 2(9's) = 29 = "SEE `-BELOW"!!!~'

BIRTH/YEAR = 19/32 = 19+32 = 51 = SON; AMERICAN ACTOR, KYLE JOHNSON was BORN in (`-51)!!!~'

KYLE JOHNSON BIRTH/DAY # `-NUMBER = 8+14+19+51 = 92 = RECIP = 29 = 2(9's) = (`-99)!!!~'

KYLE'S BIRTH/YEAR = 19+51 = 70 = WAS (`-70) YEARS of AGE for WHEN `-HIS `-MOTHER (AMERICAN ACTRESS NICHELLE NICHOLS "NYOTA UHURA from STAR TREK") `-DIED!!!~'

AMERICAN ACTRESS NICHELLE NICHOLS "NYOTA UHURA from STAR TREK" (WED) KYLE'S FATHER "FOSTER CHARLES JOHNSON" in (1951)!!!~'

FOSTER CHARLES JOHNSON `-BIRTH/DAY # `-NUMBER = 1+3+19+17 = 40

FOSTER CHARLES JOHNSON `-DEATH/DAY # `-NUMBER = 10+29+19+81 = 139 = (1+39) = 40

SON'S `-BIRTH/DAY = 8/14 = 8(1+4) = 8(5) = 8x5 = 40

NICHELLE NICHOLS `-BIRTH/DAY = 12/28 = 12+28 = 40

FOSTER CHARLES JOHNSON'S `-DEATH/DAY #`-NUMBER = 139 = 1x39 = 39 = FLIP 3 to 8 = 89 = AGE of DEATH for AMERICAN ACTRESS NICHELLE NICHOLS "NYOTA UHURA from STAR TREK"!!!~'

HE `-DIED at the `-AGE of (`-64) = 8x8 = 2(8's) = 28 = RECIP = 82 = "SEE `-ABOVE"!!!~'

DEATH/DAY # `-NUMBER in `-REVERSE = 81(-)19(-)29(-)10 = (`-23) = -a PROPHETIC # `-NUMBER!!!~'

SON KYLE'S `-BIRTH/DAY = 8/14 = 8x14 = 112 / (DIVIDED by) (`-2) = 56 = 7x8 = "FLIP 7 to 2; FLIP 8 to 3" = (`-23)!!!~'

AMERICAN ACTRESS NICHELLE NICHOLS "NYOTA UHURA from STAR TREK" BIRTH/YEAR = 32 = RECIP = 23!!!~'

FOSTER CHARLES JOHNSON'S AGE of DEATH = 64 = ('-32) X 2!!!~'

SON KYLE JOHNSON'S BIRTH/DAY # '-NUMBER = 92 = RECIP = 29 = DAY of '-FATHER'S '-DEATH!!!~'

FOSTER CHARLES JOHNSON'S '-DEATH/DAY = 10/29 = (10 + 29) = 39 = FLIP 3 to 8 = 89 = AGE of DEATH for FORMER WIFE AMERICAN ACTRESS NICHELLE NICHOLS "NYOTA UHURA from STAR TREK"!!!~'

FOSTER CHARLES JOHNSON '-BIRTH/YEAR = 19/17 = 19+17 = 36 = FLIP 3 to 8; FLIP 6 to 9 = 89 = AGE of DEATH for FORMER WIFE AMERICAN ACTRESS NICHELLE NICHOLS "NYOTA UHURA from STAR TREK"!!!~'

BIRTH/YEAR = 19/17 = (1x9)(1+7) = 98 = RECIP = 89 = AGE of DEATH for FORMER WIFE AMERICAN ACTRESS NICHELLE NICHOLS "NYOTA UHURA from STAR TREK"!!!~'

AMERICAN ACTRESS NICHELLE NICHOLS "NYOTA UHURA from STAR TREK" was '-BORN in the MONTH of ('-12); and, '-DIED in the MONTH of ('-7) = (12/7) = 1x2/7 = 27 RECIPROCAL = 72 = 8x9 = ('-89) = AGE of DEATH for AMERICAN ACTRESS NICHELLE NICHOLS "NYOTA UHURA from STAR TREK"!!!~'

SWEDISH ACTRESS INGRID BERGMAN died at the AGE of 67!!!~'

BIRTHDAY # `-NUMBER = (8/29)/1915 = 8 + 29 + 19 + 15 = 71

DEATHDAY # `-NUMBER = (8/29)/19/82 = 8 + 29 + 19 + 82 = 138

DEATH/DAY # -NUMBER = 138 = (13 + 8) = 21 = "FLIP EVERY (`-2) OVER to a (`-7)" = 71 = BIRTHDAY # `-NUMBER!!!~'

`-DEATH/DAY # `-NUMBER in `-REVERSE = 82(-)19(-)29(-)8 = 26 = FLIP 2 to 7 = 76 = RECIP = 67 = `-AGE of `-DEATH for SWEDISH ACTRESS INGRID BERGMAN that died at the AGE of 67!!!~' A `-COMMON `-PATTERN!!!~'

AMERICAN PROFESSIONAL BASKETBALL PLAYER WILLIAM FELTON RUSSELL "BILL RUSSELL" died at the AGE of 88!!!~'

`-BIRTH/DAY # `-NUMBER = 2+12+19+34 = 67

`-BIRTH/DAY # `-NUMBER = 67 = 6x7 = 42 = 20+22 = DEATH/YEAR!!!~'

`-BIRTH/DAY = 2/12 = 2x12 = 24 = RECIP = 42 = 20+22 = DEATH/YEAR!!!~'

`-DEATH/DAY # `-NUMBER = 7+31+20+22 = 80

FROM `-BIRTH-to-DEATH there are (`-169) DAYS!!!~'

(365 (-) 169) = (`-196)!!!~'

'-ENDED PLAYING CENTER for the BOSTON CELTICS in 1969!!!~'

'-69 = RECIPROCAL = '-96

'-MARRIED to MARILYN NAULT in ('-1996)

('-1969) = 19+69 = ('-88) = '-AGE of '-DEATH for AMERICAN PROFESSIONAL BASKETBALL PLAYER WILLIAM FELTON RUSSELL "BILL RUSSELL"!!!~'

FRAGMENTED '-BIRTH/DAY # '-NUMBER = 2+1+2+1+9+ 3+4 = 22

('-22) = FLIP 2 to 7 = ('-77) = WAS '-MARRIED in ('-77)!!!~'

'-BIRTH/DAY # '-NUMBER = ('-67) + ('-22) = FRAGMENTED '-BIRTH/DAY # '-NUMBER = ('-89) = '-DIED the '-VERY '-YEAR '-PRIOR at the '-AGE of ('-88)!!!~'

FRAGMENTED '-DEATH/DAY # '-NUMBER = 7+3+1+2+0+2+2 = 17 = RECIPROCAL = 71

(17 + 71) = ('-88) = '-AGE of '-DEATH for AMERICAN PROFESSIONAL BASKETBALL PLAYER WILLIAM FELTON RUSSELL "BILL RUSSELL"!!!~'

71(-)2+2 = 67 = '-BIRTH/DAY # '-NUMBER!!!~'

WIFE: MARILYN NAULT married in 1996 = (19-96) = ('-77) = MARRIED DOROTHY ANSTETT in ('-77)!!!~'

'-DEATH/DAY # '-NUMBER = 80 = DIVORCED DOROTHY ANSTETT in ('-80)!!!~'

(`-1977) = 19+77 = 96 = MARRIED MARILYN NAULT!!!~'

`-DIVORCED MARILYN NAULT in 2009 = 20x09 = 180 = 1x80 = 80 = `-DEATH/DAY # `-NUMBER for AMERICAN PROFESSIONAL BASKETBALL PLAYER WILLIAM FELTON RUSSELL "BILL RUSSELL"!!!~'

`-STARTED PLAYING CENTER for the BOSTON CELTICS in 1956!!!~'

`-MARRIED ROSE SWISHER in 1956 = (19-56) = 37 = RECIPROCAL = 73 = `-DIVORCED ROSE SWISHER in 19(`-73)!!!~'

19(-)73 = 54 = 6x9 = (`-69) = SEE `-ABOVE for `-BIRTH-to-DEATH for AMERICAN PROFESSIONAL BASKETBALL PLAYER WILLIAM FELTON RUSSELL "BILL RUSSELL"!!!~'

`-BIRTH/YEAR = 19/34 = 19+34 = 53 = RECIPROCAL = 35!!!~'

(53 + 35) = `-88 = `-AGE of `-DEATH for AMERICAN PROFESSIONAL BASKETBALL PLAYER WILLIAM FELTON RUSSELL "BILL RUSSELL"!!!~'

`-DEATH/DAY = 7/31 = 7+31 = 38 = FLIP 3 to 8 = (`-88) = `-AGE of `-DEATH for AMERICAN PROFESSIONAL BASKETBALL PLAYER WILLIAM FELTON RUSSELL "BILL RUSSELL"!!!~'

`-MARRIED TO: MARILYN NAULT from 1996 to 2009 (13 YEARS); DOROTHY ANSTETT from 1977 to 1980 (3 YEARS); ROSE SWISHER from 1956 to 1973 (17 YEARS)!!!~'

(13+3+17) = 33 = FLIP 3 to 8 = (`-88) = `-AGE of `-DEATH for AMERICAN PROFESSIONAL BASKETBALL PLAYER WILLIAM FELTON RUSSELL "BILL RUSSELL"!!!~'

THOUGHTS on & of the `-UNIVERSE:

JUST as EVERY LIVING PERSON can LOOK INSIDE the MAKING of THEIR `-OWN `-ANATOMY/`-PHYSIOLOGY to the VERY MAKEUP of THEIR CELLS & PROTEINS, FATS & CARBOHYDRATES, & WATER; on HOW this COMPLEX WORLD of a BODY EXISTS; and, is ABLE to CONTINUALLY FUNCTION; can ONLY WONDER the MIND!!!~' HERE'S a REVELATION: With the MANY TELESCOPES such as the JAMES WEBB TELESCOPE; there are BILLIONS upon BILLIONS of GALAXIES with TRILLIONS upon TRILLIONS of STARS!!!~' Within ALL of these DUST CLOUDS there are PLANETS; and, OURS is NOT the MOST ADVANCED!!!~' AS `-GOD CONTROLS `-ALL of `-US; HE too CONTROLS all of the OTHER CREATIONS, as WELL!!!~' THAT'S HOW POWERFUL `-GOD `-IS!!!~' (`-SIMULTANEOUSLY)!!!~'

AMERICAN ACTOR ANTHONY "TONY" LEE DOW from "LEAVE IT to BEAVER" died at the AGE of (`-77)!!!~'

`-BIRTH/DAY # `-NUMBER = 4+13+19+45 = 81

BIRTH/DAY = 4/13 = 43x1 = 43 = DEATH/DAY = 7/27 = 7+27 = 34 = RECIPROCAL = 43

BIRTH/DAY = 4/13 = (4+1)(3) = 5(3) = FLIP 3 to 8 = 58 = HEIGHT = 5' 8"!!!~'

BIRTH/DAY = 4/13 = FLIP 3 to 8 = 4/18 = 4/1+8 = 49 = AGE of `-SON; CHRISTOPHER DOW at the TIME of `-HIS FATHER'S `-DEATH!!!~'

`-DEATH/DAY # `-NUMBER = 7+27+20+22 = 76

`-DEATH/DAY # `-NUMBER = 76 = `-DIED the `-VERY `-NEXT `-YEAR at the `-AGE of (`-77)!!!~'

`-DEATH/DAY # `-NUMBER = 76 = 7x6 = 42 = 20+22 = DEATH/YEAR!!!~'

`-PART of `-DEATH/DAY # `-NUMBER = 7+27+20 = 54 = RECIPROCAL = 45 = `-BIRTH/YEAR!!!~'

SON; CHRISTOPHER DOW'S `-BIRTH/YEAR = 19/73 = 19(-)73 = 54 = RECIP = 45 = `-BIRTH/YEAR for `-FATHER AMERICAN ACTOR ANTHONY "TONY" LEE DOW!!!~'

`-DAY of `-DEATH = 27 = 2(7's) = (`-77) = `-AGE of `-DEATH for AMERICAN ACTOR ANTHONY "TONY" LEE DOW!!!~'

FRAGMENTED `-BIRTH/DAY # `-NUMBER = 4+1+3+1+9+4+5 = 27

FRAGMENTED `-BIRTH/DAY # `-NUMBER = 27 = `-DAY of `-DEATH = (`-27th)!!!~'

FRAGMENTED `-BIRTH/DAY # `-NUMBER = 27 = FLIP 2 to 7 = (`-77) = `-AGE of `-DEATH for AMERICAN ACTOR ANTHONY "TONY" LEE DOW!!!~'

`-BIRTH/DAY # `-NUMBER = (`-81) (-) (`-27) = FRAGMENTED `-BIRTH/DAY # `-NUMBER = 54 = "SEE `-ABOVE & `-BELOW"!!!~'

FRAGMENTED `-DEATH/DAY # `-NUMBER = 7+2+7+2+0+2+2 = 22

FRAGMENTED `-DEATH/DAY # `-NUMBER = 22 = FLIP 2 to 7 = (`-77) = `-AGE of `-DEATH for AMERICAN ACTOR ANTHONY "TONY" LEE DOW!!!~'

FRAGMENTED `-DEATH/DAY # `-NUMBER = 22 = FLIP 2 to 7 = (`-27) = FRAGMENTED `-BIRTH/DAY # `-NUMBER!!!~'

`-DEATH/DAY # `-NUMBER = (`-76) (-) (`-22) = FRAGMENTED `-DEATH/DAY # `-NUMBER = 54 = "SEE `-ABOVE & `-BELOW"!!!~'

FROM BIRTH-to-DEATH there are 105 DAYS!!!~'

(365 (-) 105) = 260 = 26+0 = 26 = FLIP 2 to 7 = 76 = `-DEATH/DAY # `-NUMBER!!!~'

YEARS `-ACTIVE = 1949 to 2022 = 73 YEARS = SON; CHRISTOPHER DOW was `-BORN in (`-73)!!!~'

BIRTH/YEAR = 19/45

`-45 = RECIPROCAL = `-54

(19 + 54) = (`-73)!!!~'

YEAR `-STARTED `-HIS `-OCCUPATIONS = 49 = 7x7 = (`-77) = `-AGE of `-DEATH for AMERICAN ACTOR ANTHONY "TONY" LEE DOW!!!~'

SON; CHRISTOPHER DOW was (`-49) YEARS of `-AGE at the TIME of `-HIS `-FATHER'S `-DEATH = (`-49) = 7x7 = (`-77) = `-AGE of `-DEATH for AMERICAN ACTOR ANTHONY "TONY" LEE DOW!!!~'

`-MARRIED to LAUREN SHULKIND from 1980 to 2022 = {42 YEARS} = (20+22) = `-DEATH/YEAR!!!~'

`-DEATH/DAY # `-NUMBER = 76 = (7x6) = (`-42)!!!~'

MARRIED to CAROL MARLOW from 1969 to 1980 = {11 YEARS}!!!~'

(42(-)11) = 31 = FLIP 3 to 8 = 81 = `-BIRTH/DAY # `-NUMBER for AMERICAN ACTOR ANTHONY "TONY" LEE DOW!!!~'

(42 + 11) = 53 = RECIPROCAL = 35

(53 + 35) = 88 = MARRIED in 1969 = (19+69) = (`-88)!!!~'

DIVORCED & MARRIED in 1980 = 19+80 = (`-99) = 9x9 = 81 = `-BIRTH/DAY # `-NUMBER for AMERICAN ACTOR ANTHONY "TONY" LEE DOW!!!~'

`-AGE of `-DEATH for AMERICAN ACTOR ANTHONY "TONY" LEE DOW = (`-77); (`-88); (`-99) = SUCCESSION of `-ORDER!!!~'

TONY & CAROL'S `-SON; CHRISTOPHER DOW `-BIRTH/DAY # `-NUMBER = 3+26+19+73 = 121 = 1+21 = 22 = FLIP 2 to 7 = 77 = `-AGE of `-DEATH for AMERICAN ACTOR & FATHER ANTHONY "TONY" LEE DOW!!!~'

`-BIRTH/DAY = 3/26 = 3+26 = 29 = 2(9's) = 99 = 9x9 = 81 = `-BIRTH/DAY # `-NUMBER for AMERICAN ACTOR ANTHONY "TONY" LEE DOW!!!~'

`-BIRTH/YEAR = 19+73 = 92 = RECIP = 29

`-29 = RECIPROCAL = `-92

(29+29) = 58 = 5' 8" in HEIGHT for AMERICAN ACTOR ANTHONY "TONY" LEE DOW!!!~'

(92+92) = 184 = BIRTH of SON; CHRISTOPHER DOW = 3/26 = FLIP 3 to 8 = 8/26 = 8/2(-)6 = 84!!!~'

92(-)29 = 63 = 6x3 = 18 = RECIPROCAL = 81 = `-BIRTH/DAY # `-NUMBER for AMERICAN ACTOR ANTHONY "TONY" LEE DOW!!!~'

92(-)29 = 63 = RECIP = 36 = 4x9 = `-AGE of SON; CHRISTOPHER DOW at the TIME of `-HIS `-FATHER'S `-DEATH = (`-49) = 7x7 = (`-77) = `-AGE of `-DEATH for AMERICAN ACTOR & FATHER ANTHONY "TONY" LEE DOW!!!~'

`-BORN in the `-MONTH of (`-4); and, `-DIED in the `-MONTH of (`-7) = (`-47) = RECIPROCAL = (`-74)!!!~'

(74(-)47) = 27 = 2(7's) = (`-77) = `-AGE of `-DEATH for AMERICAN ACTOR ANTHONY "TONY" LEE DOW!!!~'

AMERICAN ACTRESS BARBARA BILLINGSLEY from "LEAVE IT to BEAVER" died at the AGE of 94!!!~'

`-BIRTH/YEAR = 19/15 = (1x9)(1-5) = (`-94) = `-AGE of `-DEATH for AMERICAN ACTRESS BARBARA BILLINGSLEY from "LEAVE IT to BEAVER"!!!~'

`-BIRTH/DAY # `-NUMBER = 12+22+19+15 = 68

`-BIRTH/DAY # `-NUMBER = 68 = FLIP 6 to 9 = 98 / (`-DIVIDED by) (`-2) = 49 = RECIPROCAL = 94 = `-AGE of `-DEATH for AMERICAN ACTRESS BARBARA BILLINGSLEY from "LEAVE IT to BEAVER"!!!~'

`-DEATH/DAY # `-NUMBER = 10+16+20+10 = 56

`-DEATH/DAY # `-NUMBER = (`-56) = DIVORCED ROY KELLINO in (`-56)!!!~'

`-DEATH/DAY # `-NUMBER = (`-56) = 5x6 = 30 = 20+10 = `-DEATH/YEAR!!!~'

`-MARRIED ROY KELLINO in 1953 = 19+53 = 72 = 9/8 = (`-98) / (`-DIVIDED by) (`-2) = (`-49) = RECIPROCAL = (`-94) = `-AGE of `-DEATH for AMERICAN ACTRESS BARBARA BILLINGSLEY from "LEAVE IT to BEAVER"!!!~'

19(-)53 = 34 = BIRTH/DAY = 12+22 = 34 = BIRTH/YEAR = 19+15 = 34!!!~'

FRAGMENTED `-BIRTH/DAY # `-NUMBER = 1+2+2+2+1+9+1+5 = 23

`-23 = RECIPROCAL = `-32

(23+32) = (`-55) = 5' 5" in HEIGHT!!!~'

FRAGMENTED `-BIRTH/DAY # `-NUMBER = (`-23) = FLIP 2 to 7; FLIP 3 to 8 = (`-78) = WAS `-MARRIED to WILLIAM MORTENSEN in 1959 = 19+59 = (`-78)!!!~'

FRAGMENTED `-DEATH/DAY # `-NUMBER = 1+0+1+6+2+0+1+0 = 11

(23+11) = (`-34) X TIMES (`-2) = (`-68) = BIRTH/DAY # `-NUMBER!!!~'

FROM `-BIRTH-to-DEATH there are 67 DAYS = DEATH/DAY = 10+16 = 26 = FLIP 2 to 7 = 76 = RECIPROCAL = 67!!!~'

FROM `-BIRTH-to-DEATH there are 67 DAYS = FLIP 6 to 9 = 97 = 9x7 = 63 = RECIPROCAL = 36 = 9x4 = (`-94) = `-AGE of `-DEATH for AMERICAN ACTRESS BARBARA BILLINGSLEY from "LEAVE IT to BEAVER"!!!~'

(365 (-) 67) = 298 = 98 / (`-DIVIDED by) (`-2) = (`-49) = RECIPROCAL = (`-94) = `-AGE of `-DEATH for AMERICAN ACTRESS BARBARA BILLINGSLEY from "LEAVE IT to BEAVER"!!!~'

(`-298) = 29x8 = 232 = *Reciprocal-Sequencing-Numerology-RSN-'!!!~'*

`-DIVORCED GLENN BILLINGSLEY in 1947 = 19+47 = 66 = 6x6 = 36 = 9x4 = `-AGE of `-DEATH for AMERICAN ACTRESS BARBARA BILLINGSLEY from "LEAVE IT to BEAVER"!!!~'

`-DAY of `-BIRTH = (`-22) = WAS `-MARRIED to WILLIAM MORTENSEN for (`-22) YEARS from 1959 to 1981!!!~'

WAS `-MARRIED to ROY KELLINO from 1953 to 1956 for (`-3) YEARS!!!~'

WAS `-MARRIED to GLENN BILLINGSLEY from 1941 to 1947 = (`-6) YEARS!!!~'

(3/6) = 36 = 9x4 = `-AGE of `-DEATH for AMERICAN ACTRESS BARBARA BILLINGSLEY from "LEAVE IT to BEAVER"!!!~'

`-TOTAL `-YEARS `-MARRIED = (22+3+6) = (`-31) X TIMES (`-3) = 93 = FLIP 3 to 8 = 98 / (`-DIVIDED by) (`-2) = (`-49) = RECIPROCAL = (`-94) = `-AGE of `-DEATH for AMERICAN ACTRESS BARBARA BILLINGSLEY from "LEAVE IT to BEAVER"!!!~'

AMERICAN ACTOR EUGENE HUGH BEAUMONT from "LEAVE IT to BEAVER" died at the AGE of (`-73)!!!~'

PART of `-BIRTH/DAY # `-NUMBER = 2+16+19 = 37 = RECIPROCAL = 73 = `-AGE of `-DEATH for AMERICAN ACTOR EUGENE HUGH BEAUMONT from "LEAVE IT to BEAVER"!!!~'

`-BIRTH/DAY # `-NUMBER = 2+16+19+09 = 46

BIRTH/DAY = 2/16 = 2x16 = 32 = FLIP 2 to 7 = 37 = RECIPROCAL = 73 = `-AGE of `-DEATH for AMERICAN ACTOR EUGENE HUGH BEAUMONT from "LEAVE IT to BEAVER"!!!~'

BIRTH/YEAR = 19/09 = 19+09 = 28 = RECIPROCAL = 82 = `-DEATH/YEAR!!!~'

`-BIRTH/DAY # `-NUMBER = 46 = `-DEATH/DAY = 5/14 = (5+1) (4) = 64 = RECIPROCAL = 46

`-DEATH/DAY # `-NUMBER = 5+14+19+82 = 120

`-DEATH/DAY # `-NUMBER = 120 = 12+0 = 12 = RECIPROCAL = 21 = 7x3 = (`-73) = `-AGE of `-DEATH for AMERICAN ACTOR EUGENE HUGH BEAUMONT from "LEAVE IT to BEAVER"!!!~'

`-DEATH/DAY # `-NUMBER = 120 / (`-DIVIDED by) (`-2) = 60 = HEIGHT = 6' 0"!!!~'

BIRTH/DAY = 2/16 = HALF/RECIPROCAL = 2/61 = 2+61 = (`-63) = DEATH/YEAR = 19-82 = (`-63)!!!~'

FRAGMENTED `-BIRTH/DAY # `-NUMBER = 2+1+6+1+9+ 0+9 = 28

FRAGMENTED `-BIRTH/DAY # `-NUMBER = 28 = RECIPROCAL = 82 = `-DEATH/YEAR!!!~'

`-BIRTH/DAY # `-NUMBER = (`-46) + (`-28) = FRAGMENTED `-BIRTH/DAY # `-NUMBER = (`-74) = `-DIED the `-VERY `-YEAR `-PRIOR at the `-AGE of (`-73)!!!~'

FRAGMENTED `-DEATH/DAY # `-NUMBER = 5+1+4+1+9+ 8+2 = 30

(28+30) = 58 = PART of `-DEATH/DAY # `-NUMBER in `-REVERSE = 82(-)19(-)5 = 58

FROM `-BIRTH=to-DEATH there are 87 DAYS = FLIP 8 to 3 = 37 = RECIPROCAL = 73 = `-AGE of `-DEATH for AMERICAN ACTOR EUGENE HUGH BEAUMONT from "LEAVE IT to BEAVER"!!!~'

(365 (-) 87) = 278 = 27x8 = 216 = `-BIRTH/DAY = 2/16!!!~'

`-MONTH of `-BIRTH = FEBRUARY = 28 DAYS!!!~'

(28 (-) 16) – DAY of `-BIRTH = 12 = RECIPROCAL = 21 = 7x3 = (`-73) = `-AGE of `-DEATH for AMERICAN ACTOR EUGENE HUGH BEAUMONT from "LEAVE IT to BEAVER"!!!~'

JESSICA COMBS "FASTEST WOMAN ON 4 WHEELS" (39 years age of death) (BIRTH: JULY 27, 1980) (DEATH: AUGUST 27, 2019)

BIRTHDAY # `-NUMBER = (7 + 27 + 19 + 80) = 133 /|\ 13 x 3 = 39 = AGE of DEATH!!!~'

OUR DEATHS are `-KNOWN at; and, from; `-BIRTH!!!~'

JESSICA COMBS "FASTEST WOMAN ON WHEELS" BIRTH = (7+27+19+80) = 133!~'

DEATH = (8+27+20+19) = 74!~'

(133+74) = 207 = (27+0) = 27 = BORN on a (`-27ᵗʰ); AND, DIED on a (`- 27ᵗʰ)!!!~'

DIED at AGE 39 = (3x9) = 27!~'

JULY 27 = (7x27) = 189 /\ AUGUST 27 = (8x27) = 216 /|\ (216(-)189) = 27

BIRTH/DAY = 7/27 = 7 x 27 = 189 = 18 + 9 = 27

BIRTH/YEAR = 19/80 = 1 + 9 + 8 + 0 = 18 = 3 x 6 = FLIP 6 to 9 = 3 x 9 = 39 = AGE of DEATH!!!~'

BIRTH/YEAR = 19/80 = (1 x 9) (8 + 0) = 98 = RECIP = 89 = FLIP EVERY 8 to a 3 = 39 = AGE of DEATH!!!~'

DEATH/YEAR = 20/19 = 20 + 19 = 39 = AGE of DEATH!!!~'

JESSICA COMBS "FASTEST WOMAN ON 4 WHEELS" (39 years age of death) = DEATH/DAY = 8/27 = 8 / (2 + 7) = 89 = FLIP 8 to 3 = 39 = AGE of DEATH!!!~'

AUSTRALIAN ACTOR HEATH ANDREW LEDGER died at the AGE of 28!!!~'

BIRTH/DAY = 4/4 = (4 + 4) = 8 = DEATH/YEAR = (`-8)!!!~'

BIRTHDAY # `-NUMBER = 4/4/19/79 = 4 + 4 + 19 + 79 = 106

BIRTHDAY # `-NUMBER = 106 = (10 + 6) = 16 = 2x8 = (`-28) = `-AGE of `-DEATH for AUSTRALIAN ACTOR HEATH ANDREW LEDGER!!!~'

DEATHDAY # `-NUMBER = 1/22/20/08 = 1 + 22 + 20 + 08 = 51

(106 + 51) = 157 = (15 (-) 7) = 8 = DEATH/YEAR!!!~'

DEATH/DAY = 1/22 = (1 + 22) = 23 = FLIP 3 to 8 = 28 = `-AGE of `-DEATH for AUSTRALIAN ACTOR HEATH ANDREW LEDGER!!!~'

DEATH/YEAR = 20/08 = (20 + 08) = 28 = `-AGE of `-DEATH for AUSTRALIAN ACTOR HEATH ANDREW LEDGER!!!~'

FORMER U.S. REPRESENTATIVE JOHN CONYERS died at the AGE of (**90**)!!!~'

(BIRTH: MAY 16, 19**29**) (DEATH: OCTOBER 27, **2**01**9**)

WAS `-MARRIED to MONICA CONYERS for (`-**29**) YEARS & WAS `-BORN in (`-19**29**)!!!~'

MARRIED SINCE (`-19**90**)!!!~'

WAS `-MARRIED in (`-19**90**) & DIED AT THE `-AGE OF (`-**90**)!!!~'

`-BIRTH/YEAR = **29** = `-DEATH/YEAR = **2**01**9** = (29+0x1) = **29**

`-DIED (`-164) DAYS from BIRTH-TO=DEATH = (1+4)(6) = 56 = BIRTH/DAY = 5/16 = 56x1 = 56

`-DEATH/DAY = 10/27 = 10x27 = 270 / (`-DIVIDED by) (`-3) = (`-**90**) = `-AGE of `-DEATH for FORMER U.S. REPRESENTATIVE JOHN CONYERS!!!~'

`-DEATH/DAY = 10/27 = 10/2+7 = 10/9 = 10x9 = (`-**90**) = `-AGE of `-DEATH for FORMER U.S. REPRESENTATIVE JOHN CONYERS!!!~'

AMERICAN RECORD EXECUTIVE MO OSTIN died at the AGE of (`-95)!!!~'

`-BIRTH/DAY # `-NUMBER = 3+27+19+27 = 76

`-BIRTH/DAY # `-NUMBER = 76 = 7x6 = 42 = 20+22 = `-DEATH/YEAR!!!~'

`-DEATH/DAY # `-NUMBER = 7+31+20+22 = 80

76+80 = 156 = RECIPROCAL = 651 = FLIP 6 to 9 = 951 = 95x1 = (`-95) = `-AGE of `-DEATH for AMERICAN RECORD EXECUTIVE MO OSTIN!!!~'

76(-)80 = 4 = 9(-)5 = (`-95) = `-AGE of `-DEATH for AMERICAN RECORD EXECUTIVE MO OSTIN!!!~'

`-BIRTH/DAY = 3/27 = 3(-)27 = 24 = `-DEATH/DAY = 7/31 = 7(-)31 = 24 = RECIPROCAL = 42 = 20+22 = `-DEATH/YEAR!!!~'

FRAGMENTED `-BIRTH/DAY # `-NUMBER = 3+2+7+1+9+2+7 = 31

FRAGMENTED `-DEATH/DAY # `-NUMBER = 7+3+1+2+0+2+2 = 17

31(-)17 = 14 = 9+5 = (`-95) = `-AGE of `-DEATH for AMERICAN RECORD EXECUTIVE MO OSTIN!!!~'

FROM `-BIRTH-to-DEATH there are 126 DAYS = FLIP 2 to 7 = 176 = 1x76 = 76 = `-BIRTH/DAY # `-NUMBER!!!~'

(365 (-) 126) = 239 = RECIPROCAL = 932 = 9/3+2 = (`-95) = `-AGE of `-DEATH for AMERICAN RECORD EXECUTIVE MO OSTIN!!!~'

`-BIRTH/DAY = 3/27 = 3(-)27 = 24 = RECIPROCAL = 42 = 20+22 = `-DEATH/YEAR!!!~'

`-BIRTH/YEAR = 27 = FLIP 7 to 2 = 22 = `-DEATH/YEAR!!!~'

`-WAS `-BORN in the `-MONTH of (`-3); and, `-DIED in the `-MONTH of (`-7) = (`-37) = RECIPROCAL = (`-73) = DEATH/DAY = 7/31 = 73x1 = (`-73)!!!~'

BIRTH/YEAR = 19/27 = (1x9)(2-7) = (`-95) = `-AGE of `-DEATH for AMERICAN RECORD EXECUTIVE MO OSTIN!!!~'

AMERICAN SPORTSCASTER VINCENT EDWARD SCULLY died at the AGE of (`-94)!!!~'

`-BIRTH/DAY = 11/29 = HALF/RECIPROCAL = 11/92 = 1+1+92 = (`-94) = `-AGE of `-DEATH for AMERICAN SPORTSCASTER VINCENT EDWARD SCULLY!!!~'

`-WAS `-BORN in the `-MONTH of (`-11); and, `-DIED in the `-MONTH of (`-8) = (11/8) = RECIPROCAL = (8/11) = 8(1+1) = 8/2 = `-DEATH/DAY!!!~'

`-BIRTH/DAY # `-NUMBER = 11+29+19+27 = 86

`-BIRTH/DAY # `-NUMBER = 86 = FLIP 8 to 3 = 36 = 9x4 = (`-94) = `-AGE of `-DEATH for AMERICAN SPORTSCASTER VINCENT EDWARD SCULLY!!!~'

`-DEATH/DAY # `-NUMBER = 8+2+20+22 = 52

86+52 = 138 = RECIPROCAL = 831 = 83+1 = 84 = RECIPROCAL = 48 = WAS `-MARRIED to SANDRA HUNT for (`-48) YEARS!!!~'

FRAGMENTED `-BIRTH/DAY # `-NUMBER = 1+1+2+9+1+9+2+7 = 32

FRAGMENTED `-BIRTH/DAY # `-NUMBER = 32 = FLIP 3 to 8 = 8/2 = `-DEATH/DAY!!!~'

FRAGMENTED `-DEATH/DAY # `-NUMBER = 8+2+2+0+2+2 = 16

FRAGMENTED `-DEATH/DAY # `-NUMBER = 16 / (`-DIVIDED by) (`-2) = 8 = 2/8 = RECIPROCAL = 8/2 = `-DEATH/DAY!!!~'

32+16 = 48 = 8x6 = `-BIRTH/DAY # `-NUMBER!!!~'

32+16 = 48 = WAS `-MARRIED to SANDRA HUNT for (`-48) YEARS!!!~'

FROM `-BIRTH-to-DEATH there are 246 DAYS = RECIPROCAL = 642 = 64x2 = 128 = RECIPROCAL = 821 = 82x1 = 8/2 = DEATH/DAY!!!~'

FROM `-BIRTH-to-DEATH there are 246 DAYS = RECIPROCAL = 642 = 6x42 = 252 = `-DEATH/DAY # `-NUMBER = 52

(365 (-) 246) = 119 = 11/9 = `-BIRTH/DAY = 11(2)9

`-BIRTH/DAY = 11/29 = 11x29 = 319 = RECIPROCAL = 913 = 91+3 = (`-94) = `-AGE of `-DEATH for AMERICAN SPORTSCASTER VINCENT EDWARD SCULLY!!!~'

`-BIRTH/YEAR = 27 = FLIP 7 to 2 = 22 = `-DEATH/YEAR!!!~'

`-BIRTH/YEAR = 19/27 = 19+27 = 46 = 4x6 = 24 = RECIPROCAL = 42 = 20+22 = `-DEATH/YEAR!!!~'

`-BIRTH/YEAR = 1927 = (9) (1+2-7) = (`-94) = `-AGE of `-DEATH for AMERICAN SPORTSCASTER VINCENT EDWARD SCULLY!!!~'

`-WAS `-MARRIED to SANDRA HUNT from 1973 to 2021 for 48 YEARS!!!~'

`-MARRIED 19/73 = 1x9/7(-)3 = (`-94) = `-AGE of `-DEATH for `-HUSBAND AMERICAN SPORTSCASTER VINCENT EDWARD SCULLY!!!~'

`-MARRIED in 19+73 = 92 = FLIP 9 to 6 = 62 = `-MARRIED for a `-TOTAL of (`-62) YEARS to `-BOTH `-WOMEN!!!~'

`-WIFE SANDRA HUNT `-DIED in 2021 = 20+21 = 41 X TIMES (`-2) = 8/2 = `-DEATH/DAY of `-HUSBAND AMERICAN SPORTSCASTER VINCENT EDWARD SCULLY!!!~'

`-WAS `-MARRIED to JOAN CRAWFORD from 1958 to 1972 for 14 YEARS = RECIPROCAL = 41 X TIMES (`-2) = 8/2 = `-DEATH/DAY of `-HUSBAND AMERICAN SPORTSCASTER VINCENT EDWARD SCULLY!!!~'

`-MARRIED in 58 = FLIP 8 to 3 = 53 = 19-72 = 53

19+58 = 77 = FLIP 7 to 2 = 72 = DIVORCED!!!~'

`-1958 = 9/1+5+8 = 914 = 94x1 = (`-94) = `-AGE of `-DEATH for HUSBAND AMERICAN SPORTSCASTER VINCENT EDWARD SCULLY!!!~'

`-1972 = 9/1-7-2 = (`-94) = `-AGE of `-DEATH for HUSBAND AMERICAN SPORTSCASTER VINCENT EDWARD SCULLY!!!~'

`-WAS `-MARRIED for a `-TOTAL of (`-62) YEARS = FLIP 2 to 7 = 67 = CALLED (`-67) SEASONS for MAJOR LEAGUE BASEBALL'S LOS ANGELES DODGERS!!!~'

AMERICAN SINGER & ACTRESS NAOMI JUDD died at the AGE of (`-76)!!!~'

`-AGE of `-DEATH = 76 = 7x6 = 42 = 20+22 = `-DEATH/YEAR!!!~'

`-BIRTH/DAY # `-NUMBER = 1+11+19+46 = 77

`-BIRTH/DAY # `-NUMBER = (`-77) = `-DIED the `-VERY `-YEAR `-PRIOR at the `-AGE of (`-76)!!!~'

`-PART of `-BIRTH/DAY # `-NUMBER = 11+19+46 = (`-76) = `-AGE of `-DEATH for AMERICAN SINGER & ACTRESS NAOMI JUDD!!!~'

`-DEATH/DAY # `-NUMBER = 4+30+20+22 = 76

`-DEATH/DAY # `-NUMBER = (`-76) = `-AGE of `-DEATH for AMERICAN SINGER & ACTRESS NAOMI JUDD!!!~'

77+76 = 153 = 1x53 = 53 = DAUGHTER WYNONNA JUDD'S `-BIRTH/DAY = 5/30 = 5+30 = 35 = RECIPROCAL = 53

DAUGHTER WYNONNA JUDD was (`-57) YEARS of `-AGE at the `-TIME of `-HER `-MOTHER'S `-DEATH = 5x7 = 35 = RECIPROCAL = 53

FRAGMENTED `-BIRTH/DAY # `-NUMBER = 1+1+1+1+9+4+6 = 23

DAUGHTER ASHLEY JUDD'S `-BIRTH/DAY = 4/19 = 4+19 = 23

FRAGMENTED `-BIRTH/DAY # `-NUMBER = (`-23) = -a PROPHETIC # `-NUMBER!!!~'

FRAGMENTED `-DEATH/DAY # `-NUMBER = 4+3+0+2+0+ 2+2 = 13

FRAGMENTED `-DEATH/DAY # `-NUMBER = (`-13) = "A VERY PIVOTAL # `-NUMBER"!!!~'

FRAGMENTED `-DEATH/DAY # `-NUMBER = (`-13) = 7+6 = (`-76) = `-AGE of `-DEATH for AMERICAN SINGER & ACTRESS NAOMI JUDD!!!~'

FROM `-BIRTH-to-DEATH there are 109 DAYS!!!~'

(365 (-) 109) = 256 = 25+6 = 31 = RECIPROCAL = 13 = FRAGMENTED `-DEATH/DAY # `-NUMBER!!!~'

(365 (-) 109) = 256 = 2+5/6 = (`-76) = `-AGE of `-DEATH for AMERICAN SINGER & ACTRESS NAOMI JUDD!!!~'

DAUGHTER ASHLEY JUDD'S `-BIRTH/DAY = 4/19 = 4x19 = (`-76) = `-AGE of `-DEATH of `-MOTHER AMERICAN SINGER & ACTRESS NAOMI JUDD!!!~'

DAUGHTER ASHLEY JUDD'S `-BIRTH/DAY # `-NUMBER in `-REVERSE = 68(-)19(-)19(-)4 = 26 = FLIP 2 to 7 = (`-76) = `-AGE of `-DEATH of `-MOTHER AMERICAN SINGER & ACTRESS NAOMI JUDD!!!~'

`-AGE of `-DAUGHTERS WYNONNA (`-57); and, ASHLEY (`-54) at the `-TIME of `-MOTHER'S `-DEATH = 57+54 = 111 = `-MOTHER'S `-BIRTH/DAY = 1/11!!!~'

DWAYNE W. ANDERSON

MUSICIAN SOPHIE (SOPHIE XEON) `-DIES at the `-AGE of (`- 34) on (1/30/2021) = (1 + 30 + 20 + 21) = (`-72) = 9x8 = 98 = 9(1+7) = 9/17 = `-BIRTH/DAY!!!~'

`-BORN on (9/17/1986) = (9 + 17 + 19 + 86) = (`-131) = "DAY `-AFTER `-DEATH/ DAY of (1/30)"!!!~'

`-BIRTH/DAY = (9/17) = (9 x 17) = (`-153) = RECIPROCAL = (`-351) = (35 (-) 1) = (`-34) = "AGE of `-DEATH for MUSICIAN SOPHIE (SOPHIE XEON)!!!~'

`-DIED (`-135) `-DAYS after `-HER `-LAST `-BIRTH/DAY!!!~'

`-BIRTH/YEAR = 86 = RECIPROCAL = 68 / (`-DIVIDED by) (`-2) = (`-34) = `-AGE of `-DEATH of MUSICIAN SOPHIE (SOPHIE XEON)!!!~'

`-BIRTH/DAY = 9/17 = 9/1+7 = 98 = FLIP 9 to 6 = 68 / (`-DIVIDED by) (`-2) = (`-34) = `-AGE of `-DEATH of MUSICIAN SOPHIE (SOPHIE XEON)!!!~'

AMERICAN MUSICIAN & ACTOR / MEMBER of the BAND "THE MONKEES" ROBERT MICHAEL NESMITH died at the AGE of (`-78)!!!~'

`-BIRTH/DAY = 12/30 = 12+30 = 42 = 7x6 = FLIP 6 to 9 = 79 = `-DIED within `-HIS 79th YEAR of `-EXISTENCE!!!~'

`-BIRTH/DAY # `-NUMBER = 12+30+19+42 = 103

`-BIRTH/DAY # `-NUMBER = 103 = RECIPROCAL = 301 = 30(-)1 = 29 = FLIP 2 to 7 = 79 = `-DIED within `-HIS 79th YEAR of `-EXISTENCE!!!~'

`-DEATH/DAY # `-NUMBER = 12+10+20+21 = 63

`-DEATH/DAY # `-NUMBER = 63 = 7x9 = (`-79) = `-DIED within `-HIS 79th YEAR of `-EXISTENCE!!!~'

103+63 = 166 = 1(-)6/6 = 56 = 7x8 = (`-78) = `-AGE of `-DEATH for AMERICAN MUSICIAN & ACTOR / MEMBER of the BAND "THE MONKEES" ROBERT MICHAEL NESMITH!!!~'

FRAGMENTED `-BIRTH/DAY # `-NUMBER = 1+2+3+0+1+9+ 4+2 = 22

FRAGMENTED `-DEATH/DAY # `-NUMBER = 1+2+1+0+ 2+0+2+1 = 9

22+9 = 31 = RECIPROCAL = 13 = `-BIRTH/DAY # `-NUMBER = 103 = 10+3 = 13

22(-)9 = 13 = `-BIRTH/DAY # `-NUMBER = 103 = 10+3 = 13

FROM `-BIRTH-to-DEATH there are 20 DAYS = `-TOTAL of (`-20) YEARS `-MARRIED!!!~'

(365 (-) 20) = 345 = FLIP 3 to 8 = 8/4+5 = 89 = RECIPROCAL = 98 = FLIP 9 to 6; FLIP 8 to 3 = 63 = `-DEATH/DAY # `-NUMBER!!!~'

`-BIRTH/YEAR = 1942 = 9(-)2/1(-)4 = 73 = FLIP 3 to 8 = (`-78) = `-AGE of `-DEATH for AMERICAN MUSICIAN & ACTOR / MEMBER of the BAND "THE MONKEES" ROBERT MICHAEL NESMITH!!!~'

`-DEATH/YEAR = 2021 = 20+21 = 41 X TIMES (`-2) = 82 = RECIPROCAL = 28 = FLIP 2 to 7 = (`-78) = `-AGE of `-DEATH for AMERICAN MUSICIAN & ACTOR / MEMBER of the BAND "THE MONKEES" ROBERT MICHAEL NESMITH!!!~'

'-WAS '-MARRIED to KATHRYN BILD from 1976 to 1988 for 12 YEARS!!!~'

76 = FLIP 6 to 9 = 79 = '-DIED within '-HIS 79ᵗʰ YEAR of '-EXISTENCE!!!~'

1988 = 1+9+8/8 = 18/8 = 1(-)8/8 = ('-78) = '-AGE of '-DEATH for HUSBAND AMERICAN MUSICIAN & ACTOR / MEMBER of the BAND "THE MONKEES" ROBERT MICHAEL NESMITH!!!~'

'-WAS '-MARRIED to PHYLLIS BARBOUR NESMITH from 1964 to 1972 for 8 YEARS!!!~'

'-TOTAL of ('-20) YEARS '-MARRIED!!!~'

'-YEARS '-MARRIED = 12/8 = 1x2/8 = 2/8 = FLIP 2 to 7 = ('-78) = '-AGE of '-DEATH for HUSBAND AMERICAN MUSICIAN & ACTOR / MEMBER of the BAND "THE MONKEES" ROBERT MICHAEL NESMITH!!!~'

'-MOTHER BETTE NESMITH GRAHAM died at the AGE of ('-56) = 7x8 = ('-78) = '-AGE of '-DEATH for SON AMERICAN MUSICIAN & ACTOR / MEMBER of the BAND "THE MONKEES" ROBERT MICHAEL NESMITH!!!~'

'-SON; JASON NESMITH was '-BORN in 1968 = 19+68 = 87 = RECIPROCAL = ('-78) = '-AGE of '-DEATH for FATHER AMERICAN MUSICIAN & ACTOR / MEMBER of the BAND "THE MONKEES" ROBERT MICHAEL NESMITH!!!~'

ENGLISH MUSICIAN & DRUMMER of the ROLLING STONES CHARLES ROBERT WATTS died at the AGE of (`-80)!!!~'

`-WAS `-BORN in the `-MONTH of (`-6); and, `-DIED in the `-MONTH of (`-8) = (`-68) = `-BIRTH/DAY # `-NUMBER = "SEE `-BELOW"!!!~'

`-BIRTH/YEAR = 41 = 20+21 = `-DEATH/YEAR!!!~'

`-BIRTH/DAY # `-NUMBER = 6+2+19+41 = 68

`-BIRTH/DAY # `-NUMBER = 68 = `-DEATH/DAY = 8/24 = 8/2+4 = 86 = RECIPROCAL = 68

`-DEATH/DAY = 8/24 = HALF/RECIPROCAL = 8/42 = 8(-)42 = 34 X TIMES (`-2) = (`-68)!!!~'

`-DAUGHTER SERAPHINA WATTS was `-BORN in (`-68)!!!~'

`-DEATH/DAY # `-NUMBER = 8+24+20+21 = 73

68+73 = 141 = 1+1/4 = 24 = 8x3 = 83 = `-DAYS from `-BIRTH-to-DEATH!!!~'

6+8+7+3 = 24 = 8x3 = 83 = `-DAYS from `-BIRTH-to-DEATH!!!~'

FRAGMENTED `-BIRTH/DAY # `-NUMBER = 6+2+1+9+4+1 = 23

FRAGMENTED `-BIRTH/DAY # `-NUMBER = 23 = FLIP 2 to 7 = 73 = `-DEATH/DAY # `-NUMBER!!!~'

FRAGMENTED `-BIRTH/DAY # `-NUMBER = 23 = `-DEATH/DAY = 8+24 = 32 = RECIPROCAL = 23

FRAGMENTED `-DEATH/DAY # `-NUMBER = 8+2+4+2+0+2+1 = 19

23+19 = 42 = RECIPROCAL = 24 = 8x3 = 83 = `-DAYS from `-BIRTH-to-DEATH!!!~'

FROM `-BIRTH-to-DEATH there are 83 DAYS = "SEE `-ABOVE & `-BELOW"!!!~'

(365 (-) 83) = 282 = 2(-)82 = (`-80) = `-AGE of `-DEATH for ENGLISH MUSICIAN & DRUMMER of the ROLLING STONES CHARLES ROBERT WATTS!!!~'

(`-38) = RECIPROCAL = (`-83)!!!~'

`-DAUGHTER SERAPHINA WATTS was `-BORN on 3/18 = 38x1 = (`-38) = RECIPROCAL = (`-83)!!!~'

{3x18} = 54 = `-SHE is `-CURRENTLY (`-54) YEARS of `-AGE / RIGHT AFTER `-HER `-FATHER'S `-DEATH!!!~'

`-WIFE SHIRLEY ANN SHEPHERD was `-BORN in (`-38); and, was (`-8{3) years of age some 18} days after her husband's death = (1x8) = 8+0 = DAYS AWAY from the `-TIME of `-HER `-HUSBANDS `-DEATH / ENGLISH MUSICIAN & DRUMMER of the ROLLING STONES CHARLES ROBERT WATTS at the AGE of (`-80) = 8x10 = 8+10 = 18!!!~'

AMERICAN POLITICIAN JACQUELINE R. WALORSKI died at the AGE of (`-58)!!!~'

`-BIRTH/DAY # `-NUMBER = 8+17+19+63 = 107

`-BIRTH/DAY # `-NUMBER = 107 = 10+7 = 17 = FRAGMENTED `-DEATH/DAY # `-NUMBER!!!~'

`-DEATH/DAY # `-NUMBER = 8+3+20+22 = 53

`-DEATH/DAY # `-NUMBER = 53 = FLIP 3 to 8 = (`-58) = `-AGE of `-DEATH for AMERICAN POLITICIAN JACQUELINE R. WALORSKI!!!~'

107+53 = 160 = 1(-)60 = 59 = `-DIED within HER (`-59th) YEAR of EXISTENCE!!!~'

FRAGMENTED `-BIRTH/DAY # `-NUMBER = 8+1+7+1+9+6+3 = 35

FRAGMENTED `-BIRTH/DAY # `-NUMBER = 35 = RECIPROCAL = 53 = `-DEATH/DAY # `-NUMBER!!!~'

`-BIRTH/DAY # `-NUMBER = 107 (+) 35 = FRAGMENTED `-BIRTH/DAY # `-NUMBER = (`-142) = 1x42 = 42 = 20+22 = `-DEATH/YEAR!!!~'

FRAGMENTED `-DEATH/DAY # `-NUMBER = 8+3+2+0+2+2 = 17

FRAGMENTED `-DEATH/DAY # `-NUMBER = 17 = `-BIRTH/DAY # `-NUMBER = 107 = 10+7 = 17

35+17 = 52 = `-BIRTH/DAY = 8+17 = 25 = RECIPROCAL = 52!!!~'

`-BIRTH/DAY = 8/17 = 8/1+7 = 8/8

`-DEATH/DAY = 8/3 = FLIP 3 to 8 = 8/8

`-BIRTH/DAY = 8/17 = 8/1+7 = 8/8 = FLIP 8 to 3 = 8/3 = `-DEATH/DAY!!!~'

`-REPRESENTATIVE in 2$^{ND}$ DISTRICT SINCE 2013 = 20+13 = 33 = FLIP 3 to 8 = 8/3 = `-DEATH/DAY!!!~'

`-REPRESENTATIVE in 2$^{ND}$ DISTRICT SINCE 2013 = 20+13 = 33 = FLIP 3 to 8 = 8/8 = `-BIRTH/DAY = 8/1+7!!!~'

`-BIRTH/DAY = 8x17 = 136 = 1x36 = 36 = RECIPROCAL = 63 = `-BIRTH/YEAR!!!~'

`-DEATH/DAY = 8x3 = 24 = RECIPROCAL = 42 = 20+22 = `-DEATH/YEAR!!!~'

FROM `-BIRTH-to-DEATH there are 14 DAYS = `-MARRIED in 1995 to DEAN SWIHART = 19+95 = 114 = 1x14 = 14!!!~'

FROM `-BIRTH-to-DEATH there are 14 DAYS = 2x7 = 27 = `-MARRIED for (`-27) YEARS!!!~'

`-MARRIED in 95 = RECIPROCAL = 59 = `-DIED within HER (`-59th) YEAR of EXISTENCE!!!~'

`-MARRIED in 19/95 = 19-95 = 76 = 7x6 = 42 = 20+22 = `-DEATH/YEAR!!!~'

(365 (-) 14) = 351 = 35x1 = 35 = FRAGMENTED `-BIRTH/DAY # `-NUMBER = RECIPROCAL = 53 = `-DEATH/DAY # `-NUMBER!!!~'

`-BIRTH/YEAR = 1963 = 1+9+6/3 = 16/3 = 1(-)6/3 = 53 = `-DEATH/DAY # `-NUMBER!!!~'

`-BIRTH/YEAR = 1963 = 1+9+6/3 = 16/3 = 16(-)3 = 13 = 5+8 = (`-58) = `-AGE of `-DEATH for AMERICAN POLITICIAN JACQUELINE R. WALORSKI!!!~'

`-WAS `-BORN in the `-MONTH of (`-8); and, `-DIED in the `-MONTH of (`-8) = (`-88) = 2(8's) = 28 = RECIPROCAL = 82 = BIRTH/YEAR = 19+63 = 82!!!~'

AMERICAN ACTOR/OPERA SINGER PAUL ANTHONY SORVINO died at the AGE of (`-83)!!!~'

`-AGE of `-DEATH = 83 = 8x3 = 24 = RECIPROCAL = 42 = 20+22 = DEATH/YEAR!!!~'

`-BIRTH/DAY # `-NUMBER = 4+13+19+39 = 75

`-BIRTH/DAY # `-NUMBER = 75 = DEATH/DAY = 7(2)5

`-BIRTH/DAY = 4/13 = 4x13 = 52 = RECIPROCAL = 25 = `-DAY of `-DEATH (`-25th)!!!~'

`-BIRTH/DAY = 4/13 = 4/1+3 = (`-44) = `-SON; AMERICAN ACTOR, MICHAEL ERNEST SORVINO was (`-44) YEARS of `-AGE at the `-TIME of `-HIS `-FATHER'S `-DEATH!!!~'

`-BIRTH/DAY = 4/13 = 4(-)1/3 = 3/3 = 33 = FLIP 3 to 8 = (`-83) = `-AGE of `-DEATH for AMERICAN ACTOR/OPERA SINGER PAUL ANTHONY SORVINO!!!~'

`-DEATH/DAY # `-NUMBER = 7+25+20+22 = 74

`-DEATH/DAY = 7/25 = 7x25 = 175 = 1x75 = 75 = `-BIRTH/DAY # `-NUMBER!!!~'

`-DEATH/DAY = 7/25 = FLIP 7 to 2 = 2/25 = RECIPROCAL = 52/2 = 52+2 = (`-54) = `-DAUGHTER; AMERICAN ACTRESS, MIRA KATHERINE SORVINO was (`-54) YEARS of `-AGE at the `-TIME of `-HER `-FATHER'S `-DEATH!!!-'

75+74 = 149 = 14+9 = (`-23) = "SEE `-SON & `-DAUGHTER & `-BELOW"!!!-'

75+74 = 149 = FLIP 9 to 6 = 146 = 1(-)6/4 = (`-54) = `-DAUGHTER; AMERICAN ACTRESS, MIRA KATHERINE SORVINO was (`-54) YEARS of `-AGE at the `-TIME of `-HER `-FATHER'S `-DEATH!!!-'

FRAGMENTED `-BIRTH/DAY # `-NUMBER = 4+1+3+1+9+3+9 = 30

FRAGMENTED `-DEATH/DAY # `-NUMBER = 7+2+5+2+0+2+2 = 20

30+20 = 50 = DEATH/DAY = 7/25 = FLIP 7 to 2 = 2/25 = 2x25 = (`-50)!!!-'

30/20 = HALF/RECIPROCAL = 3(00)2 = `-DEATH/DAY = 7/25 = 7+25 = (`-32)!!!-'

FROM `-BIRTH-to-DEATH there are 103 DAYS = 10+3 = (`-13) = "A VERY `-PIVOTAL `-NUMBER"!!!-'

FROM `-BIRTH-to-DEATH there are 103 DAYS = 10x3 = 30 = FRAGMENTED `-BIRTH/DAY # `-NUMBER!!!-'

(365 (-) 103) = 262 = HEIGHT was 6' 2"!!!-'

(365 (-) 103) = 262 = 26x2 = 52 = RECIPROCAL = 25 = `-DAY of `-DEATH (`-25th)!!!-'

(365 (-) 103) = 262 = 2x62 = 124 = 1(-)24 = (`-23) = "SEE `-ABOVE & `-BELOW"!!!~'

`-BIRTH/YEAR = 1939 = 1-9/3+9 = 8/12 = 8/1+2 = (`-83) = `-AGE of `-DEATH for AMERICAN ACTOR/OPERA SINGER PAUL ANTHONY SORVINO!!!~'

`-DAUGHTER; AMERICAN ACTRESS, MIRA KATHERINE SORVINO has a `-BIRTH/DAY # `-NUMBER of = 9+28+19+67 = (`-123) = FLIP 2 to 7 = 173 = 1+7/3 = (`-83) = `-AGE of `-DEATH for `-FATHER AMERICAN ACTOR/OPERA SINGER PAUL ANTHONY SORVINO!!!~'

`-HER `-BIRTH/YEAR = 19/67 = 1-9/6+7 = 8/13 = 83x1 = (`-83) = `-AGE of `-DEATH for `-FATHER AMERICAN ACTOR/ OPERA SINGER PAUL ANTHONY SORVINO!!!~'

`-WAS `-MARRIED to DEE DEE BENKIE from 2014 to 2022 for (`-8) `-YEARS!!!~'

`-WAS `-MARRIED to VANESSA ARICO from 1991 to 1996 for (`-5) `-YEARS!!!~'

`-WAS `-MARRIED to LORRAINE DAVIS from 1966 to 1988 for (`-22) `-YEARS!!!~'

`-MARRIED for (`-35) `-YEARS `-TOTAL = RECIPROCAL = (`-53)!!!~'

35+53 = (`-88) = FLIP 8 to 3 = (`-83) = `-AGE of `-DEATH for `-HUSBAND AMERICAN ACTOR/OPERA SINGER PAUL ANTHONY SORVINO!!!~'

(`-35) = 7x5 = (`-75) = `-BIRTH/DAY # `-NUMBER!!!~'

`-DIVORCED `-LORRAINE DAVIS in (`-88) = FLIP 8 to 3 = (`-83) = `-AGE of `-DEATH for `-HUSBAND AMERICAN ACTOR/ OPERA SINGER PAUL ANTHONY SORVINO!!!~'

`-SON'S; `-BIRTH/DAY = 11+21 = (`-32) = RECIPROCAL = (`-23)!!!~'

`-SON; AMERICAN ACTOR, MICHAEL ERNEST SORVINO has a `-BIRTH/DAY # `-NUMBER of = 11+21+19+77 = 128 = RECIPROCAL = 821 = 82+1 = (`-83) = `-AGE of `-DEATH for `-FATHER AMERICAN ACTOR/OPERA SINGER PAUL ANTHONY SORVINO!!!~'

`-SON; AMERICAN ACTOR, MICHAEL ERNEST SORVINO has a `-BIRTH/DAY # `-NUMBER of = 11+21+19+77 = (`-128) = {FLIP 8 to 3} = (`-123) = `-DAUGHTER; AMERICAN ACTRESS, MIRA KATHERINE SORVINO has a `-BIRTH/DAY # `-NUMBER of = 9+28+19+67 = (`-123)!!!~'

AMERICAN IFBB PROFESSIONAL BODYBUILDER CEDRIC MCMILLAN died at the AGE of (`-44)!!!~'

`-PARTIAL `-BIRTH/DAY # `-NUMBER in `-REVERSE = 77(-)19(-)17 = 41 = `-FIRST `-PART of `-DEATH/DAY!!!~'

`-BIRTH/DAY # `-NUMBER = 8+17+19+77 = 121

`-DAY of `-BIRTH = 17 = `-DAY of `-DEATH = 12 = FLIP 2 to 7 = 17

`-BIRTH/DAY = 8/17 = 8+17 = 25 = `-DEATH/DAY = 4/12 = HALF RECIPROCAL = 4/21 = 4+21 = (`-25)!!!~'

`-BIRTH/YEAR = 19/77 = 19-77 = 58 = `-DEATH/DAY # `-NUMBER = (`-58)!!!~'

`-DEATH/DAY # `-NUMBER = 4+12+20+22 = 58

121+58 = 179 = `-BIRTH/DAY = 8/17 = HALF RECIPROCAL = 8/71 = 8+71 = 79 = 1x79 = (`-179)!!!~'

`-DEATH/DAY = 4/12 = 4+12 = 16 = 4x4 = (`-44) = `-AGE of `-DEATH for AMERICAN IFBB PROFESSIONAL BODYBUILDER CEDRIC MCMILLAN!!!~'

FRAGMENTED `-BIRTH/DAY # `-NUMBER = 8+1+7+1+9+7+7 = 40

FRAGMENTED `-BIRTH/DAY # `-NUMBER = 40 = 5x8 = (`-58) = `-DEATH/DAY # `-NUMBER!!!~'

FRAGMENTED `-DEATH/DAY # `-NUMBER = 4+1+2+2+0+2+2 = 13

`-DEATH/DAY # `-NUMBER = (`-58) (-) (`-13) = FRAGMENTED `-DEATH/DAY # `-NUMBER = (`-45) = `-DIED the `-VERY `-YEAR `-PRIOR at the `-AGE of (`-44)!!!~'

FRAGMENTED `-DEATH/DAY # `-NUMBER = 13 = `-BIRTH/DAY # `-NUMBER = 121 = 1/2+1 = 13

40/13 = 4+0/1+3 = (`-44) = `-AGE of `-DEATH for AMERICAN IFBB PROFESSIONAL BODYBUILDER CEDRIC MCMILLAN!!!~'

40+13 = 53 = FLIP 3 to 8 = 58 = `-DEATH/DAY # `-NUMBER = (`-58)!!!~'

FROM `-BIRTH-to-DEATH there are 127 DAYS = 12x7 = 84 = RECIPROCAL = 48 = `-DEATH/DAY = 4x12 = 48!!!~'

(365 (-) 127) = 238 = 2x38 = 76 = 7x6 = 42 = 20+22 = `-DEATH/YEAR!!!~'

(365 (-) 127) = 238 = 2+38 = 40 = FRAGMENTED `-BIRTH/DAY # `-NUMBER = (`-40)!!!~'

(`-40) = 4+0 = (`-4) = `-DIED at the `-AGE of (`-44) with having (`-4) `-CHILDREN!!!~'

FROM `-BIRTH-to-DEATH there are 127 DAYS = 12x7 = 84 = `-WAS `-BORN in the `-MONTH of (`-8); and, `-DIED in the `-MONTH of (`-4)!!!~'

`-BIRTH/YEAR = 1977 = 1+9/7+7 = 10/14 = 10+14 = 24 = RECIPROCAL = 42 = 20+22 = `-DEATH/YEAR!!!~'

`-BIRTH/YEAR = 1977 = 1+9/7+7 = 10/14 = 10+14 = 24 = 2(4's) = (`-44) = `-AGE of `-DEATH for AMERICAN IFBB PROFESSIONAL BODYBUILDER CEDRIC MCMILLAN!!!~'

GERMAN-BORN AMERICAN ACTOR GEORGE BARTENIEF died at the AGE of (`-89)!!!~'

`-AGE of `-DEATH = (`-89) = 8x9 = (`-72) = FLIP 2 to 7 = (`-77) = `-BIRTH/DAY # `-NUMBER!!!~'

`-BIRTH/DAY # `-NUMBER = 1+24+19+33 = 77

`-BIRTH/DAY # `-NUMBER = 77 = 7+7 = 14 = 7x2 = 72 = 8x9 = (`-89) = `-AGE of `-DEATH for GERMAN-BORN AMERICAN ACTOR GEORGE BARTENIEF!!!~'

`-BIRTH/YEAR = 1933 = 19-33 = 14 = 7x2 = 72 = 8x9 = (`-89) = `-AGE of `-DEATH for GERMAN-BORN AMERICAN ACTOR GEORGE BARTENIEF!!!~'

`-BIRTH/DAY # `-NUMBER = 77 = 7x7 = 49 = RECIPROCAL = 94 = `-WAS `-MARRIED to KAREN MALPEDE in (`-94)!!!~'

`-BIRTH/DAY = 1/24 = 1+24 = 25 = RECIPROCAL = 52 = 19+33 = `-BIRTH/YEAR!!!~'

`-BIRTH/DAY = 1/24 = HALF RECIPROCAL = 1/42 = 1+42 = 43 X TIMES (`-2) = 86 = FLIP 6 to 9 = (`-89) = `-AGE of `-DEATH for GERMAN-BORN AMERICAN ACTOR GEORGE BARTENIEF!!!~'

`-DEATH/DAY # `-NUMBER = 7+30+20+22 = 79

`-DEATH/DAY # `-NUMBER = 79 = 7+9 = 16 = FRAGMENTED `-DEATH/DAY # `-NUMBER!!!~'

`-DEATH/DAY # `-NUMBER = 79 = 7x9 = 63 = RECIPROCAL = 36 = 4x9 = 49 = 7x7 = 77 = `-BIRTH/DAY # `-NUMBER!!!~'

77+79 = 156 = RECIPROCAL = 651 = 6x51 = 306 = 30+6 = 36 = FLIP 3 to 8; FLIP 6 to 9 = (`-89) = `-AGE of `-DEATH for GERMAN-BORN AMERICAN ACTOR GEORGE BARTENIEF!!!~'

`-DEATH/DAY = 7/30 = 7(-)30 = (`-23) = FRAGMENTED `-BIRTH/DAY # `-NUMBER = (`-23)!!!~'

FRAGMENTED `-BIRTH/DAY # `-NUMBER = 1+2+4+1+9+3+3 = 23

FRAGMENTED `-BIRTH/DAY # `-NUMBER = 23 = FLIP 2 to 7; FLIP 3 to 8 = (`-78) = "SEE `-BELOW on `-BIRTH-to-DEATH # `-NUMBERS"!!!~'

FRAGMENTED `-BIRTH/DAY # `-NUMBER = 23 = `-DEATH/DAY = 7/30 = FLIP 7 to 2 = 2/30 = 2+30 = (`-32) = RECIPROCAL = (`-23)!!!~'

FRAGMENTED `-BIRTH/DAY # `-NUMBER = 23 = `-DEATH/DAY = 7/30 = 7+30 = 37 = RECIPROCAL = 73 = FLIP 7 to 2 = (`-23)!!!~'

FRAGMENTED `-DEATH/DAY # `-NUMBER = 7+3+0+2+0+2+2 = 16

(`-16) = RECIPROCAL = (`-61)

16+61 = (`-77) = `-BIRTH/DAY # `-NUMBER!!!~'

23+16 = 39 = FLIP 3 to 8 = (`-89) = `-AGE of `-DEATH for GERMAN-BORN AMERICAN ACTOR GEORGE BARTENIEF!!!~'

FROM `-BIRTH-to-DEATH there are 187 DAYS = RECIPROCAL = 781 = 7/8+1 = (`-79) = `-DEATH/DAY # `-NUMBER!!!~'

FROM `-BIRTH-to-DEATH there are 187 DAYS = 1+87 = 88 = 2(8's) = 28 = `-FROM MARRIAGE to KAREN MALPEDE for 28 `-YEARS since `-1994!!!~'

FROM `-BIRTH-to-DEATH there are 187 DAYS = 1+87 = 88 = `-BIRTH/YEAR = (`-33) = FLIP 3 to 8 = (`-88)!!!~'

(365 (-) 187) = 178 = `-BIRTH/DAY # `-NUMBER (`-77) (+) (`-79) = `-DEATH/DAY # `-NUMBER = 156 / (`-DIVIDED by) (`-2) = (`-78) = 1x78 = (`-178)!!!~'

FROM `-BIRTH-to-DEATH there are 187 DAYS = 1(-)87 = 86 = FLIP 6 to 9 = (`-89) = `-AGE of `-DEATH for GERMAN-BORN AMERICAN ACTOR GEORGE BARTENIEF!!!~'

BRITISH/AUSTRALIAN SINGER/ACTRESS OLIVIA NEWTON-JOHN died at the AGE of (`-73)!!!~'

`-WAS `-BORN in the `-MONTH of (`-9); and, `-DIED in the `-MONTH of (`-8) = (`-98) = RECIPROCAL = (`-89) = FLIP 9 to 6 = (`-86) = `-BIRTH/YEAR of `-DAUGHTER CHLOE ROSE LATTANZI!!!~'

`-AGE of `-DEATH = 73 = FLIP 7 to 2; FLIP 3 to 8 = 28 = 2(8's) = (`-88) = `-DEATH/DAY!!!~'

`-BIRTH/DAY # `-NUMBER = 9+26+19+48 = 102

`-BIRTH/DAY # `-NUMBER = 102 = RECIPROCAL = 201 = 20+1 = 21 = 7x3 = (`-73) = `-AGE of `-DEATH for BRITISH/AUSTRALIAN SINGER/ACTRESS OLIVIA NEWTON-JOHN!!!~'

`-DEATH/DAY # `-NUMBER = 8+8+20+22 = 58

`-HUSBAND JOHN EASTERLING's `-BIRTH/DAY # `-NUMBER = 4+10+19+52 = 85 = RECIPROCAL = 58

`-FORMER `-HUSBAND MATT LATTANZI `-BIRTH/YEAR = 1959 = 19(-)59 = 40 = 5x8 = `-DEATH/DAY # `-NUMBER!!!~'

`-BIRTH/DAY = 9/26 = 9+26 = 35 = RECIPROCAL = 53 = FLIP 3 to 8 = (`-58) = `-DEATH/DAY # `-NUMBER!!!~'

102+58 = 160 = 16+0 = 16 = 8+8 = `-DEATH/DAY!!!~'

102(-)58 = 44 = 4x4 = 16 = 8+8 = `-DEATH/DAY!!!~'

FRAGMENTED `-BIRTH/DAY # `-NUMBER = 9+2+6+1+9+4+8 = 39

FRAGMENTED `-BIRTH/DAY # `-NUMBER = 39 = 3x9 = 27 = RECIPROCAL = 72 = 7/1+1 = RECIPROCAL = 1/17 = DAUGHTER'S `-BIRTH/DAY!!!~'

`-BIRTH/DAY # `-NUMBER = 102 (-) 39 = FRAGMENTED `-BIRTH/DAY # `-NUMBER = (`-63) = "SEE `-ABOVE & `-BELOW"!!!~'

FRAGMENTED `-BIRTH/DAY # `-NUMBER = (`-39) = FLIP 9 to 6 = (`-36) = RECIPROCAL = (`-63)!!!~'

FRAGMENTED `-DEATH/DAY # `-NUMBER = 8+8+2+0+2+2 = 22

FRAGMENTED `-DEATH/DAY # `-NUMBER = 22 = FLIP 2 to 7 = 72 = 7/1+1 = RECIPROCAL = 1/17 = DAUGHTER'S `-BIRTH/DAY!!!~'

`-DEATH/DAY # `-NUMBER = 58 (-) 22 = FRAGMENTED `-DEATH/DAY # `-NUMBER = (`-36) = "SEE `-ABOVE & BELOW"!!!~'

(`-63) = RECIPROCAL = (`-36)!!!~'

39(-)22 = 17 = `-DAUGHTER'S `-DAY of `-BIRTH = (`-17th)!!!~'

39+22 = 61 = RECIPROCAL = 16 = 8+8 = `-DEATH/DAY!!!~'

`-BIRTH/DAY = 9/26 = 9(-)26 = 17 = `-DAUGHTER'S `-DAY of `-BIRTH = (`-17ᵗʰ)!!!~'

FROM `-BIRTH-to-DEATH there are 49 DAYS = `-DAUGHTER'S `-BIRTH/DAY # `-NUMBER in `-REVERSE = 86(-)19(-)17(-)1 = (`-49)!!!~'

FROM `-BIRTH-to-DEATH there are 49 DAYS = 4x9 = 36 = `-AGE of `-DAUGHTER at `-HER (MOTHER'S) `-TIME of `-DEATH BRITISH/AUSTRALIAN SINGER/ACTRESS OLIVIA NEWTON-JOHN!!!~'

FROM `-BIRTH-to-DEATH there are 49 DAYS = 4x9 = 36 = RECIPROCAL = 63 = `-AGE of `-FORMER `-HUSBAND MATT LATTANZI at the `-TIME of `-HIS `-FORMER WIFE'S `-DEATH!!!~'

(365 (-) 49) = 316 = 3x16 = (`-48) = `-BIRTH/YEAR!!!~'

(365 (-) 49) = 316 = 36x1 = 36 = `-AGE of `-DAUGHTER at `-HER (MOTHER'S) `-TIME of `-DEATH BRITISH/AUSTRALIAN SINGER/ACTRESS OLIVIA NEWTON-JOHN!!!~'

(365 (-) 49) = 316 = 36x1 = 36 = RECIPROCAL = 63 = `-AGE of `-FORMER `-HUSBAND MATT LATTANZI at the `-TIME of `-HIS `-FORMER WIFE'S `-DEATH!!!~'

(`-36) = RECIPROCAL = (`-63) = `-AGE of `-FATHER & `-DAUGHTER at `-TIME of `-FORMER `-WIFE & `-MOTHER'S `-DEATH BRITISH/AUSTRALIAN SINGER/ACTRESS OLIVIA NEWTON-JOHN!!!~'

(365 (-) 49) = 316 = 31x6 = 186 = 1x86 = 86 = `-BIRTH/YEAR of `-DAUGHTER!!!~'

`-DAUGHTER'S `-BIRTH/YEAR = (`-86) = FLIP 8 to 3 = (`-36) = AT `-AGE of `-HER `-MOTHER'S `-DEATH!!!~'

`-BIRTH/YEAR = 1948 = 1(-)8/9+4 = 7/13 = 73x1 = (`-73) = `-AGE of `-DEATH for BRITISH/AUSTRALIAN SINGER/ACTRESS OLIVIA NEWTON-JOHN!!!~'

`-BIRTH/YEAR = 1948 = 19+48 = (67) = 6x7 = 42 = 20+22 = `-DEATH/YEAR!!!~'

`-DAUGHTER `-BIRTH/YEAR = 1986 = 19-86 = 67

`-DIVORCED MATT LATTANZI in 1995 = 19(-)95 = 76 = RECIPROCAL = 67

6{7x3} = 201 = RECIPROCAL = 102 = `-BIRTH/DAY # `-NUMBER of BRITISH/AUSTRALIAN SINGER/ACTRESS OLIVIA NEWTON-JOHN!!!~"

`-DAUGHTER CHLOE ROSE LATTANZI's `-BIRTH/DAY # `-NUMBER = 1+17+19+86 = (`-123) = 1x23 = 23 = FLIP 2 to 7 = (`-73) = `-AGE of `-DEATH of `-MOTHER BRITISH/AUSTRALIAN SINGER/ACTRESS OLIVIA NEWTON-JOHN!!!~"

`-DAUGHTER CHLOE ROSE LATTANZI's `-BIRTH/DAY # `-NUMBER = 1+17+19+86 = (`-123) = 12x3 = (`-36) = `-AGE at `-TIME of `-MOTHER'S `-DEATH!!!~'

`-BIRTH/DAY = 9/26 = 9/2+6 = 98 = 9x8 = 72 = 7/1+1 = RECIPROCAL = 1/17 = DAUGHTER'S `-BIRTH/DAY!!!~'

DEATH/MONTH = AUGUST = 31 DAYS

(31(-)8) – DAY of DEATH = 23 = FLIP 2 to 7 = (`-73) = `-AGE of `-DEATH for BRITISH/AUSTRALIAN SINGER/ACTRESS OLIVIA NEWTON-JOHN!!!~'

`-WAS `-MARRIED to JOHN EASTERLING from 2008 to 2022 for 14 YEARS!!!~'

(`-2008) = 20+08 = 28 = 2(8's) = (`-8/8) = `-DEATH/DAY!!!~'

`-WAS `-MARRIED to MATT LATTANZI from 1984 to 1995 for 11 YEARS!!!~'

(`-84) = RECIPROCAL = (`-48) = `-BIRTH/YEAR!!!~'

MATT LATTANZI `-BIRTH/YEAR = 1959 = 19+59 = 78 = FLIP 8 to 3 = (`-73) = `-AGE of `-DEATH for `-FORMER `-WIFE BRITISH/AUSTRALIAN SINGER/ACTRESS OLIVIA NEWTON-JOHN!!!~'

MATT LATTANZI `-BIRTH/DAY = 2/1 = (`-21) = 7x3 = (`-73) = `-AGE of `-DEATH for `-FORMER `-WIFE BRITISH/AUSTRALIAN SINGER/ACTRESS OLIVIA NEWTON-JOHN!!!~'

`-MARRIED for a `-TOTAL of (14+11) YEARS = (`-25) = 2x5 = 10 = 7+3 = (`-73) = `-AGE of `-DEATH for `-WIFE BRITISH/AUSTRALIAN SINGER/ACTRESS OLIVIA NEWTON-JOHN!!!~'

AMERICAN AUTHOR-NARRATOR-HISTORIAN DAVID GAUB MCCULLOUGH died at the AGE of (`-89)!!!~'

`-WAS `-BORN in the `-MONTH of (`-7); and, `-DIED in the `-MONTH of (`-8) = (`-78) = RECIPROCAL = (`-8/7) = `-DEATH/DAY!!!~'

`-BIRTH/DAY # `-NUMBER = 7+7+19+33 = 66

`-BIRTH/DAY # `-NUMBER = 66 = 6x6 = 36 = FLIP 3 to 8; FLIP 6 to 9 = (`-89) = `-AGE of `-DEATH for AMERICAN AUTHOR-NARRATOR-HISTORIAN DAVID GAUB MCCULLOUGH!!!~'

`-BIRTH/DAY = 7/7 = 7x7 = 49 = 4x9 = 36 = FLIP 3 to 8; FLIP 6 to 9 = (`-89) = `-AGE of `-DEATH for AMERICAN AUTHOR-NARRATOR-HISTORIAN DAVID GAUB MCCULLOUGH!!!~'

`-BIRTH/YEAR = 19/33 = 19x33 = 627 = 6+2/7 = (`-8/7) = `-DEATH/DAY!!!~'

`-DEATH/DAY # `-NUMBER = 8+7+20+22 = 57

`-BIRTH/YEAR = 1933 = 19+33 = 52 = FLIP 2 to 7 = 57 = `-DEATH/DAY # `-NUMBER!!!~'

66+57 = 123 = "PROPHETIC-LINEAR-PROGRESSION-PLP"!!!~'

66+57 = 123 = 1+2/3 = (`-33) = `-BIRTH/YEAR!!!~'

FRAGMENTED `-BIRTH/DAY # `-NUMBER = 7+7+1+9+3+3 = 30

FRAGMENTED `-BIRTH/DAY # `-NUMBER = 30 = 3+0 = (`-3) `-KIDS/CHILDREN!!!~'

`-BIRTH/DAY # `-NUMBER = (`-66) (-) (`-30) = FRAGMENTED `-BIRTH/DAY # `-NUMBER = (`-36) = FLIP 3 to 8; FLIP 6 to 9 = (`-89) = `-AGE of `-DEATH for AMERICAN

AUTHOR-NARRATOR-HISTORIAN DAVID GAUB MCCULLOUGH!!!~'

FRAGMENTED `-DEATH/DAY # `-NUMBER = 8+7+2+0+ 2+2 = 21

FRAGMENTED `-DEATH/DAY # `-NUMBER = 21 = 2+1 = (`-3) `-KIDS/CHILDREN!!!~'

`-DEATH/DAY # `-NUMBER = (`-57) (-) (`-21) = FRAGMENTED `-DEATH/DAY # `-NUMBER = (`-36) = FLIP 3 to 8; FLIP 6 to 9 = (`-89) = `-AGE of `-DEATH for AMERICAN AUTHOR-NARRATOR-HISTORIAN DAVID GAUB MCCULLOUGH!!!~'

30(-)21 = 9 = 3+6 = 36 = FLIP 3 to 8; FLIP 6 to 9 = (`-89) = `-AGE of `-DEATH for AMERICAN AUTHOR-NARRATOR-HISTORIAN DAVID GAUB MCCULLOUGH!!!~'

FROM `-BIRTH-to-DEATH there are 31 DAYS = RECIPROCAL = 13 = 4+9 = 49 = 7x7 = 7/7 = `-BIRTH/DAY!!!~'

(365 (-) 31) = 334 = FLIP 3 to 8 = 8/34 = 8/3+4 = 8/7 = `-DEATH/ DAY!!!~'

`-AGE of `-DEATH = (`-89) = 8x9 = 72 = FLIP 2 to 7 = (`-7/7) = `-BIRTH/DAY!!!~'

`-BIRTH/YEAR = (`-33) = FLIP 3 to 8 = (`-88) = `-WAS this `-AGE of (`-88) in `-HIS `-YEAR of `-DEATH!!!~'

`-MONTH of `-BIRTH was JULY with 31 DAYS....

(31 (-) 7) – DAY of `-BIRTH = 24 = RECIPROCAL = 42 = 20+22 = `-DEATH/YEAR!!!~'

`-BIRTH/YEAR = 19/33 = 1(-)9/3x3 = (`-89) = `-AGE of `-DEATH for AMERICAN AUTHOR-NARRATOR-HISTORIAN DAVID GAUB MCCULLOUGH!!!~'

AMERICAN SINGER-SONGWRITER LAMONT HERBERT DOZIER died at the AGE of (`-81)!!!~'

`-BIRTH/DAY # `-NUMBER = 6+16+19+41 = 82

`-BIRTH/DAY # `-NUMBER = 82 = `-DIED within (`-82) YEARS of `-EXISTING `-DYING the `-VERY `-YEAR `-PRIOR!!!~'

`-BIRTH/DAY # `-NUMBER = 82 = RECIPROCAL = 28 = 2(8's) = (`-88) = `-DEATH/DAY!!!~'

`-BIRTH/DAY # `-NUMBER = 82 = 8x2 = 16 = 8+8 = 8/8 = `-DEATH/DAY!!!~'

`-BIRTH/DAY = 6x16 = 96 = FLIP 6 to 9 = 99 = 9x9 = (`-81) = `-AGE of `-DEATH for AMERICAN SINGER-SONGWRITER LAMONT HERBERT DOZIER!!!~'

`-BIRTH/DAY = 6/16 = HALF RECIPROCAL = 6/61 = 6+61 = 67 = 6x7 = 42 = 20+22 = `-DEATH/YEAR!!!~'

`-BIRTH/DAY = 6/16 = 6/1+6 = 6/7 = 6x7 = 42 = 20+22 = `-DEATH/YEAR!!!~'

`-DEATH/DAY # `-NUMBER = 8+8+20+22 = 58

`-DEATH/DAY # `-NUMBER = 58 = 5x8 = 40 X TIMES (`-2) = (`-80) = (`-53) DAYS from = FLIP 3 to 8 = (`-58)

`-DEATH/DAY = 8/8 = 8+8 = 16 = `-DAY of `-BIRTH = 16ᵗʰ!!!~'

82+58 = 140 = 14+0 = 14 = RECIPROCAL = 41 = `-BIRTH/ YEAR!!!~'

82(-)58 = 24 = RECIPROCAL = 42 = 20+22 = `-DEATH/YEAR!!!~'

FRAGMENTED `-BIRTH/DAY # `-NUMBER = 6+1+6+1+9+4+1 = 28

FRAGMENTED `-BIRTH/DAY # `-NUMBER = 28 = 2(8's) = (`-88) = `-DEATH/DAY!!!~'

FRAGMENTED `-BIRTH/DAY # `-NUMBER = 28 = RECIPROCAL = (`-82) = `-DIED within (`-82) YEARS of `-EXISTING `-DYING the `-VERY `-YEAR `-PRIOR!!!~'

FRAGMENTED `-DEATH/DAY # `-NUMBER = 8+8+2+0+ 2+2 = 22

`-DEATH/DAY # `-NUMBER = (`-58) (-) (`-22) = FRAGMENTED `-DEATH/DAY # `-NUMBER = (`-36) = 3x6 = (`-18) = RECIPROCAL = (`-81) = `-AGE of `-DEATH for AMERICAN SINGER-SONGWRITER LAMONT HERBERT DOZIER!!!~'

`-DEATH/DAY # `-NUMBER = (`-58) (+) (`-22) = FRAGMENTED `-DEATH/DAY # `-NUMBER = (`-80) = `-DIED the `-VERY `-YEAR `-AFTER at the `-AGE of (`-81)!!!~'

FRAGMENTED `-DEATH/DAY # `-NUMBER = 22 = `-BIRTH/ DAY = 6+16 = 22

28+22 = 50 = `-MARRIED for SOME (`-51) YEARS!!!~'

28(-)22 = 6 = FLIP 6 to 9 = 9 = 8+1 = (`-81) = `-AGE of `-DEATH for AMERICAN SINGER-SONGWRITER LAMONT HERBERT DOZIER!!!~'

FROM `-BIRTH-to-DEATH there are 53 DAYS = FLIP 3 to 8 = (`-58) = `-DEATH/DAY # `-NUMBER!!!~'

(365 (-) 53) = 312 = 3+1/2 = (`-42) = `-WAS `-MARRIED to BARBARA ULLMAN DOZIER for (`-42) YEARS!!!~'

(365 (-) 53) = 312 = 3+1/2 = (`-42) = 20+22 = `-DEATH/YEAR!!!~'

(365 (-) 53) = 312 = 3x12 = 36 = 3x6 = 18 = RECIPROCAL = (`-81) = `-AGE of `-DEATH for AMERICAN SINGER-SONGWRITER LAMONT HERBERT DOZIER!!!~'

`-WAS `-MARRIED to BARBARA ULLMAN DOZIER from 1980 to 2022 for 42 YEARS!!!~'

42 = 20+22 = `-DEATH/YEAR!!!~'

1980 = 1(-)9/8+0 = 8/8 = `-DEATH/DAY!!!~'

`-WAS `-MARRIED to ELIZABETH ANN DOZIER from 1959 to 1968 for 9 YEARS!!!~'

1959 = 19(-)59 = 40 X TIMES (`-2) = (`-80) = `-NEXT `-MARRIAGE!!!~'

(`-9) = 8+1 = (`-81) = `-AGE of `-DEATH for AMERICAN SINGER-SONGWRITER LAMONT HERBERT DOZIER!!!~'

`-WAS `-BORN in the `-MONTH of (`-6); and, `-DIED in the `-MONTH of (`-8) = (`-68) = `-DIVORCED ELIZABETH ANN DOZIER in (`-68)!!!~'

`-BIRTH/DAY = 6/16 = 6/1x6 = 6/6

`-DEATH/DAY = 8/8

`-MARRIED for a `-TOTAL of SOME (`-51) YEARS!!!~'

42(-)9 = 33 = FLIP 3 to 8 = 8/8 = `-DEATH/DAY!!!~'

(`-51) = 5+1 = 6 = FLIP 6 to 9 = 9 = 8+1 = (`-81) = `-AGE of `-DEATH for AMERICAN SINGER-SONGWRITER LAMONT HERBERT DOZIER!!!~'

JAPANESE FASHION DESIGNER ISSEY MIYAKE died at the AGE of (`-84)!!!~'

`-WAS `-BORN in the `-MONTH of (`-4); and, `-DIED in the `-MONTH of (`-8) = (`-48) = RECIPROCAL = (`-84) = `-AGE of `-DEATH for JAPANESE FASHION DESIGNER ISSEY MIYAKE!!!~'

`-BIRTH/YEAR = (`-38) = RECIPROCAL = (`-83) = `-BIRTH/ DAY # `-NUMBER!!!~'

`-BIRTH/YEAR = 3x8 = 8x3 = 24 = RECIPROCAL = 42 = 20+22 = `-DEATH/YEAR!!!~'

`-BIRTH/DAY # `-NUMBER = 4+22+19+38 = 83

`-BIRTH/DAY # `-NUMBER = 83 = `-WAS (`-83) / 105 DAYS `-PRIOR before `-DEATH!!!~'

`-BIRTH/DAY # `-NUMBER = (`-83) = `-DIED the `-VERY `-NEXT `-YEAR `-AFTER at the `-AGE of (`-84)!!!~'

`-BIRTH/DAY = 4/22 = 4/2(-)2 = 4/0 = `-DEATH/DAY = 8/5 = 8x5 = (`-40)!!!-'

`-BIRTH/DAY = 4/22 = 4(-)22 = 18 = FLIP 8 to 3 = 13 = `-DEATH/DAY = 8+5 = 13

`-DEATH/DAY # `-NUMBER = 8+5+20+22 = 55

`-AGE of `-DEATH = 84 = 8x4 = (`-32) + RECIPROCAL (`-23) = (`-55)!!!-'

83+55 = 138 = 1x38 = (`-38) = `-BIRTH/YEAR!!!-'

83(-)55 = 28 = `-BIRTH/DAY = 4/22 = RECIPROCAL = 22/4 = 2/2x4 = (`-28)!!!-'

FRAGMENTED `-BIRTH/DAY # `-NUMBER = 4+2+2+1+9+3+8 = 29

FRAGMENTED `-DEATH/DAY # `-NUMBER = 8+5+2+0+2+2 = 19

29+19 = 48 = RECIPROCAL = (`-84) = `-AGE of `-DEATH for JAPANESE FASHION DESIGNER ISSEY MIYAKE!!!-'

29(-)19 = 10 = 5+5 = (`-55) = `-DEATH/DAY # `-NUMBER!!!-'

FROM `-BIRTH-to-DEATH there are 105 DAYS!!!-'

(365 (-) 105) = 260 = 26+0 = 26 = `-BIRTH/DAY = 4+22 = 26

`-MONTH of `-DEATH is AUGUST with 31 DAYS

(31 (-) 5) – DAY of DEATH = 26 = "SEE `-ABOVE for FROM `-BIRTH-to-DEATH"!!!-'

`-BIRTH/DAY = 4/22 = 4x22 = 88 = FLIP 8 to 3 = 38 = `-BIRTH/YEAR!!!~'

`-BIRTH/YEAR = 1938 = 1+9+3/8 = 13/8 = 1+3/8 = (`-48) = RECIPROCAL = (`-84) = `-AGE of `-DEATH for JAPANESE FASHION DESIGNER ISSEY MIYAKE!!!~'

MONTH of `-BIRTH was APRIL with 30 DAYS

(30 (-) 22) – DAY of `-BIRTH = (`-8) = `-MONTH of `-DEATH!!!~'

AMERICAN COMEDIC ACTOR ROBERT "BOB" OSBOURNE DENVER "GILLIGAN'S ISLAND" died at the AGE of (`-70)!!!~'

`-BIRTH/YEAR = (`-35) X TIMES (`-2) = (`-70) = `-AGE of `-DEATH for AMERICAN COMEDIC ACTOR ROBERT "BOB" OSBOURNE DENVER "GILLIGAN'S ISLAND"!!!~'

`-DIVORCED JEAN WEBBER in (`-70); and, `-DIED at the `-AGE of (`-70)!!!~'

`-BIRTH/DAY = 1/9 = RECIPROCAL = 9/1 = `-DIED the `-VERY `-NEXT `-DAY on 9/2!!!~'

`-BIRTH/DAY # `-NUMBER = 1+9+19+35 = 64

`-DEATH/DAY # `-NUMBER = 9+2+20+05 = 36

64+36 = 100 = `-YEAR `-MARRIAGE `-ENDED & `-DEATH `-OCCURRED = 2005 = 20x05 = 100!!!~'

64(-)36 = 28 = FRAGMENTED `-BIRTH/DAY # `-NUMBER!!!~'

FRAGMENTED `-BIRTH/DAY # `-NUMBER = 1+9+1+9+ 3+5 = 28

FRAGMENTED `-DEATH/DAY # `-NUMBER = 9+2+2+0+ 0+5 = 18

28+18 = 46 = RECIPROCAL = 64 = `-BIRTH/DAY # `-NUMBER!!!~'

FROM `-BIRTH-to-DEATH there are 236 DAYS = 23+6 = 29 = RECIPROCAL = 9/2 = `-DEATH/DAY!!!~'

(365 (-) 236) = 129 = RECIPROCAL = 921 = 92x1 = 9/2 = `-DEATH/DAY!!!~'

(365 (-) 236) = 129 = FLIP 2 to 7 = 179 = 7/1+9 = 7/10 = 7x10 = (`-70) = `-AGE of `-DEATH for AMERICAN COMEDIC ACTOR ROBERT "BOB" OSBOURNE DENVER "GILLIGAN'S ISLAND"!!!~'

`-WAS `-MARRIED to DREAMA PERRY DENVER from 1979 to 2005 for 26 YEARS!!!~'

`-MARRIAGE `-BEGAN = 1979 = 1+9+7+9 = 26 = `-YEARS of `-MARRIAGE!!!~'

`-MARRIAGE `-ENDED in 2005 = 2+5/00 = 7/00 = 70+0 = (`-70) = `-AGE of `-DEATH for AMERICAN COMEDIC ACTOR ROBERT "BOB" OSBOURNE DENVER "GILLIGAN'S ISLAND"!!!~'

`-MONTH of `-DEATH was `-SEPTEMBER with 30 `-DAYS!!!~'

(30 (-) 2) – DAY of `-DEATH = 28 = `-FRAGMENTED `-BIRTH/ DAY # `-NUMBER!!!~'

`-BIRTH/YEAR = 1935 = 1+9/35 = 10/35 = 10(-)35 = 25 = `-DEATH/ YEAR = 20+05 = 25!!!~'

`-WAS `-BORN in the `-MONTH of (`-1); and, `-DIED in the `-MONTH of (`-9) = (`-1/9) = `-BIRTH/DAY!!!~'

AMERICAN ACTRESS DAWN ELBERTA WELLS "GILLIGAN'S ISLAND" died at the AGE of (`-82)!!!~'

`-BIRTH/DAY = 10/18 = 10+18 = 28 = RECIPROCAL = (`-82) = `-AGE of `-DEATH for AMERICAN ACTRESS DAWN ELBERTA WELLS "GILLIGAN'S ISLAND"!!!~'

`-BIRTH/DAY # `-NUMBER = 10+18+19+38 = 85

`-BIRTH/DAY # `-NUMBER = 85 = 8x5 = 40 = 20+20 = `-DEATH/ YEAR!!!~'

`-DEATH/DAY # `-NUMBER = 12+30+20+20 = 82

`-DEATH/DAY # `-NUMBER = (`-82) = `-AGE of `-DEATH for AMERICAN ACTRESS DAWN ELBERTA WELLS "GILLIGAN'S ISLAND"!!!~'

`-DEATH/DAY = 12/30 = 12(-)30 = 18 = `-DAY of `-BIRTH = 18th!!!~'

85+82 = 167 = 1x67 = (`-67) = `-DIVORCED LARRY ROSEN in (`-67)!!!~'

85+82 = 167 = 1x67 = (`-67) = `-FATHER JOE WELLS `-DIED in (`-67)!!!~'

FRAGMENTED `-BIRTH/DAY # `-NUMBER = 1+0+1+8+1+9+ 3+8 = 31

`-BIRTH/MONTH is `-OCTOBER with 31 `-DAYS!!!~'

(31 (-) 18) – DAY of `-BIRTH = 13 = RECIPROCAL = 31 = `-FRAGMENTED `-BIRTH/DAY # `-NUMBER!!!~'

FRAGMENTED `-DEATH/DAY # `-NUMBER = 1+2+3+0+2+0+2+0 = 10

FRAGMENTED `-DEATH/DAY # `-NUMBER = 10 = 8+2 = (`-82) = `-AGE of `-DEATH for AMERICAN ACTRESS DAWN ELBERTA WELLS "GILLIGAN'S ISLAND"!!!~'

31+10 = 41 X TIMES (`-2) = (`-82) = `-AGE of `-DEATH for AMERICAN ACTRESS DAWN ELBERTA WELLS "GILLIGAN'S ISLAND"!!!~'

31(-)10 = 21 = 7x3 = (`-73) = `-DAYS from `-BIRTH-to-DEATH!!!~'

FROM `-BIRTH-to-DEATH there are 73 DAYS = "SEE `-ABOVE"!!!~'

(365 (-) 73) = 292 = 29x2 = 58 = RECIPROCAL = 85 = `-BIRTH/ DAY # `-NUMBER!!!~'

(365 (-) 73) = 292 = 29+2 = (`-31) = `-FRAGMENTED `-BIRTH/ DAY # `-NUMBER!!!~'

`-HEIGHT = 5' 4" = 5x4 = (`-20) = `-DEATH/YEAR!!!~'

`-BIRTH/YEAR = 1938 = 1(-)9/3+8 = 8/11 = 8/1+1 = (`-82) = `-AGE of `-DEATH for AMERICAN ACTRESS DAWN ELBERTA WELLS "GILLIGAN'S ISLAND"!!!~'

`-BIRTH/YEAR = 1938 = 1(-)9/3+8 = 8/11 = 8x11 = 88 = 2(8's) = 28 = RECIPROCAL = (`-82) = `-AGE of `-DEATH for AMERICAN ACTRESS DAWN ELBERTA WELLS "GILLIGAN'S ISLAND"!!!~'

`-MARRIED LARRY ROSEN from 1962 to 1967 for (`-5) YEARS!!!~'

1962 = 19+62 = 81 = `-DIED the `-VERY `-NEXT `-YEAR of `-AGE at (`-82)!!!~'

(`-62) = FLIP 2 to 7 = (`-67)!!!~'

(`-5) = "The `-HAND of `-GOD"!!!~'

`-BIRTH/YEAR = (`-38) = RECIPROCAL = (`-83) = `-DIED within (`-83) `-YEARS of `-EXISTENCE!!!~'

AMERICAN ACTRESS NATALIE SCHAFER "GILLIGAN'S ISLAND" died at the AGE Of (`-90)!!!~'

`-DEATH/DAY # `-NUMBER in `-REVERSE = 91(-)19(-)10(-)4 = 58 = RECIPROCAL = 85 = FLIP 8 to 3 = (`-35) = `-BIRTH/DAY # `-NUMBER!!!~'

`-BIRTH/DAY # `-NUMBER = 11+5+19+00 = 35

`-BIRTH/DAY = 11/5 = 11(-)5 = 6 = FLIP 6 to 9 = 9 = "JUST `-ADD a `-ZERO" = (`-90) = `-AGE of `-DEATH for AMERICAN ACTRESS NATALIE SCHAFER "GILLIGAN'S ISLAND"!!!~'

`-DEATH/DAY # `-NUMBER = 4+10+19+91 = 124

`-DEATH/DAY = 4/10 = 4(-)10 = 6 = FLIP 6 to 9 = 9 = "JUST `-ADD a `-ZERO" = (`-90) = `-AGE of `-DEATH for AMERICAN ACTRESS NATALIE SCHAFER "GILLIGAN'S ISLAND"!!!~'

35+124 = 159 = 1+59 = (`-60) = FLIP 6 to 9 = (`-90) = `-AGE of `-DEATH for AMERICAN ACTRESS NATALIE SCHAFER "GILLIGAN'S ISLAND"!!!~'

124(-)35 = 89 = `-FORMER `-HUSBAND'S LOUIS CALHERN `-BIRTH/DAY = 2/19 = HALF RECIPROCAL = 2/91 = 2(-)91 = (`-89)!!!~'

FRAGMENTED `-BIRTH/DAY = 1+1+5+1+9+0+0 = 17

FRAGMENTED `-DEATH/DAY = 4+1+0+1+9+9+1 = 25

`-BIRTH/MONTH was NOVEMBER with 30 DAYS

(30 (-) 5) – DAY of `-BIRTH = 25 = FRAGMENTED `-DEATH/ DAY # `-NUMBER!!!~'

17+25 = 42 = `-DEATH/DAY # `-NUMBER = 124 = RECIPROCAL = 421 = 42x1 = (`-42)!!!~'

FROM `-BIRTH-to-DEATH there are 156 DAYS = 15x6 = (`-90) = `-AGE of `-DEATH for AMERICAN ACTRESS NATALIE SCHAFER "GILLIGAN'S ISLAND"!!!~'

FROM `-BIRTH-to-DEATH there are 156 DAYS = 1x56 = (`-56) = `-FORMER `-HUSBAND LOUIS CALHERN `-DIED in (`-56)!!!~'

(365 (-) 156) = 209 = 20x9 = 180 (`-DIVIDED by) (`-2) = (`-90) = `-AGE of `-DEATH for AMERICAN ACTRESS NATALIE SCHAFER "GILLIGAN'S ISLAND"!!!~'

(365 (-) 156) = 209 = RECIPROCAL = 902 = 90+2 = (`-92) = `-DEATH/DAY # `-NUMBER of `-FORMER `-HUSBAND LOUIS CALHERN = 5+12+19+{56} = (`-92)!!!~'

`-YEARS `-ACTIVE from 1927 to 1990 = 63 YEARS = 6+3 = 9 = "JUST `-ADD a `-ZERO" = (`-90) = `-AGE of `-DEATH for AMERICAN ACTRESS NATALIE SCHAFER "GILLIGAN'S ISLAND"!!!~'

`-BIRTH/YEAR = 1900 = 1x90+0 = (`-90) = `-AGE of `-DEATH for AMERICAN ACTRESS NATALIE SCHAFER "GILLIGAN'S ISLAND"!!!~'

`-DEATH/YEAR = 1991 = 1x9/9+1 = 9/10 = 9x10 = (`-90) = `-AGE of `-DEATH for AMERICAN ACTRESS NATALIE SCHAFER "GILLIGAN'S ISLAND"!!!~'

`-WAS `-MARRIED to LOUIS CALHERN from 1933 to 1942 for (`-9) `-YEARS = "JUST `-ADD a `-ZERO" = (`-90) = `-AGE of `-DEATH for AMERICAN ACTRESS NATALIE SCHAFER "GILLIGAN'S ISLAND"!!!~'

`-MARRIAGE = 1933 = 19+33 = 52 = RECIPROCAL = 25 = 1+1/5 = 11/5 = `-BIRTH/DAY!!!~'

`-MARRIAGE = 1933 = 19(-)33 = 14 = RECIPROCAL = 4/1 = "JUST `-ADD a `-ZERO" = (4/10) = `-DEATH/DAY!!!~'

`-DIVORCE = 1942 = 19+42 = 61 = RECIPROCAL = 16 = `-BIRTH/DAY = 11/5 = 1/1+5 = 1/6

`-FORMER `-HUSBAND LOUIS CALHERN `-BIRTH/DAY # `-NUMBER in `-REVERSE = 95(-)18(-)19(-)2 = (`-56)!!!~'

'-FORMER '-HUSBAND LOUIS CALHERN '-DEATH/YEAR = ('-56)!!!~'

AMERICAN ACTRESS NATALIE SCHAFER "GILLIGAN'S ISLAND" FROM '-BIRTH-to-DEATH there are 156 DAYS = 1x56 = ('-56)!!!~'

'-WAS '-BORN in the '-MONTH of ('-11); and, '-DIED in the '-MONTH of ('-4) = (11/4) = RECIPROCAL = 4/11 = '-DIED the '-DAY '-PRIOR on ('-4/10)!!!~'

AMERICAN ACTOR JAMES GILMORE BACKUS "GILLIGAN'S ISLAND" / "MISTER MAGOO" died at the AGE of ('-76)!!!~'

'-PARTIAL '-DEATH/DAY # '-NUMBER in '-REVERSE = 89(-)19(-)3 = 67 = RECIPROCAL = ('-76) = '-AGE of '-DEATH for AMERICAN ACTOR JAMES GILMORE BACKUS "GILLIGAN'S ISLAND" / "MISTER MAGOO"!!!~'

'-BIRTH/DAY # '-NUMBER = 2+25+19+13 = 59

'-BIRTH/DAY = 2/25 = 2/2+5 = 2/7 = RECIPROCAL = 7/2 = 8x9 = ('-89) = '-DEATH/YEAR!!!~'

'-BIRTH/DAY = 2/25 = 2/2+5 = 2/7 = RECIPROCAL = 7/2 = '-DIED the '-VERY '-NEXT '-DAY on ('-7/3)!!!~'

'-BIRTH/YEAR = 19/13 = 19+13 = 32 = RECIPROCAL = 23 = FLIP 2 to 7 = ('-7/3) = '-DEATH/DAY!!!~'

'-DEATH/DAY # '-NUMBER = 7+3+19+89 = 118

59+118 = 177 = 1(-)77 = (`-76) = `-AGE of `-DEATH for AMERICAN ACTOR JAMES GILMORE BACKUS "GILLIGAN'S ISLAND" / "MISTER MAGOO"!!!~'

118(-)59 = (`-59) = `-BIRTH/DAY # `-NUMBER!!!~'

`-BIRTH/DAY # `-NUMBER (`-59) = ½ = `-DEATH/DAY # `-NUMBER (`-118)!!!~'

FRAGMENTED `-BIRTH/DAY # `-NUMBER = 2+2+5+1+9+ 1+3 = 23

FRAGMENTED `-BIRTH/DAY # `-NUMBER = 23 = `-BIRTH/ DAY = 2/25 = 2(-)25 = (`-23)!!!~'

FRAGMENTED `-DEATH/DAY # `-NUMBER = 7+3+1+9+ 8+9 = 37

FRAGMENTED `-DEATH/DAY # `-NUMBER = 37 = RECIPROCAL = 7/3 = `-DEATH/DAY!!!~'

23+37 = 60 = `-DEATH/DAY # `-NUMBER in `-REVERSE = 89(-)19(-)3(-)7 = (`-60)!!!~'

23(-)37 = 14 = `-BIRTH/DAY = 2/25 = 2/2+5 = 2/7 = 2x7 = (`-14)!!!~'

FROM `-BIRTH-to-DEATH there are 128 DAYS = 1x28 = 28 = `-DEATH/DAY # `-NUMBER = 118 = 1+1/8 = (`-28)!!!~'

FROM `-BIRTH-to-DEATH there are 128 DAYS = RECIPROCAL = 821 = 82+1 = 83 = `-BIRTH/YEAR = 19/13 = 1(-)9/1x3 = (`-83)!!!~'

(365 (-) 128) = 237 = FLIP 3 to 8 = 287 = 2+87 = (`-89) = `-DEATH/ YEAR!!!~'

(365 (-) 128) = 237 = FLIP 3 to 8 = 287 = 2(-)8/7 = 67 = RECIPROCAL = (`-76) = `-AGE of `-DEATH for AMERICAN ACTOR JAMES GILMORE BACKUS "GILLIGAN'S ISLAND" / "MISTER MAGOO"!!!~'

(365 (-) 128) = 237 = RECIPROCAL = 732 = 7(-)3/2 = (`-42) = 7x6 = (`-76) = `-AGE of `-DEATH for AMERICAN ACTOR JAMES GILMORE BACKUS "GILLIGAN'S ISLAND" / "MISTER MAGOO"!!!~'

`-BIRTH/YEAR = 19/13 = 19+13 = 32 = RECIPROCAL = 23 = FRAGMENTED `-BIRTH/DAY # `-NUMBER!!!~'

`-YEARS `-ACTIVE from 1948 to 1984 = 36 YEARS = RECIPROCAL = 63 = FLIP 6 to 9 = (`-93) = `-FORMER `-WIFE HENNY BACKUS `-LIVED to be (`-93) `-YEARS of `-AGE!!!~'

`-WIFE HENNY BACKUS was `-BORN in the `-MONTH of (`-3); and, `-DIED in the `-MONTH of (`-12) = (3x12) = (`-36)!!!~'

3/12 = HALF RECIPROCAL = 3/21

`-HER `-BIRTH/DAY was (`-3/21) = 3x21 = (`-63) = RECIPROCAL = (`-36)!!!~'

`-BIRTH/DAY # `-NUMBER = 3+21+19+11 = (`-54)!!!~'

`-DEATH/DAY # `-NUMBER = 12+9+20+04 = (`-45)!!!~'

(`-54) = RECIPROCAL = (`-45)!!!~'

`-FORMER `-HUSBAND'S `-BIRTH/DAY # `-NUMBER = 59 = 5x9 = (`-45)!!!~'

`-WAS `-MARRIED to HENNY BACKUS from 1943 to 1989 for (`-46) `-YEARS!!!~'

1989 = 19+89 = 108 = `-DEATH/DAY of HENNY BACKUS = 12/9 = 12x9 = 108

108+108 = 216 = FLIP 2 to 7 = 716 = 76x1 = (`-76) = `-AGE of `-DEATH for AMERICAN ACTOR JAMES GILMORE BACKUS "GILLIGAN'S ISLAND" / "MISTER MAGOO"!!!~'

`-YEARS `-ACTIVE from 1948 to 1984 = 36 YEARS = FLIP 3 to 8; FLIP 6 to 9 = (`-89) = `-DEATH/YEAR!!!~'

(`-48) = RECIPROCAL = (`-84)

4x8 = 8x4 = 32 = RECIPROCAL = (`-23) = FRAGMENTED `-BIRTH/DAY # `-NUMBER!!!~'

`-WAS `-BORN in the `-MONTH of (`-2); and, `-DIED in the `-MONTH of (`-7) = (`-27) = RECIPROCAL = (`-72) = 8x9 = `-DEATH/YEAR!!!~'

`-FORMER `-WIFE BETTY KEAN `-LIVED to BE (`-70) `-YEARS of `-AGE!!!~'

`-FORMER `-WIFE HENNY BACKUS `-LIVED to BE (`-93) `-YEARS of `-AGE!!!~'

70+93 = 163 = 1x63 = 63 = RECIPROCAL = 36 = `-SEE `-ABOVE & `-YEARS `-ACTIVE from 1948 to 1984 = 36 YEARS!!!~'

`-FORMER `-WIFE BETTY KEAN was `-BORN in the `-MONTH of (`-12); and, `-DIED in the `-MONTH of (`-9) = 12/9 = `-DEATH/ DAY of `-FORMER `-WIFE HENNY BACKUS = 12/9!!!~'

`-FORMER `-WIFE BETTY KEAN `-DEATH/DAY # `-NUMBER = 9+29+19+86 = 143 = 1x43 = (`-43) = `-MARRIED `-WIFE HENNY BACKUS in (`-43)!!!~'

`-FORMER `-WIFE BETTY KEAN `-BIRTH/YEAR = 19/15 = 19+15 = (`-34) = RECIPROCAL = (`-43) = `-MARRIED `-WIFE HENNY BACKUS in (`-43)!!!~'

`-FORMER `-WIFE BETTY KEAN `-DIED in 1986 = 19(-)86 = 67 = RECIPROCAL = (`-76) = `-AGE of `-DEATH for AMERICAN ACTOR `-FORMER `-HUSBAND JAMES GILMORE BACKUS "GILLIGAN'S ISLAND" / "MISTER MAGOO"!!!~'

AMERICAN ACTOR ALAN HALE JR. "GILLIGAN'S ISLAND" died at the AGE of (`-68)!!!~'

`-DEATH/DAY # `-NUMBER in `-REVERSE = 90(-)19(-)2(-)1 = (`-68) = `-AGE of `-DEATH for AMERICAN ACTOR ALAN HALE JR. "GILLIGAN'S ISLAND"!!!~'

`-BIRTH/YEAR = 21 = RECIPROCAL = (`-1/2) = `-DEATH/DAY!!!~'

`-BIRTH/DAY # `-NUMBER = 3+8+19+21 = 51

`-DEATH/DAY # `-NUMBER = 1+2+19+90 = 112

`-DEATH/DAY # `-NUMBER = 112 = 1x12 = (`-1/2) = `-DEATH/DAY!!!~'

`-DEATH/YEAR = 19/90 = 19(-)90 = 71 = RECIPROCAL = 1/7 = FLIP 7 to 2 = (`-1/2) = `-DEATH/DAY!!!~'

51+112 = 163 = 1x63 = 63 = `-DIVORCED BETTINA REED DOERR in (`-63)!!!~'

`-MARRIED BETTINA REED DOEER in 1943 = 19(-)43 = 24 = `-BIRTH/DAY = 3x8 = (`-24)!!!~'

51+112 = 163 = 1x63 = 63 = FLIP {3 to 8} = (`-68) = `-AGE of `-DEATH for AMERICAN ACTOR ALAN HALE JR. "GILLIGAN'S ISLAND"!!!~'

FRAGMENTED `-BIRTH/DAY # `-NUMBER = 3+8+1+9+ 2+1 = 24

FRAGMENTED `-BIRTH/DAY # `-NUMBER = 24 = `-BIRTH/ DAY = 3/8 = 3x8 = (`-24)!!!~'

FRAGMENTED `-DEATH/DAY # `-NUMBER = 1+2+1+9+ 9+0 = 22

`-DEATH/DAY # `-NUMBER = (`-112) (+) (`-22) = FRAGMENTED `-DEATH/DAY # `-NUMBER = (`-134) = 1x34 = (`-34) = X TIMES (`-2) = (`-68) = `-AGE of `-DEATH for AMERICAN ACTOR ALAN HALE JR. "GILLIGAN'S ISLAND"!!!~'

24(-)22 = (`-2) = `-JUST `-ADD a `-ZERO = (`-20) = `-WAS `-MARRIED to BETTINA REED DOERR for (`-20) `-YEARS!!!~'

24+22 = 46 = RECIPROCAL = 64 = `-MARRIED NAOMI GRACE INGRAM in (`-64)!!!~'

FROM `-BIRTH-to-DEATH there are 65 DAYS!!!~'

(365 (-) 65) = 300 = 30+0 = 30 = 5x6 = (`-56) X TIMES (`-2) = 112 = `-DEATH/DAY # `-NUMBER!!!~'

`-HEIGHT = 6' 2" = 6x2 = (`-1/2) = `-DEATH/DAY!!!~'

`-WAS `-BORN in the `-MONTH (`-3); and, `-DIED in the `-MONTH of (`-1) = (`-31) = RECIPROCAL = (1/3) = = `-DIED the `-DAY `-PRIOR on (1/2)!!!~'

`-BIRTH/YEAR = 19/21 = 19+21 = 40 = 8x5 = (`-85) = `-AGE of `-DEATH of `-FORMER `-WIFE NAOMI GRACE INGRAM!!!~'

AMERICAN ACTOR RUSSELL DAVID JOHNSON "GILLIGAN'S ISLAND" died at the AGE of (`-89)!!!~'

`-BIRTH/DAY # `-NUMBER = 11+10+19+24 = 64

`-BIRTH/DAY # `-NUMBER = 64 = 8x8 = (`-88) = `-DIED the `-VERY `-NEXT `-YEAR of `-AGE at (`-89)!!!~'

`-BIRTH/DAY = 11/10 = 11+10 = 21 = RECIPROCAL = 12 = `-DEATH/DAY = 1+16 = 17 = FLIP 7 to 2 = (`-12)!!!~'

`-DEATH/DAY # `-NUMBER = 1+16+20+14 = 51

64+51 = 115 = 1/15 = `-DIED the `-VERY `-NEXT `-DAY on 1/16!!!~'

64(-)51 = 13 = 6+7 = (`-67) = `-DAYS from `-BIRTH-to-DEATH!!!~'

FRAGMENTED `-BIRTH/DAY # `-NUMBER = 1+1+1+0+1+9+2+4 = 19

`-BIRTH/DAY # `-NUMBER = (`-64) (+) (`-19) = FRAGMENTED `-BIRTH/DAY # `-NUMBER = (`-83) = FLIP 3 to 8 = (`-88) = `-DIED the `-VERY `-NEXT `-YEAR of `-AGE at (`-89)!!!~'

FRAGMENTED `-DEATH/DAY # `-NUMBER = 1+1+6+2+0+ 1+4 = 15

FRAGMENTED `-DEATH/DAY # `-NUMBER = 15 = RECIPROCAL = 51 = `-DEATH/DAY # `-NUMBER!!!~'

(15 + 51) = 66 = 6x6 = (`-36) = FLIP 3 to 8; FLIP 6 to 9 = (`-89) = `-AGE of `-DEATH for AMERICAN ACTOR RUSSELL DAVID JOHNSON "GILLIGAN'S ISLAND"!!!~'

`-DEATH/MONTH was JANUARY with 31 DAYS

(31 (-) 16) – DAY of `-DEATH = 15 = FRAGMENTED `-DEATH/ DAY # `-NUMBER!!!~'

19+15 = (`-34) X TIMES (`-2) = (`-68) = RECIPROCAL = 86 = FLIP 6 to 9 = (`-89) = `-AGE of `-DEATH for AMERICAN ACTOR RUSSELL DAVID JOHNSON "GILLIGAN'S ISLAND"!!!~'

FROM `-BIRTH-to-DEATH there are 67 DAYS = `-WAS `-DIVORCED from EDITH CAHOON in 1948 = 19+48 = (`-67)!!!~'

FROM `-BIRTH-to-DEATH there are 67 DAYS = 6+7 = 13 = `-DEATH/DAY = 1/16 = HALF RECIPROCAL = 1/61 = 1+61 = 62 (`-DIVIDED by) (`-2) = 31 = RECIPROCAL = (`-13)!!!~'

(365 (-) 67) = 298 = RECIPROCAL = 892 = (`-89) X TIMES (`-2) = (`-89) = `-AGE of `-DEATH for AMERICAN ACTOR RUSSELL DAVID JOHNSON "GILLIGAN'S ISLAND"!!!~'

`-WAS `-BORN in the `-MONTH of (`-11); and, `-DIED in the `-MONTH of (`-1) = (11/1) = `-FIRST `-THREE # `-NUMBERS of `-BIRTH/DAY = 11/10 = 111+0 = (`-111)!!!~'

`-BIRTH/DAY # `-NUMBER = 64 = 6x4 = (`-**24**)!!!-'

`-WAS `-MARRIED to EDITH CAHOON in 1943 = 19(-)43 = (`-**24**)!!!-'

`-BIRTH/YEAR = (`-**24**) = `-DEATH/YEAR = **2**01**4** = 24+0x1 = (`-**24**)!!!-'

`-WAS `-MARRIED to CONSTANCE DANE from 1982 to 2014 for (`-**32**) `-YEARS!!!-'

1982 = 19(-)82 = 63 = FLIP 3 to 8 = (`-68) = RECIPROCAL = 86 = FLIP 6 to 9 = (`-89) = `-AGE of `-DEATH for AMERICAN ACTOR RUSSELL DAVID JOHNSON "GILLIGAN'S ISLAND"!!!-'

`-WAS `-MARRIED to KAY LEVEY from 1949 to 1980 for (`-**31**) `-YEARS!!!-'

`-WAS `-MARRIED in 1949!!!-'

1949 = 19+49 = 68 = RECIPROCAL = 86 = FLIP 6 to 9 = (`-89) = `-AGE of `-DEATH for AMERICAN ACTOR RUSSELL DAVID JOHNSON "GILLIGAN'S ISLAND"!!!-'

`-WAS `-MARRIED to EDITH CAHOON from 1943 to 1948 for (`-**5**) `-YEARS!!!-'

`-MARRIED = (`-43) = FLIP 3 to 8 = (`-48) = `-DIVORCED!!!-'

(`-43) X TIMES (`-2) = (`-86) = FLIP 6 to 9 = (`-89) = `-AGE of `-DEATH for AMERICAN ACTOR RUSSELL DAVID JOHNSON "GILLIGAN'S ISLAND"!!!-'

`-MARRIED for a `-TOTAL of (`-**68**) YEARS = (32+31+5) = (`-**68**)!!!-'

`-DEATH/YEAR = 20/14 = 20+14 = (`-34) X TIMES (`-2) = (`-68) = RECIPROCAL = 86 = FLIP 6 to 9 = (`-89) = `-AGE of `-DEATH for AMERICAN ACTOR RUSSELL DAVID JOHNSON "GILLIGAN'S ISLAND"!!!~'

`-BIRTH/YEAR = 19/24 = 19+24 = (`-43) X TIMES (`-2) = (`-86) = FLIP 6 to 9 = (`-89) = `-AGE of `-DEATH for AMERICAN ACTOR RUSSELL DAVID JOHNSON "GILLIGAN'S ISLAND"!!!~'

NEWS ANCHOR (KTVU) SAN FRANCISCO LESLIE RAY GRIFFITH died at the AGE of (`-66)!!!~'

`-PARTIAL `-BIRTH/DAY # `-NUMBER = 1+1+19 = 21 = RECIPROCAL = 12 = 6+6 = (`-66) = `-AGE of `-DEATH for NEWS ANCHOR (KTVU) LESLIE RAY GRIFFITH!!!~'

`-BIRTH/YEAR = 56 = RECIPROCAL = 65 = `-DIED the `-VERY `-NEXT `-YEAR of `-AGE at (`-66)!!!~'

`-BIRTH/DAY # `-NUMBER = 1+1+19+56 = 77

`-BIRTH/DAY # `-NUMBER = 77 = 7x7 = 49 = 4x9 = (`-36) = 6x6 = (`-66) = `-AGE of `-DEATH for NEWS ANCHOR (KTVU) LESLIE RAY GRIFFITH!!!~'

`-DEATH/DAY # `-NUMBER = 8+10+20+22 = 60

`-DEATH/DAY = 8/10 = 8(-)10 = (`-2) = `-BIRTH/DAY = 1/1 = 1+1 = (`-2)

77+60 = 137 = 1(-)37 = (`-36) = 6x6 = (`-66) = `-AGE of `-DEATH for NEWS ANCHOR (KTVU) LESLIE RAY GRIFFITH!!!~'

77+60 = 137 = 1x37 = `-BIRTH/YEAR = 19(-)56 = (`-37)!!!~'

77+60 = 137 = 1+37 = 38 = 3x8 = 24 = RECIPROCAL = 42 = 20+22 = `-DEATH/YEAR!!!~'

77(-)60 = 17 = 1+7 = (`-8) = `-DEATH/MONTH!!!~'

`-DEATH/MONTH is AUGUST with 31 DAYS

(31 (-) 10) – DAY of `-DEATH = (`-**21**) = 3x7 = (`-37) = FLIP 3 to 8 = 87 = 8x7 = (`-56) = `-BIRTH/YEAR!!!~'

`-BIRTH/MONTH is JANUARY with 31 DAYS

(31 (-) 1) – DAY of `-BIRTH = 30 = 5x6 = (`-56) = `-BIRTH/YEAR!!!~'

`-BIRTH/YEAR = 56 = 5+6 = 1/1 = `-BIRTH/DAY!!!~'

FRAGMENTED `-BIRTH/DAY # `-NUMBER = 1+1+1+9+5+6 = 23

FRAGMENTED `-BIRTH/DAY # `-NUMBER = 23 = -a PROPHETIC # `-NUMBER!!!~'

FRAGMENTED `-BIRTH/DAY # `-NUMBER = (`-23) X TIMES (`-3) = 69 = FLIP 9 to 6 = (`-66) = `-AGE of `-DEATH for NEWS ANCHOR (KTVU) LESLIE RAY GRIFFITH!!!~'

FRAGMENTED `-DEATH/DAY # `-NUMBER = 8+1+0+2+0+2+2 = 15

`-DEATH/DAY # `-NUMBER = (`-60) (+) (1+5) = FRAGMENTED `-DEATH/DAY # `-NUMBER = (`-66) = `-AGE of `-DEATH for NEWS ANCHOR (KTVU) LESLIE RAY GRIFFITH!!!~'

23+15 = 38 = 3x8 = 24 = RECIPROCAL = 42 = 20+22 = `-DEATH/
YEAR!!!~'

23(-)15 = (`-8) = `-DEATH/MONTH!!!~'

FROM `-BIRTH-to-DEATH there are 221 DAYS = 2x21 = 42 =
20+22 = `-DEATH/YEAR!!!~'

FROM `-BIRTH-to-DEATH there are 221 DAYS = 2+21 = 23
= FLIP 2 to 7; FLIP 3 to 8 = (`-78) = 7x8 = (`-56) = `-BIRTH/
YEAR!!!~'

(365 (-) 221) = 144 = 14x4 = (`-56) = `-BIRTH/YEAR!!!~'

`-BIRTH/YEAR = 19/56 = 1+9+5/6 = 15/6 = 1+5/6 = (`-66) = `-AGE
of `-DEATH for NEWS ANCHOR (KTVU) SAN FRANCISCO'S
LESLIE RAY GRIFFITH!!!~'

AMERICAN ACTRESS ANNE CELESTE HECHE died at the
AGE of (`-53)!!!~'

`-Was `-BORN in the `-MONTH of (`-5); and, `-DIED in the
`-MONTH of (`-8) = (`-58) = FLIP 8 to 3 = (`-53) = `-AGE of
`-DEATH for AMERICAN ACTRESS ANNE CELESTE
HECHE!!!~'

`-BIRTH/DAY = 5/25 = 5/2(-)5 = (`-53) = `-AGE of `-DEATH for
AMERICAN ACTRESS ANNE CELESTE HECHE!!!~'

`-BIRTH/DAY = 5/25 = HALF RECIPROCAL = 5/52 = 5+52 =
57 = 5x7 = 35 = RECIPROCAL = (`-53) = `-AGE of `-DEATH for
AMERICAN ACTRESS ANNE CELESTE HECHE!!!~'

`-BIRTH/DAY # `-NUMBER in `-REVERSE = 69(-)19(-)25(-)5 = (`-20) = `-AGE of `-SON HOMER LAFFOON at the `-TIME of `-HIS `-MOTHER'S `-DEATH!!!~'

`-BIRTH/DAY # `-NUMBER = 5+25+19+69 = 118

`-BIRTH/DAY # `-NUMBER = 118 / (`-DIVIDED by) (`-2) = 59 = 5x9 = 45 = RECIPROCAL = 54 = `-DIED within (`-54) `-YEARS of `-EXISTENCE at the `-AGE of (`-53)!!!~'

(`-35) = RECIPROCAL = (`-53)!!!~'

`-BIRTH/DAY # `-NUMBER = 118 = 11x8 = 88 = 53+35 = (`-53) = `-AGE of `-DEATH for AMERICAN ACTRESS ANNE CELESTE HECHE!!!~'

`-BIRTH/YEAR = 19/69 = 19+69 = (`-88) = 53+35 = (`-53) = `-AGE of `-DEATH for AMERICAN ACTRESS ANNE CELESTE HECHE!!!~'

`-BIRTH/DAY # `-NUMBER of (`-MOTHER) NANCY PRICKETT HECHE = 3+10+19+37 = (`-69) = `-DAUGHTER'S `-BIRTH/YEAR = 6x9 = (`-54) = `-DAUGHTER `-DIED within this `-AMOUNT of `-TIME!!!~'

`-DEATH/DAY # `-NUMBER = 8+12+20+22 = 62

`-DEATH/DAY # `-NUMBER = 62 / (`-DIVIDED by) (`-2) = 31 = RECIPROCAL = 13 = 5+8 = (`-58) = FLIP 8 to 3 = (`-53) = `-AGE of `-DEATH for AMERICAN ACTRESS ANNE CELESTE HECHE!!!~'

`-DEATH/DAY = 8/12 = 8x12 = 96 = RECIPROCAL = 69 = `-BIRTH/YEAR!!!~'

118+62 = 180 = 18+0 = 18 = 5+13 = 53x1 = (`-53) = `-AGE of `-DEATH for AMERICAN ACTRESS ANNE CELESTE HECHE!!!~'

118(-)62 = 56 = FLIP 6 to 9 = 59 = 5x9 = 45 = RECIPROCAL = 54 = `-DIED within (`-54) `-YEARS of `-EXISTENCE at the `-AGE of (`-53)!!!~'

FRAGMENTED `-BIRTH/DAY # `-NUMBER = 5+2+5+1+9+6+9 = 37

FRAGMENTED `-BIRTH/DAY # `-NUMBER = 37 = `-MOTHER of ANNE CELESTE HECHE (NANCY PRICKETT HECHE) was `-BORN in (`-37); and, `-WAS (`-85) YEARS of `-AGE at the `-TIME of `-HER `-DAUGHTER'S `-DEATH = RECIPROCAL = 58 = FLIP 8 to 3 = (`-53) = `-AGE of `-DEATH for `-DAUGHTER AMERICAN ACTRESS ANNE CELESTE HECHE!!!~'

FRAGMENTED `-DEATH/DAY # `-NUMBER = 8+1+2+2+0+2+2 = 17

37(-)17 = (`-20) = `-AGE of `-SON HOMER LAFFOON at the `-TIME of `-HER `-DEATH!!!~'

37+17 = 54 = `-DIED within (`-54) `-YEARS of `-EXISTENCE at the `-AGE of (`-53)!!!~'

37+17 = 54 = ANNE CELESTE HECHE `-BIRTH/YEAR = (`-69) = 6x9 = (`-54)!!!~'

FROM `-BIRTH-to-DEATH there are 79 DAYS = `-DEATH/DAY = 8/12 = 8+1/2 = 9/2 = RECIPROCAL = 2/9 = FLIP 2 to 7 = (`-79)!!!~'

(365 (-) 79) = 286 = 2x86 = 172 = 1+72 = (`-73) = RECIPROCAL = (`-37) = FRAGMENTED `-BIRTH/DAY # `-NUMBER!!!~'

(365 (-) 79) = 286 = 28x6 = 168 = 1+68 = (`-69) = `-BIRTH/ YEAR!!!~'

(365 (-) 79 = 286 = 2+86 = (`-88) = 53+35 = (`-53) = `-AGE of `-DEATH for AMERICAN ACTRESS ANNE CELESTE HECHE!!!~'

`-WAS `-MARRIED to COLEMAN LAFFOON from 2001 to 2009 for (`-8) `-YEARS!!!~'

(`-8) = 5+3 = (`-53) = `-AGE of `-DEATH for `-FORMER `-WIFE AMERICAN ACTRESS ANNE CELESTE HECHE!!!~'

2001 = 20+01 = 21 = 3x7 = (`-37) = FRAGMENTED `-BIRTH/ DAY # `-NUMBER!!!~'

`-FORMER `-HUSBAND COLEMAN LAFOON's `-BIRTH/ DAY # `-NUMBER in `-REVERSE = 73(-)19(-)7(-)10 = (`-37) = RECIPROCAL = (`-73) = `-BIRTH/YEAR!!!~'

2009 = 20/09 = RECIPROCAL = 90/02 = 90(-)02 = (`-88) = 53+35 = (`-53) = `-AGE of `-DEATH for `-FORMER `-WIFE AMERICAN ACTRESS ANNE CELESTE HECHE!!!~'

`-AT `-TIME of `-DEATH ANNE CELESTE HECHE'S `-SON ATLAS HECHE TUPPER was (`-13) YEARS of `-AGE; and, `-SON HOMER LAFFOON was (`-20) YEARS of `-AGE!!!~'

(`-13) = 5+8 = (`-58) = FLIP 8 to 3 = (`-53) = `-AGE of `-DEATH for `-MOTHER AMERICAN ACTRESS ANNE CELESTE HECHE!!!~'

`-SON `-BORN in (`-20/09) = RECIPROCAL = 90/02 = 90(-)02 = (`-88) = 53+35 = (`-53) = `-AGE of `-DEATH for AMERICAN ACTRESS ANNE CELESTE HECHE!!!~'

`-SON ATLAS HECHE TUPPER's `-FATHER = JAMES TUPPER = `-AGE at TIME of `-DEATH = (`-57) = 5x7 = (`-35) = RECIPROCAL = (`-53) = `-AGE of `-DEATH for AMERICAN ACTRESS ANNE CELESTE HECHE!!!~'

JAMES TUPPER `-BIRTH/DAY = 8/4/19/65!!!~'

`-BIRTH/YEAR = 19+65 = 84 = 8/4 = `-BIRTH/DAY!!!~'

1965 = 1x5/9(-)6 = (`-53) = `-AGE of `-DEATH for AMERICAN ACTRESS ANNE CELESTE HECHE!!!~'

LAFOON'S `-SON = (`-20) = 5x4 = (`-54) = `-DIED within (`-54) `-YEARS of `-EXISTENCE at the `-AGE of (`-53)!!!~'

ANNE CELESTE HECHE `-BIRTH/YEAR = (`-69) = 6x9 = (`-54)!!!~'

`-SON HOMER LAFFOON's `-BIRTH/DAY = 3/2/20/02 = HALF RECIPROCAL = 3/2/20/20 = 3+2+20+20 = 45 = RECIPROCAL = (`-54)!!!~'

`-BIRTH/YEAR = (`-02) = RECIPROCAL = (`-20) = "SEE `-ABOVE" & "`-AGE at `-TIME of `-MOTHER'S `-DEATH"!!!~'

`-BIRTH/YEAR = (`-02) = RECIPROCAL = (`-20) = 02(-)20 = 18 = 5+13 = 53x1 = (`-53) = `-AGE of `-DEATH for `-MOTHER AMERICAN ACTRESS ANNE CELESTE HECHE!!!~'

ANNE CELESTE HECHE `-BIRTH/YEAR = 19/69 = 1(-)9/9+6 = 8/15 = 8/1x5 = 8/5 = RECIPROCAL = 5/8 = FLIP 8 to 3 = (`-53) = `-AGE of `-DEATH for AMERICAN ACTRESS ANNE CELESTE HECHE!!!~'

`-FATHER of ANNE CELESTE HECHE (DONALD JOE HECHE) was `-BORN in (`-38); and, `-DIED in (`-83)!!!~'

(`-38) = RECIPROCAL = (`-83)!!!~'

83(-)38 = 45 = RECIPROCAL = 54 = `-DAUGHTER `-DIED within (`-54) `-YEARS of `-EXISTENCE at the `-AGE of (`-53)!!!~'

`-DEATH/DAY # `-NUMBER = 3+3+19+83 = 108 / (`-DIVIDED by) (`-2) = 54 = `-DAUGHTER `-DIED within (`-54) `-YEARS of `-EXISTENCE at the `-AGE of (`-53)!!!~'

`-DEATH/DAY # `-NUMBER in `-REVERSE = 83(-)19(-)3(-)3 = (`-58) = FLIP 8 to 3 = (`-53) = `-AGE of `-DEATH for `-DAUGHTER AMERICAN ACTRESS ANNE CELESTE HECHE!!!~'

`-DEATH/DAY = 3/3 = FLIP 3 to 8 = 8/8 = (`-88) = 53+35 = (`-53) = `-AGE of `-DEATH for `-DAUGHTER AMERICAN ACTRESS ANNE CELESTE HECHE!!!~'

COMEDIAN TEDDY RAY died at the AGE of (`-32)!!!~'

`-WAS `-BORN in the `-MONTH of (`-7); and, `-DIED within the `-MONTH of (`-8) = (7/8) = 7x8 = (`-56) = `-BIRTH/DAY # `-NUMBER = 146 = 1+4/6 = (`-56)!!!~'

`-BIRTH/DAY # `-NUMBER = 7+30+19+90 = 146

`-BIRTH/DAY # `-NUMBER = 146 = 1x46 = (`-46) / (`-DIVIDED by) (`-2) = (`-23) = RECIPROCAL = (`-32) = `-AGE of `-DEATH for COMEDIAN TEDDY RAY!!!~'

`-BIRTH/DAY # `-NUMBER = 146 = 14x6 = 84 = FLIP 8 to 3 = (`-34) = `-BIRTH/DAY # `-NUMBER in `-REVERSE = 90(-)19 (-)30(-)7 = (`-34)!!!~'

`-AGE of `-DEATH = (`-32) = FLIP 3 to 8; FLIP 2 to 7 = (`-87) = 8x7 = (`-56) = `-BIRTH/DAY # `-NUMBER = 146 = 1+4/6 = (`-56)!!!~'

`-DEATH/DAY # `-NUMBER = 8+12+20+22 = 62

`-DEATH/DAY # `-NUMBER = 62 = FLIP 2 to 7 = 67 = 6x7 = 42 = 20+22 = `-DEATH/YEAR!!!~'

`-DEATH/DAY # `-NUMBER = 62 / (`-DIVIDED by) (`-2) = 31 = RECIPROCAL = 13 = DAYS from `-BIRTH-to-DEATH!!!~'

146(-)62 = 84 = 8x4 = (`-32) = `-AGE of `-DEATH for COMEDIAN TEDDY RAY!!!~'

146+62 = 208 = 20+8 = 28 = 14x2 = 1(-)4/2 = (`-32) = `-AGE of `-DEATH for COMEDIAN TEDDY RAY!!!~'

146+62 = 208 = 20+8 = 28 = RECIPROCAL = 82 = FLIP 8 to 3 = (`-32) = `-AGE of `-DEATH for COMEDIAN TEDDY RAY!!!~'

FRAGMENTED `-BIRTH/DAY # `-NUMBER = 7+3+0+1+9+9+0 = 29

FRAGMENTED `-DEATH/DAY # `-NUMBER = 8+1+2+2+0+2+2 = 17

`-DEATH/DAY # `-NUMBER = (`-62) (+) (`-17) = FRAGMENTED `-DEATH/DAY # `-NUMBER = (`-79) = FLIP 7 to 2 = (`-29) = FRAGMENTED `-BIRTH/DAY # `-NUMBER!!!~'

29+17 = 46 = / (`-DIVIDED by) (`-2) = (`-23) = RECIPROCAL = (`-32) = `-AGE of `-DEATH for COMEDIAN TEDDY RAY!!!~'

29+17 = 46 = `-BIRTH/DAY # `-NUMBER = 146 = 1x46 = (`-46)!!!~'

29(-)17 = 12 = 6x2 = (`-62) = `-DEATH/DAY # `-NUMBER!!!~'

FROM `-BIRTH-to-DEATH there are 13 DAYS = "A VERY PIVOTAL # `-NUMBER"!!!~'

(365 (-) 13) = 352 = 35+2 = (`-37) = FLIP 7 to 2 = (`-32) = `-AGE of `-DEATH for COMEDIAN TEDDY RAY!!!~'

(365 (-) 13) = 352 = RECIPROCAL = 253 = 25+3 = 28 = RECIPROCAL = 82 = FLIP 8 to 3 = (`-32) = `-AGE of `-DEATH for COMEDIAN TEDDY RAY!!!~'

`-BIRTH/DAY = 7/30 = 7+30 = 37 = FLIP 7 to 2 = (`-32) = `-AGE of `-DEATH for COMEDIAN TEDDY RAY!!!~'

`-DEATH/DAY = 8/12 = FLIP 8 to 3 = 3/12 = 32x1 = (`-32) = `-AGE of `-DEATH for COMEDIAN TEDDY RAY!!!~'

`-BIRTH/DAY = 7/30 = 7+30 = 37 = FLIP 3 to 8; FLIP 7 to 2 = (`-8/2) = `-DEATH/DAY = 8/12 = 82x1 = (`-82) = FLIP 8 to 3 = (`-32) = `-AGE of `-DEATH for COMEDIAN TEDDY RAY!!!~'

`-BIRTH/DAY = 7/30 = 7(-)30 = (`-23) = RECIPROCAL = (`-32) = `-AGE of `-DEATH for COMEDIAN TEDDY RAY!!!~'

`-DEATH/DAY = 8/12 = 8x12 = 96 / (`-DIVIDED by) (`-3) = (`-32) = `-AGE of `-DEATH for COMEDIAN TEDDY RAY!!!~'

AMERICAN AUTHOR MELISSA SUSAN BANK died at the AGE of (`-61)!!!~'

`-BIRTH/YEAR = (`-60) = `-DIED the `-VERY `-NEXT `-YEAR of `-AGE at the `-AGE of (`-61)!!!~'

`-BIRTH/DAY # `-NUMBER = 10+11+19+60 = 100

`-BIRTH/DAY # `-NUMBER = 100 = 50x2 = 50+2 = (`-52) = `-DEATH/DAY # `-NUMBER!!!~'

`-DEATH/DAY # `-NUMBER = 8+2+20+22 = 52

`-DEATH/DAY = 8/2 = 8x2 = 16 = RECIPROCAL = (`-61) = `-AGE of `-DEATH for AMERICAN AUTHOR MELISSA SUSAN BANK!!!~'

`-DEATH/DAY # `-NUMBER = 52 = 5+2 = (`-7) = 6+1 = (`-61) = `-AGE of `-DEATH for AMERICAN AUTHOR MELISSA SUSAN BANK!!!~'

`-PARTIAL `-DEATH/DAY # `-NUMBER = 8+2+20 = 30 = X TIMES (`-2) = (`-60) = `-BIRTH/YEAR!!!~'

100(-)52 = 48 = 4+8 = 12 = RECPROCAL = 21 = `-BIRTH/DAY = 10+11 = (`-21)!!!~'

`-BIRTH/DAY = 10+11 = 21 = X TIMES (`-2) = 42 = 20+22 = `-DEATH/YEAR!!!~'

100+52 = 152 = 1+5/2 = (`-62) = `-DIED the `-VERY `-PREVIOUS `-YEAR of `-AGE at the `-AGE of (`-61)!!!~'

100+52 = 152 = 15x2 = 30 = X TIMES (`-2) = 60 = `-BIRTH/ YEAR!!!~'

FRAGMENTED `-BIRTH/DAY # `-NUMBER = 1+0+1+1+1+9+ 6+0 = 19

FRAGMENTED `-BIRTH/DAY # `-NUMBER = 19 = FLIP 9 to 6 = 16 = RECIPROCAL = (`-61) = `-AGE of `-DEATH for AMERICAN AUTHOR MELISSA SUSAN BANK!!!~'

FRAGMENTED `-DEATH/DAY # `-NUMBER = 8+2+2+0+ 2+2 = 16

FRAGMENTED `-BIRTH/DAY # `-NUMBER = 19 = FLIP 9 to 6 = 16 = FRAGMENTED `-DEATH/DAY # `-NUMBER!!!~'

FRAGMENTED `-DEATH/DAY # `-NUMBER = 16 = RECIPROCAL = (`-61) = `-AGE of `-DEATH for AMERICAN AUTHOR MELISSA SUSAN BANK!!!~'

19+16 = 35 = X TIMES (`-2) = (`-70) = `-TIME from `-BIRTH-to-DEATH!!!~'

FROM BIRTH-to-DEATH there are 70 DAYS = "SEE `-RIGHT `-ABOVE for `-CALCULATION"!!!~'

(365 (-) 70) = 295 = 29(-)5 = 24 = RECIPROCAL = 42 = 20+22 = `-DEATH/YEAR!!!~'

(365 (-) 70) = 295 = 2x95 = 190 = 19+0 = 19 = RECIPROCAL = 91 = FLIP 9 to 6 = (`-61) = `-AGE of `-DEATH for AMERICAN AUTHOR MELISSA SUSAN BANK!!!~'

`-BIRTH/YEAR = 19/60 = 19(-)60 = 41 = X TIMES (`-2) = 8/2 = `-DEATH/DAY!!!~'

`-BIRTH/YEAR = 19/60 = 1+9+0/6 = 10/6 = 10+6 = 16 = RECIPROCAL = (`-61) = `-AGE of `-DEATH for AMERICAN AUTHOR MELISSA SUSAN BANK!!!~'

`-BIRTH/YEAR = 19/60 = 19+60 = 79 = 7+9 = 16 = RECIPROCAL = (`-61) = `-AGE of `-DEATH for AMERICAN AUTHOR MELISSA SUSAN BANK!!!~'

`-DEATH/MONTH was AUGUST with 31 DAYS

(31 (-) 2) – DAY of `-DEATH = 29 = RECIPROCAL = 92 = FLIP 9 to 6 = (`-62) = `-DIED the `-VERY `-PREVIOUS `-YEAR of `-AGE at the `-AGE of (`-61)!!!~'

`-WAS `-BORN in the `-MONTH of (`-10); and, `-DIED within the `-MONTH of (`-8) = (10/8) = 10+8 = (`-18) = RECIPROCAL = (`-81)!!!~'

(81(-)18) = 63 = 7x9 = (`-79) = 19+60 = `-BIRTH/YEAR!!!~'

(`-18) = 1(-)8 = 7 = 6+1 = (`-61) = `-AGE of `-DEATH for AMERICAN AUTHOR MELISSA SUSAN BANK!!!~'

INDIAN-BORN BRITISH BUSINESS EXECUTIVE ANSHUMAN JAIN died at the AGE of (`-59)!!!~'

`-BIRTH/DAY # `-NUMBER = 1+7+19+63 = 90

`-BIRTH/DAY # `-NUMBER = 90 / (`-DIVIDED by) (`-2) = (`-45) = 5X9 = (`-59) = `-AGE of `-DEATH for INDIAN-BORN BRITISH BUSINESS EXECUTIVE ANSHUMAN!!!~'

`-DEATH/DAY # `-NUMBER = 8+12+20+22 = 62

`-DAY of `-DEATH 12th = FLIP 2 to 7 = 1/7 = `-BIRTH/DAY!!!~'

`-DEATH/DAY # `-NUMBER = 62 = FLIP 2 to 7 = 67 = 6x7 = 42 = 20+22 = `-DEATH/YEAR!!!~'

90+62 = 152 = 1+5/2 = 62 = `-DEATH/DAY # `-NUMBER!!!~'

90+62 = 152 = 15+2 = 17 = FRAGMENTED `-DEATH/DAY # `-NUMBER!!!~'

90(-)62 = 28 = X TIMES (`-2) = 56 = FLIP 6 to 9 = 59 = `-AGE of `-DEATH for INDIAN-BORN BRITISH BUSINESS EXECUTIVE ANSHUMAN!!!~'

FRAGMENTED `-BIRTH/DAY # `-NUMBER = 1+7+1+9+ 6+3 = 27

FRAGMENTED `-BIRTH/DAY # `-NUMBER = 27 = PARTIAL `-BIRTH/DAY # `-NUMBER = 1+7+19 = (`-27)!!!~'

FRAGMENTED `-DEATH/DAY # `-NUMBER = 8+1+2+2+0+ 2+2 = 17

FRAGMENTED `-DEATH/DAY # `-NUMBER = 17 = 1/7 = `-BIRTH/DAY!!!~'

27+17 = 44 = 4+4 = 8 = `-BIRTH/DAY = 1/7 = 1+7 = (`-8)!!!~'

27+17 = 44 = `-BIRTH/YEAR = 19(-)63 = (`-44)!!!~'

FROM `-BIRTH-to-DEATH there are 148 DAYS = 1+4/8 = 58 = `-DIED the `-VERY `-NEXT `-YEAR of `-AGE at the `-AGE of (`-59)!!!~'

FROM `-BIRTH-to-DEATH there are 148 DAYS = RECIPROCAL = 841 = 84x1 = 84 = `-DIVIDED by (`-2) = 42 = 20+22 = `-DEATH/ YEAR!!!~'

(365 (-) 148) = 217 = 21+7 = 28 = X TIMES (`-2) = 56 = FLIP 6 to 9 = 59 = `-AGE of `-DEATH for INDIAN-BORN BRITISH BUSINESS EXECUTIVE ANSHUMAN!!!~'

`-BIRTH/MONTH was JANUARY with 31 DAYS

(31 (-) 7) – DAY of `-BIRTH = 24 = RECIPROCAL = 42 = 20+22 = `-DEATH/YEAR!!!~'

`-WAS `-MARRIED to GEETIKA JAIN from 1986 to 2022 = 36 YEARS!!!~'

(`-36) = FLIP 3 to 8 = (`-86) was `-MARRIED in this `-YEAR of (`-86)!!!~'

1986 = 19(-)86 = 67 = 6x7 = 42 = 20+22 = `-DEATH/YEAR!!!~'

`-BIRTH/DAY # `-NUMBER in `-REVERSE = 63(-)19(-)7(-)1 = (`-36)!!!~'

`-BIRTH/YEAR = (`-63) = RECIPROCAL = (`-36)!!!~'

`-BIRTH/YEAR = 63 = RECIPROCAL = 36 = FLIP 3 to 8 = (`-86) = `-MARRIED in this `-YEAR of (`-86)!!!~'

`-BIRTH/YEAR = 1963 = 19+63 = (`-82) = `-DEATH/DAY = 8/12 = 82x1 = (`-82)!!!~'

`-DEATH/DAY = 8/12 = FLIP 2 to 7 = 8/17 = 8x17 = (`-136) = 1x36 = (`-36) = RECIPROCAL = (`-63) = `-BIRTH/YEAR!!!~'

`-BIRTH/YEAR = 1963 = 9/1+6+3 = 9/10 = 9x10 = 90 / (`-DIVIDED by) (`-2) = (`-45) = 5X9 = (`-59) = `-AGE of `-DEATH for INDIAN-BORN BRITISH BUSINESS EXECUTIVE ANSHUMAN!!!~'

`-WAS `-BORN in the `-MONTH of (`-1); and, `-DIED within the `-MONTH of (`-8) = (1/8) = (`-18) = 6x3 = (`-63) = `-BIRTH/YEAR!!!~'

AMERICAN STAND-UP COMEDIAN & ACTOR GILBERT JEREMY GOTTFRIED died at the AGE of (`-67)!!!~'

`-AGE of `-DEATH = (`-67) = 6x7 = (`-42) = 20+22 = `-DEATH/YEAR!!!~'

`-BIRTH/DAY # `-NUMBER = 2+28+19+55 = 104

`-BIRTH/DAY # `-NUMBER = 104 / (`-DIVIDED by) (`-2) = (`-52) = `-AGE of `-WIFE DARA KRAVITZ at `-TIME of `-HER `-HUSBAND'S `-DEATH AMERICAN STAND-UP COMEDIAN & ACTOR GILBERT JEREMY GOTTFRIED!!!~'

`-BIRTH/DAY = 2/28 = HALF RECIPROCAL = 2/82 = 2+82 = (`-84) = / (`-DIVIDED by) (`-2) = 42 = 20+22 = `-DEATH/YEAR!!!~'

`-BIRTH/DAY = 2/28 = 2(-)28 = 26 = RECIPROCAL = 62 = FLIP 2 to 7 = (`-67) = `-AGE of `-DEATH for AMERICAN STAND-UP COMEDIAN & ACTOR GILBERT JEREMY GOTTFRIED!!!~'

`-DEATH/DAY # `-NUMBER = 4+12+20+22 = 58

`-DEATH/DAY # `-NUMBER = 58 = 5x8 = 40 = `-BIRTH/DAY # `-NUMBER = 104 = RECIPROCAL = 401 = 40x1 = (`-40)!!!~'

`-BIRTH/DAY = 2/28 = HALF RECIPROCAL = 2/82 = 2(-)82 = (`-80) = / (`-DIVIDED by) (`-2) = (`-40) = "SEE `-ABOVE"!!!~'

104+58 = 162 = 1x62 = (`-62) = FLIP 2 to 7 = (`-67) = `-AGE of `-DEATH for AMERICAN STAND-UP COMEDIAN & ACTOR GILBERT JEREMY GOTTFRIED!!!~'

104(-)58 = 46 = / (`-DIVIDED by) (`-2) = 23 = RECIPROCAL = (`-32) = FRAGMENTED `-BIRTH/DAY # `-NUMBER!!!~'

`-DEATH/DAY = 4/12 = 4+1/2 = (`-52) = `-AGE of `-WIFE DARA KRAVITZ at `-TIME of `-HER `-HUSBAND'S `-DEATH AMERICAN STAND-UP COMEDIAN & ACTOR GILBERT JEREMY GOTTFRIED!!!~'

`-DEATH/DAY = 4/12 = HALF RECIPROCAL = 4/21 = 4+21 = 25 = RECIPROCAL = (`-52) = `-AGE of `-WIFE DARA KRAVITZ at `-TIME of `-HER `-HUSBAND'S `-DEATH AMERICAN STAND-UP COMEDIAN & ACTOR GILBERT JEREMY GOTTFRIED!!!~'

`-DEATH/DAY = 4/12 = 42x1 = 42 = 20+22 = `-DEATH/YEAR!!!~'

`-DEATH/DAY = 4/12 = 4x12 = 48 = RECIPROCAL = 84 / (`-DIVIDED by) (`-2) = 42 = 20+22 = `-DEATH/YEAR!!!~'

FRAGMENTED `-BIRTH/DAY # `-NUMBER = 2+2+8+1+9+5+5 = 32

FRAGMENTED `-BIRTH/DAY # `-NUMBER = 32 = -a PROPHETIC # `-NUMBER!!!~'

FRAGMENTED `-BIRTH/DAY # `-NUMBER = 32 = FLIP 3 to 8; FLIP 2 to 7 = (`-87)

`-DAUGHTER `-BORN in 2007 = 20+07 = (`-27)!!!~'

`-SON `-BORN in 2009 = 20+09 = (`-29)!!!~'

27+29 = (`-56) = 8x7 = "SEE `-ABOVE for `-BIRTH/DAY # `-NUMBER `-CONVERSION"!!!~'

`-BIRTH/DAY = for AMERICAN STAND-UP COMEDIAN & ACTOR GILBERT JEREMY GOTTFRIED = 2/28 = 2x28 = (`-56) = CHILDREN'S `-BIRTHS `-ADDED `-UP `-TOGETHER!!!~'

FRAGMENTED `-DEATH/DAY # `-NUMBER = 4+1+2+2+0+ 2+2 = 13

FRAGMENTED `-DEATH/DAY # `-NUMBER = 13 = "A VERY `-PIVOTAL # `-NUMBER"!!!~'

`-DEATH/DAY # `-NUMBER = (`-58) (+) (1+3) = FRAGMENTED `-DEATH/DAY # `-NUMBER = (`-62) = FLIP 2 to 7 = (`-67) = `-AGE of `-DEATH for AMERICAN STAND-UP COMEDIAN & ACTOR GILBERT JEREMY GOTTFRIED!!!~'

FRAGMENTED `-DEATH/DAY # `-NUMBER = 13 = 6+7 = (`-67) = `-AGE of `-DEATH for AMERICAN STAND-UP COMEDIAN & ACTOR GILBERT JEREMY GOTTFRIED!!!~'

32+13 = 45 / (`-DIVIDED by) (`-3) = (`-15) = `-WAS `-MARRIED for (`-15) `-YEARS!!!~'

FROM `-BIRTH-to-DEATH there are 43 DAYS = FLIP 3 to 8 = 48 = RECIPROCAL = 84 / (`-DIVIDED by) (`-2) = 42 = 20+22 = `-DEATH/YEAR!!!~'

FROM `-BIRTH-to-DEATH there are 43 DAYS = FLIP 3 to 8 = 48 = `-DEATH/DAY = 4x12 = (`-48)!!!~'

(365 (-) 43) = 322 = 3+2/2 = (`-52) = `-AGE of `-WIFE DARA KRAVITZ at `-TIME of `-HER `-HUSBAND'S `-DEATH AMERICAN STAND-UP COMEDIAN & ACTOR GILBERT JEREMY GOTTFRIED!!!~'

`-WAS `-MARRIED to DARA KRAVITZ from 2007 to 2022 for 15 YEARS!!!~'

`-DAUGHTER LILY ASTER GOTTFRIED was (`-15) `-YEARS of `-AGE at the `-TIME of `-HER `-FATHER'S `-DEATH!!!~'

`-MARRIED = 2007 = 20(-)07 = (`-13) = FRAGMENTED `-DEATH/DAY # `-NUMBER for AMERICAN STAND-UP COMEDIAN & ACTOR GILBERT JEREMY GOTTFRIED!!!~'

`-SON MAX AARON GOTTFRIED was (`-13) YEARS of `-AGE at the `-TIME of `-HIS `-FATHER'S `-DEATH!!!~'

`-WIFE DARA KRAVITZ `-BIRTH/DAY # `-NUMBER = 2/24/19/70!!!~'

`-WIFE's `-BIRTH/DAY = 2/24 = 2+24 = 26 = RECIPROCAL = 62 = FLIP 2 to 7 = (`-67) = `-AGE of `-DEATH for `-HUSBAND AMERICAN STAND-UP COMEDIAN & ACTOR GILBERT JEREMY GOTTFRIED!!!~'

`-WIFE's `-BIRTH/DAY = 2/24 = 2x24 = 48 = RECIPROCAL = 84 = / (`-DIVIDED by) (`-2) = 42 = 20+22 = `-DEATH/YEAR for `-HUSBAND AMERICAN STAND-UP COMEDIAN & ACTOR GILBERT JEREMY GOTTFRIED!!!~'

`-WIFE's `-BIRTH/DAY = 2/24 = 2x24 = 48 = `-HUSBAND'S `-DEATH/DAY = 4x12 = (`-48)!!!~'

`-WIFE's `-DAY of `-BIRTH = 24<sup>th</sup> / `-HUSBAND'S `-DAY of `-BIRTH = 28th / (24+28) = (`-52) = `-AGE of `-WIFE DARA KRAVITZ at `-TIME of `-HER `-HUSBAND'S `-DEATH AMERICAN STAND-UP COMEDIAN & ACTOR GILBERT JEREMY GOTTFRIED!!!~'

`-WIFE's `-BIRTH/DAY # `-NUMBER in `-REVERSE = 70(-)19(-)24(-)2 = 25 = RECIPROCAL = (`-52) = `-AGE of `-WIFE DARA KRAVITZ at `-TIME of `-HER `-HUSBAND'S `-DEATH AMERICAN STAND-UP COMEDIAN & ACTOR GILBERT JEREMY GOTTFRIED!!!~'

`-YEARS `-ACTIVE in the `-BUSINESS from 1970 to 2022 = (52) YEARS = `-AGE of `-WIFE DARA KRAVITZ at `-TIME of `-HER `-HUSBAND'S `-DEATH AMERICAN STAND-UP COMEDIAN & ACTOR GILBERT JEREMY GOTTFRIED!!!~'

`-WAS `-BORN in the `-MONTH of (`-2); and, `-DIED in the `-MONTH of (`-4) = (`-24) = RECIPROCAL = (`-42) = 20+22 = `-DEATH/YEAR!!!~'

`-**BIRTH/YEAR**:-

(`-24) = FLIP 2 to 7 = (`-74) = `-BIRTH/YEAR = 19+55 = (`-74)!!!~'

42(-)24 = (`-18)

DEATH/MONTH of APRIL with 30 DAYS

30 (-) 12) – DAY of `-DEATH = (`-18) = "SEE `-ABOVE & `-BELOW"!!!~'

1**8**+1**8** = 36 = `-**BIRTH/YEAR** = 19(-)55 = (`-**36**)!!!~'

`-SIBLING ARLENE HARRIET GOTTFRIED was `-**BORN** in the `-MONTH of (`-**8**); and, `-**DIED** in the `-MONTH of (`-**8**) with a `-**DEATH/DAY** of = (`-**8/8**)!!!~'

`-SHE `-DIED (`-**18**) `-DAYS `-AWAY from `-**BIRTH-to-DEATH from `-TURNING `-AGE (`-67)!!!~'**

AMERICAN BASKETBALL COACH PETER JOSEPH CARRIL died at the AGE of (`-92)!!!~'

`-AGE of `-DEATH = (`-92) = 9(-)2 = (`-7) = `-BIRTH/MONTH!!!~'

`-PARTIAL `-BIRTH/DAY # `-NUMBER = 7+10+19 = 36 = `-DAYS from `-BIRTH-to-DEATH!!!~'

`-BIRTH/DAY # `-NUMBER = 7+10+19+30 = 66

`-BIRTH/DAY `-NUMBER = 66 = 2(6's) = 26 = RECIPROCAL = 62 = FLIP 6 to 9 = (`-92) = `-AGE of `-DEATH for AMERICAN BASKETBALL COACH PETER JOSEPH CARRIL!!!~'

`-BIRTH/DAY # `-NUMBER = 66 = FLIP 6 to 9 = (`-99) = 2(9's) = 29 = RECIPROCAL = (`-92) = `-AGE of `-DEATH for AMERICAN BASKETBALL COACH PETER JOSEPH CARRIL!!!~'

`-DEATH/DAY # `-NUMBER = 8+15+20+22 = 65

`-DEATH/DAY # `-NUMBER = 65 = 6+5 = (`-11) = 9+2 = (`-92) = `-AGE of `-DEATH for AMERICAN BASKETBALL COACH PETER JOSEPH CARRIL!!!~'

66+65 = 131 = 1x31 = (`-31) = RECIPROCAL = (`-13)

31(-)13 = 18 = 3x6 = (`-36) = `-DAYS from `-BIRTH-to-DEATH!!!~'

`-BIRTH/DAY # `-NUMBER = (`-66) = 6x6 = (`-36) = `-DAYS from `-BIRTH-to-DEATH!!!~'

`-BIRTH/YEAR = 19/30 = 19+30 = 49 = 4x9 = (`-36) = `-DAYS from `-BIRTH-to-DEATH!!!~'

`-DEATH/DAY = 8/15 = 8+15 = (`-23) = X TIMES (`-4) = (`-92) = `-AGE of `-DEATH for AMERICAN BASKETBALL COACH PETER JOSEPH CARRIL!!!~'

`-BIRTH/DAY = 7/10 = 7x10 = 70 / (`-DIVIDED by) (`-2) = 35 = FLIP 3 TO 8 = (`-85) = `-DEATH/DAY = 8/15 = 85x1 = (`-85)!!!~'

`-DEATH/YEAR = 20/22 = FLIP 2 to 7 = 20/72 = 20+72 = (`-92) = `-AGE of `-DEATH for AMERICAN BASKETBALL COACH PETER JOSEPH CARRIL!!!~'

FRAGMENTED `-BIRTH/DAY # `-NUMBER = 7+1+0+1+9+3+0 = 21

`-BIRTH/MONTH was JULY with 31 DAYS

(31 (-) 10) – DAY of `-BIRTH = 21

FRAGMENTED `-DEATH/DAY # `-NUMBER = 8+1+5+2+0+2+2 = 20

21x20 = 420 = 42+0 = (`-42) = 6x7 = FLIP 6 to 9; FLIP 7 to 2 = (`-92) = `-AGE of `-DEATH for AMERICAN BASKETBALL COACH PETER JOSEPH CARRIL!!!~'

21+20 = 41 = X TIMES (`-3) = 123 = 1x23 = (`-23) = X TIMES (`-4) = (`-92) = `-AGE of `-DEATH for AMERICAN BASKETBALL COACH PETER JOSEPH CARRIL!!!~'

FROM `-BIRTH-to-DEATH there are 36 DAYS = RECIPROCAL = 63 = FLIP 6 to 9 = (`-93) = `-DIED the `-PREVIOUS `-YEAR of `-AGE at `-TIME of `-DEATH of (`-92)!!!~'

(365 (-) 36) = 329 = 3(-)29 = 26 = RECIPROCAL = 62 = FLIP 6 to 9 = (`-92) = `-AGE of `-DEATH for AMERICAN BASKETBALL COACH PETER JOSEPH CARRIL!!!~'

(365 (-) 36) = 329 = 3+29 = (`-32) = RECIPROCAL = (`-23) = X TIMES (`-4) = (`-92) = `-AGE of `-DEATH for AMERICAN BASKETBALL COACH PETER JOSEPH CARRIL!!!~'

`-DEATH/MONTH was AUGUST with 31 DAYS

(31 (-) 15) – DAY of `-DEATH = 16 = RECIPROCAL = 61 = FLIP 6 to 9 = (`- 91) = `-DIED the `-VERY `-NEXT `-YEAR of `-AGE at the `-TIME of `-DEATH of (`-92)!!!~'

`-BIRTH/YEAR = 19/30 = 1x9/3+0 = (`-93) = `-DIED the `-PREVIOUS `-YEAR of `-AGE at `-TIME of `-DEATH of (`-92)!!!~'

`-BIRTH/YEAR = 19/30 = 19(-)30 = (`-11) = 9+2 = (`-92) = `-AGE of `-DEATH for AMERICAN BASKETBALL COACH PETER JOSEPH CARRIL!!!~'

`-BIRTH/YEAR = 19/30 = 9+0/1(-)3 = (`-92) = `-AGE of `-DEATH for AMERICAN BASKETBALL COACH PETER JOSEPH CARRIL!!!~'

'-HAD a '-COACHING CAREER from 1954 to 2011 = 57 YEARS = 5x7 = ('-35) = FLIP 3 to 8 = ('-85) = '-DEATH/DAY = 8/15 = 85x1 = ('-85)!!!~'

1954 = 19(-)54 = ('-35) = FLIP 3 to 8 = ('-85) = '-DEATH/DAY = 8/15 = 85x1 = ('-85)!!!~'

'-WAS '-BORN in the '-MONTH of ('-7); and, '-DIED in the '-MONTH of ('-8) = (7/8) = FLIP 7 to 2; FLIP 8 to 3 = ('-23) = '-DEATH/DAY = 8/15 = 8+15 = ('-23)!!!~'

'-WAS '-BORN in the '-MONTH of ('-7); and, '-DIED in the '-MONTH of ('-8) = (7/8) = FLIP 7 to 2; FLIP 8 to 3 = ('-23) = X TIMES ('-4) = ('-92) = '-AGE of '-DEATH for AMERICAN BASKETBALL COACH PETER JOSEPH CARRIL!!!~'

'-DEATH/YEAR = 20/22 = 20+22 = 42 = 6x7 = ('-67) = FLIP 6 to 9; FLIP 7 to 2 = ('-92) = '-AGE of '-DEATH for AMERICAN BASKETBALL COACH PETER JOSEPH CARRIL!!!~'

GERMAN FILM DIRECTOR "THE PERFECT STORM" WOLFGANG PETERSEN died at the AGE of ('-81)!!!~'

'-WAS '-BORN in the '-MONTH ('-3); and, '-DIED in the '-MONTH of ('-8) = ('-38) = 3x8 = 24 = RECIPROCAL = 42 = 20+22 = '-DEATH/YEAR!!!~'

'-BIRTH/YEAR = 41 = X TIMES ('-2) = ('-82) = DEATH/DAY = 8/12 = 82x1 = ('-82)!!!~'

'-BIRTH/YEAR = 41 = X TIMES ('-2) = ('-82) = DIED the '-VERY '-YEAR of '-AGE '-PREVIOUS at the '-AGE of ('-81))!!!~'

`-BIRTH/DAY = 3/14 = 3x14 = 42 = 20+22 = `-DEATH/YEAR!!!~'

`-BIRTH/DAY = 3/14 = 3+14 = 17 = 1x7 = (`-7) = 8(-)1 = (`-81) = `-AGE of `-DEATH for GERMAN FILM DIRECTOR "THE PERFECT STORM" WOLFGANG PETERSEN!!!~'

`-BIRTH/DAY # `-NUMBER = 3+14+19+41 = 77

`-BIRTH/DAY # `-NUMBER = 77 = `-BIRTH/YEAR = 19(-)41 = 22 = FLIP 2 to 7 = (`-77)

`-BIRTH/DAY # `-NUMBER = 77 = `-SON DANIEL PETERSEN `-BIRTH/YEAR = 19(-)68 = 49 = 7x7 = 77

`-DEATH/DAY # `-NUMBER = 8+12+20+22 = 62

`-DEATH/DAY # `-NUMBER = 62 / (`-DIVIDED by) (`-2) = (`-31) = FLIP 3 to 8 = (`-81) = `-AGE of `-DEATH for GERMAN FILM DIRECTOR "THE PERFECT STORM" WOLFGANG PETERSEN!!!~'

77+62 = 139 = 13x9 = 117 = 11x7 = (`-77) = `-BIRTH/DAY # `-NUMBER!!!~'

77(-)62 = 15 = 5x3 = (`-53) = `-AGE of `-SON DANIEL PETERSEN at the `-TIME of `-HIS `-FATHER'S `-DEATH!!!~'

77(-)62 = 15 = `-FORMER `-WIFE URSULA SIEG'S `-BIRTH/DAY = 8/7 = 8+7 = (`-15)!!!~'

`-DEATH/DAY = 8/12 = 8x12 = 96 = FLIP 6 to 9 = 99 = 9x9 = (`-81) = `-AGE of `-DEATH for GERMAN FILM DIRECTOR "THE PERFECT STORM" WOLFGANG PETERSEN!!!~'

`-FORMER `-WIFE URSULA SIEG'S `-BIRTH/DAY = 8/7 = FLIP 7 to 2 = 8/2 = `-DEATH/DAY = 8/12 = 82x1 = (`-82)!!!~'

`-PARTIAL `-DEATH/DAY # `-NUMBER = 8+12+20 = 40 = 8x5 = (`-85) = `-AGE of `-FORMER `-WIFE URSULA SIEG at the `-TIME of `-HER `-FORMER `-HUSBAND'S `-DEATH!!!~'

`-DEATH/DAY = 8/12 = 82(-)1 = (`-81) = `-AGE of `-DEATH for GERMAN FILM DIRECTOR "THE PERFECT STORM" WOLFGANG PETERSEN!!!~'

FRAGMENTED `-BIRTH/DAY # `-NUMBER = 3+1+4+1+9+4+1 = 23

FRAGMENTED `-BIRTH/DAY # `-NUMBER = 23 = -a `-PROPHETIC # `-NUMBER!!!~'

FRAGMENTED `-BIRTH/DAY # `-NUMBER = 23 = RECIPROCAL = 32 = FLIP 3 to 8 = (`-82) = `-DEATH/DAY = 8/12 = 82x1 = (`-82)!!!~'

FRAGMENTED `-BIRTH/DAY # `-NUMBER = 23 = RECIPROCAL = 32 = FLIP 3 to 8 = (`-82) = DIED the `-VERY `-YEAR of `-AGE `-PREVIOUS at the `-AGE of (`-81))!!!~'

FRAGMENTED `-BIRTH/DAY # `-NUMBER = 23 = RECIPROCAL = 32 = FLIP 3 to 8; FLIP 2 to 7 = (`-87) = `-SON DANIEL PETERSEN `-BIRTH/YEAR = 19+68 = (`-87) = `-BIRTH/DAY (8/7) of `-MOTHER URSULA SIEG & `-FORMER `-WIFE of WOLFGANG PETERSEN!!!~'

FRAGMENTED `-DEATH/DAY # `-NUMBER = 8+1+2+2+0+2+2 = 17

FRAGMENTED `-DEATH/DAY # `-NUMBER = 17 = `-BIRTH/
DAY = 3/14 = 3+14 = 17

`-BIRTH/MONTH was MARCH with 31 DAYS

(31 (-) 14) – DAY of `-BIRTH = 17 = FRAGMENTED `-DEATH/
DAY # `-NUMBER!!!~'

23 = RECIPROCAL = 32+17 = 49 = 7x7 = (`-77) = `-BIRTH/DAY
# `-NUMBER!!!~'

23 = RECIPROCAL = 32(-)17 = 15 = 5x3 = (`-53) = `-AGE of
`-SON DANIEL PETERSEN at the `-TIME of `-HIS `-FATHER'S
`-DEATH!!!~'

23 = RECIPROCAL = 32(-)17 = 15 = `-FORMER `-WIFE URSULA
SIEG'S `-BIRTH/DAY = 8/7 = 8+7 = (`-15)!!!~'

23+17 = 40 = 8x5 = (`-85) = `-AGE of `-FORMER `-WIFE URSULA
SIEG at the `-TIME of `-HER `-FORMER `-HUSBAND'S
`-DEATH!!!~'

FROM `-BIRTH-to-DEATH there are 151 DAYS = 15x1 = (`-15)
= `-SEE `-ABOVE for `-FORMER `-WIFE URSULA SIEG and
`-THEIR `-SON DANIEL PETERSEN!!!~'

(365 (-) 151) = 214 = 2x14 = 28 = RECIPROCAL = 82 = DIED the
`-VERY `-YEAR of `-AGE `-PREVIOUS at the `-AGE of (`-81))!!!~'

`-WAS `-MARRIED to MARIA BORGEL-PETERSEN from
1978 to 2022 for 44 YEARS = `-BIRTH/DAY = 3/14 = HALF
RECIPROCAL = 3/41 = 3+41 = (`-44)!!!~'

`-BIRTH/DAY = 3/14 = 3+1/4 = (`-44)!!!~'

44+44 = 88 = `-WAS `-BORN in the `-MONTH (`-3); and, `-DIED in the `-MONTH of (`-8) = (`-38) = FLIP 3 to 8 = (`-88)!!!~'

1978 = 1+9+7/8 = 17/8 = 1+7/8 = (`-88)!!!~'

`-BIRTH/YEAR of `-WOLFGANG PETERSEN = 19(-)41 = 22 = `-YEAR of `-DEATH = (`-22)!!!~'

22+22 = (`-44) = `-YEARS OF `-MARRIAGE to `-MARIA BORGEL-PETERSEN from 1978 to 2022 for 44 YEARS!!!~'

1978 = 19+78 = 97 = FLIP 9 to 6 = 67 = 6x7 = 42 = 20+22 = `-DEATH/YEAR!!!~'

ONE `-MARRIAGE `-BEGAN & ONE `-MARRIAGE `-ENDED in (`-19/78)!!!~'

(`-78) = RECIPROCAL = (`-87) = `-FORMER `-WIFE URSULA SIEG'S `-BIRTH/DAY = (`-8/7)!!!~'

`-FORMER `-WIFE URSULA SIEG'S `-BIRTH/DAY # `-NUMBER = 8+7+19+37 = (`-71) = RECIPROCAL = (`-17) = FRAGMENTED `-DEATH/DAY # `-NUMBER for FORMER HUSBAND GERMAN FILM DIRECTOR "THE PERFECT STORM" WOLFGANG PETERSEN!!!~'

`-FORMER `-WIFE URSULA SIEG was (`-85) at the `-TIME of `-HER `-FORMER `-HUSBAND'S `-DEATH!!!~'

(`-85) = 8+5 = 13 = RECIPROCAL = (`-31) = FLIP 3 to 8 = (`-81) = `-AGE of `-DEATH for `-FORMER `-HUSBAND GERMAN FILM DIRECTOR "THE PERFECT STORM" WOLFGANG PETERSEN!!!~'

(`-85) = RECIPROCAL = (`-58) = FLIP 8 to 3 = (`-53) = `-AGE of `-SON DANIEL PETERSEN at the `-TIME of `-HIS `-FATHER'S `-DEATH!!!~'

`-FORMER `-WIFE URSULA SIEG'S `-BIRTH/YEAR = 19(-)37 = 18 = RECIPROCAL = (`-81) = `-AGE of `-DEATH for `-FORMER `-HUSBAND GERMAN FILM DIRECTOR "THE PERFECT STORM" WOLFGANG PETERSEN!!!~'

`-SON DANIEL PETERSEN'S `-BIRTH/DAY = 10/21 = 10+21 = (`-31) = FLIP 3 to 8 = (`-81) = `-AGE of `-DEATH for `-FATHER GERMAN FILM DIRECTOR "THE PERFECT STORM" WOLFGANG PETERSEN!!!~'

JAPANESE FASHION DESIGNER HANAE MORI died at the AGE of (`-96)!!!~'

`-WAS `-BORN in the `-MONTH of (`-1); and, `-DIED in the `-MONTH of (`-8) = (`-1/8) = `-BIRTH/DAY & = (RECIPROCAL) = `-DEATH/DAY!!!~'

`-BIRTH/DAY = 1/8 = RECIPRICAL = 8/11 = `-DEATH/DAY = 8/11 = 8/1x1 = 8/1

`-BIRTH/DAY # `-NUMBER = 1+8+19+26 = 54

`-BIRTH/DAY # `-NUMBER = 54 = 9x6 = (`-96) = `-AGE of `-DEATH for JAPANESE FASHION DESIGNER HANAE MORI!!!~'

`-DEATH/DAY # `-NUMBER = 8+11+20+22 = 61

54+61 = 5+4/6x1 = (`-96) = `-AGE of `-DEATH for JAPANESE FASHION DESIGNER HANAE MORI!!!~'

54+61 = 115 = 1x15 = (`-15) = 9+6 = (`-96) = `-AGE of `-DEATH for JAPANESE FASHION DESIGNER HANAE MORI!!!~'

FRAGMENTED `-BIRTH/DAY # `-NUMBER = 1+8+1+9+ 2+6 = 27

`-BIRTH/DAY # `-NUMBER = (`-54) (+) (`-27) = FRAGMENTED `-BIRTH/DAY # `-NUMBER = 81 = RECIPROCAL = (`-18) = `-WAS `-BORN in the `-MONTH of (`-1); and, `-DIED in the `-MONTH of (`-8) = (`-1/8)!!!~'

FRAGMENTED `-BIRTH/DAY # `-NUMBER = 27 = RECIPROCAL = 72 = `-CHILD AKIRA MORI was (`-73) `-YEARS of `-AGE at the `-TIME of `-MOTHER'S `-DEATH!!!~'

FRAGMENTED `-DEATH/DAY # `-NUMBER = 8+1+1+2+0+ 2+2 = 16

FRAGMENTED `-DEATH/DAY # `-NUMBER = 16 = RECIPROCAL = 61 = `-DEATH/DAY # `-NUMBER!!!~'

27+16 = 43 = RECIPROCAL = 34

43+34 = (`-77) = 2(7's) = (`-27) = FRAGMENTED `-BIRTH/DAY # `-NUMBER!!!~'

FROM `-BIRTH-to-DEATH there are 215 DAYS = 21+5 = (`-26) = `-BIRTH/YEAR!!!~'

FROM `-BIRTH-to-DEATH there are 215 DAYS = 21(-)5 = 16 = FRAGMENTED `-DEATH/DAY # `-NUMBER = RECIPROCAL = 61 = `-DEATH/DAY # `-NUMBER!!!~'

(365 (-) 215) = 150 = 15+0 = (`-15) = 9+6 = (`-96) = `-AGE of `-DEATH for JAPANESE FASHION DESIGNER HANAE MORI!!!~'

`-WAS `-MARRIED to KEN MORI from 1948 to 1996 for 48 YEARS!!!~'

`-MARRIAGE `-ENDED in (`-96) = `-AGE of `-DEATH for JAPANESE FASHION DESIGNER HANAE MORI!!!~'

`-MARRIAGE `-BEGAN in (`-48); and, `-LASTED for (`-48) YEARS = X TIMES (`-2) = (`-96) = `-AGE of `-DEATH for JAPANESE FASHION DESIGNER HANAE MORI!!!~'

`-BIRTH/MONTH was JANUARY with 31 DAYS

(31 (-) 8) – DAY of `-BIRTH = (`-23) = RECIPROCAL = (`-32) = 4x8 = (`-48) = `-YEARS of `-MARRIAGE!!!~'

(31 (-) 8) – DAY of `-BIRTH = (`-23) = FLIP 2 to 7 = (`-73) = `-AGE of `-CHILD AKIRA MORI at `-TIME of `-MOTHER'S `-DEATH!!!~'

`-CHILD AKIRA MORI was `-BORN in 1949 = 9/1(-)4(-)9 = (`-96) = `-AGE of `-DEATH for `-MOTHER JAPANESE FASHION DESIGNER HANAE MORI!!!~'

`-CHILD AKIRA MORI `-BIRTH/DAY # `-NUMBER = 6+3+19+49 = (`-77)!!!~'

JAPANESE FASHION DESIGNER HANAE MORI `-DEATH/DAY # `-NUMBER = 61 = RECIPROCAL = 16 = FRAGMENTED `-DEATH/DAY # `-NUMBER....

61+16 = (`-77)!!!~'

61(-)16 = (`-45)!!!~'

HANAE MORI FRAGMENTED `-BIRTH/DAY # `-NUMBER = 27 = 2(7's) = (`-77)!!!~'

HANAE MORI `-BIRTH/YEAR = 19/26 = 19+26 = 45 = RECIPROCAL = 54

45+54 = 99 = FLIP 9 to 6 = (`-96) = `-AGE of `-DEATH for JAPANESE FASHION DESIGNER HANAE MORI!!!~'

`-BIRTH/YEAR = (`-26) = RECIPROCAL = (`-62) = FLIP 6 to 9; FLIP 2 to 7 = (`-97) = `-DIED the `-VERY `-YEAR `-PRIOR at the `-AGE of (`-96)!!!~'

AMERICAN ARTIST "BIG EYES" MARGARET D. H. KEANE died at the AGE of (`-94)!!!~'

`-BIRTH/DAY = 9/15 = 9/1(-)5 = (`-94) = `-AGE of `-DEATH for AMERICAN ARTIST "BIG EYES" MARGARET D. H. KEANE!!!~'

`-DEATH/DAY = 6/26 = FLIP 6 to 9 = 9/26 = 9/2(-)6 = (`-94) = `-AGE of `-DEATH for AMERICAN ARTIST "BIG EYES" MARGARET D. H. KEANE!!!~'

`-BIRTH/DAY # `-NUMBER = 9+15+19+27 = 70

`-BIRTH/DAY = 9/15 = 9+15 = 24 = RECIPROCAL = 42 = 20+22 = `-DEATH/YEAR!!!~'

`-BIRTH/DAY = 9/15 = HALF RECIPROCAL = 9/51 = 9(-)51 = 42 = 20+22 = `-DEATH/YEAR!!!~'

`-DEATH/DAY # `-NUMBER = 6+26+20+22 = 74

70+74 = 144 = 14x4 = 56 = 5x6 = ('-30) = `-TOTAL `-YEARS of `-MARRIAGE!!!~'

70+74 = 144 = 14+4 = 18 = RECIPROCAL = 81 = DAYS from `-BIRTH-to-DEATH!!!~'

70(-)74 = 4

`-DEATH/MONTH was JUNE with 30 DAYS

(30 (-) 26) – DAY of `-DEATH = ('-4)

FRAGMENTED `-BIRTH/DAY # `-NUMBER = 9+1+5+1+9+2+7 = 34

`-BIRTH/DAY # `-NUMBER = 70 (-) 34 = FRAGMENTED `-BIRTH/DAY # `-NUMBER = 36 = 9x4 = ('-94) = `-AGE of `-DEATH for AMERICAN ARTIST "BIG EYES" MARGARET D. H. KEANE!!!~'

FRAGMENTED `-BIRTH/DAY # `-NUMBER = 34 = FLIP 3 to 8 = 84 / ('-DIVIDED by) ('-2) = 42 = 20+22 = `-DEATH/YEAR!!!~'

FRAGMENTED `-DEATH/DAY # `-NUMBER = 6+2+6+2+0+2+2 = 20

`-DEATH/DAY # `-NUMBER = 74 (+) 20 = FRAGMENTED `-DEATH/DAY # `-NUMBER = ('-94) = `-AGE of `-DEATH for AMERICAN ARTIST "BIG EYES" MARGARET D. H. KEANE!!!~'

`-DEATH/DAY = 6/26 = 6/2+6 = ('-68) / ('-DIVIDED by) ('-2) = ('-34) = FRAGMENTED `-BIRTH/DAY # `-NUMBER!!!~'

FRAGMENTED `-DEATH/DAY # `-NUMBER = 20 = `-DEATH/ DAY = 6/26 = 6(-)26 = 20

34+20 = 54 = 5x4 = 20 = FRAGMENTED `-DEATH/DAY # `-NUMBER!!!~'

34+20 = 54 = 9x6 = `-WAS `-BORN in the `-MONTH of (`-9); and, `-DIED in the `-MONTH of (`-6)!!!~'

34(-)20 = 14 = 6+8 = (`-68) = `-DEATH/DAY = 6/26 = 6/2+6 = (`-68)!!!~'

`-DEATH/DAY = 6/26 = FLIP 6 to 9 = 9/2/6 = "9 to 6" = `-FROM `-BIRTH/MONTH (`-9) to `-DEATH/MONTH (`-6)!!!~'

`-BIRTH/DAY = 9/15 = 9/1+5 = 9/6 = `-WAS `-BORN in the `-MONTH of (`-9); and, `-DIED in the `-MONTH of (`-6)!!!~'

FROM `-BIRTH-to-DEATH there are 81 DAYS = FLIP 8 to 3 = 31 = RECIPROCAL = 13 = 9+4 = (`-94) = `-AGE of `-DEATH for AMERICAN ARTIST "BIG EYES" MARGARET D. H. KEANE!!!~'

(365 (-) 81) = 284 = 2(-)8/4 = 6/4 = FLIP 6 to 9 = (`-94) = `-AGE of `-DEATH for AMERICAN ARTIST "BIG EYES" MARGARET D. H. KEANE!!!~'

(365 (-) 81) = 284 = 2x84 = 168 = 1x68 = 68 = `-DEATH/DAY = 6/26 = 6/2+6 = (`-68)!!!~'

(365 (-) 81) = 284 = 2(-)8/4 = 6/4 = (`-64) = `-DIVORCED in 1983 = 19(-)83 = (`-64) = FLIP 6 to 9 = (`-94) `-AGE of `-DEATH for AMERICAN ARTIST "BIG EYES" MARGARET D. H. KEANE!!!~'

`-MARRIED in 1970 = 19+70 = 89 = RECIPROCAL = 98 = FLIP 9 to 6 = (`-68) = `-DEATH/DAY = 6/26 = 6/2+6 = (`-68)!!!~'

`-MARRIED in 1970 = 19+70 = 89 = FLIP 8 to 3; FLIP 9 to 6 = (`-36) = 9x4 = (`-94) = `-AGE of `-DEATH for AMERICAN ARTIST "BIG EYES" MARGARET D. H. KEANE!!!~'

`-MARRIAGE `-ENDED in 1983 = 9/1(-)8(-)3 = (`-94) = `-AGE of `-DEATH for AMERICAN ARTIST "BIG EYES" MARGARET D. H. KEANE!!!~'

`-WAS `-MARRIED to DAN MCGUIRE from 1970 to 1983 for 13 YEARS = 9+4 = (`-94) = `-AGE of `-DEATH for AMERICAN ARTIST "BIG EYES" MARGARET D. H. KEANE!!!~'

`-WAS `-MARRIED to WALTER KEANE from 1955 to 1965 for 10 YEARS!!!~'

`-MARRIED in 1955 = 19+55 = 74 = `-DEATH/DAY # `-NUMBER!!!~'

`-MARRIED in 1955 = 19(-)55 = 36 = 9x4 = (`-94) = `-AGE of `-DEATH for AMERICAN ARTIST "BIG EYES" MARGARET D. H. KEANE!!!~'

`-DIVORCED in 1965 = 19+65 = 84 = FLIP 8 to 3 = (`-34) = FRAGMENTED `-BIRTH/DAY # `-NUMBER!!!~'

`-DIVORCED in 1965 = 19(-)65 = 46 = RECIPROCAL = 64 = FLIP 6 to 9 = (`-94) = `-AGE of `-DEATH for AMERICAN ARTIST "BIG EYES" MARGARET D. H. KEANE!!!~'

`-WAS `-MARRIED to FRANK ULBRICH from 1948 to 1955 for 7 YEARS!!!~'

`-MARRIED in (`-48) = RECIPROCAL = (`-84) = FLIP 8 to 3 = (`-34) = FRAGMENTED `-BIRTH/DAY # `-NUMBER!!!-'

`-MARRIED in 1948 = 19(-)48 = 29 = FLIP 9 to 6 = 26 = `-DAY of `-DEATH!!!-'

`-MARRIED in 1948 = 19+48 = 67 = 6x7 = 42 = 20+22 = `-DEATH/YEAR!!!-'

`-DIVORCED in 1955 = 19+55 = 74 = `-DEATH/DAY # `-NUMBER!!!-'

`-DIVORCED in 1955 = 19(-)55 = 36 = 9x4 = (`-94) = `-AGE of `-DEATH for AMERICAN ARTIST "BIG EYES" MARGARET D. H. KEANE!!!-'

`-TOTAL `-YEARS of `-MARRIAGE = (13+10+7) = 30 YEARS = 5x6 = (`-56) = `-DEATH/DAY = 6/26 = HALF RECIPROCAL = 6/62 = 6(-)62 = (`-56)!!!-'

`-DEATH/DAY = 6/26 = 6x26 = 156 = 1x56 = (`-56) = 5x6 = (`-30) = `-TOTAL `-YEARS of `-MARRIAGE!!!-'

`-BIRTH/YEAR = 1927 = 19+27 = 46 = 4x6 = 24 = RECIPROCAL = 42 = 20+22 = `-DEATH/YEAR!!!-'

`-BIRTH/YEAR = 19/27 = 9/1+2(-)7 = (`-94) = `-AGE of `-DEATH for AMERICAN ARTIST "BIG EYES" MARGARET D. H. KEANE!!!-'

`-BIRTH/YEAR = 1927 = 19+27 = 46 = RECIPROCAL = 64 = FLIP 6 to 9 = (`-94) = `-AGE of `-DEATH for AMERICAN ARTIST "BIG EYES" MARGARET D. H. KEANE!!!-'

The COMPLEXITY of OUR CREATION, is BEYOND; `-OUR `-IMAGINATION!!!~'

AMERICAN ACTOR JAMES GARNER died at the AGE of (`-86)!!!~'

`-WAS `-BORN in the `-MONTH of (`-4); and, `-DIED in the `-MONTH of (`-7) = (`-47) = `-BIRTH/DAY = (`-4/7) = `-BIRTH/YEAR = 19+28 = (`-47)!!!~'

`-AGE of `-DEATH = (`-86) = 8+6 = (`-14) = `-DEATH/YEAR!!!~'

`-PARTIAL `-BIRTH/DAY # `-NUMBER = 4+7+19 = 30 = X TIMES (`-2) = (`-60) = `-DEATH/DAY # `-NUMBER!!!~'

`-BIRTH/DAY # `-NUMBER = 4+7+19+28 = 58

`-BIRTH/DAY # `-NUMBER = 58 = RECIPROCAL = 85 = `-DIED the `-VERY `-NEXT `-YEAR of `-AGE at (`-86)!!!~'

`-PARTIAL `-DEATH/DAY # `-NUMBER = 7+19+20 = 46 = `-SERVED in the `-MERCHANT MARINES from 1944 to 1946!!!~'

`-PARTIAL `-DEATH/DAY # `-NUMBER = 7+19+20 = 46 = `-WAS `-BORN the `-VERY `-NEXT `-DAY = (`-4/7)!!!~'

`-PARTIAL `-DEATH/DAY # `-NUMBER = 7+19+20 = 46 = FLIP 6 to 9 = 49 = RECIPROCAL = 94 = (47+47) = `-SEE `-ABOVE = (`-94)!!!~'

`-DEATH/DAY = 7/19 = 7/1(-)9 = 7/8 = FLIP 7 to 2 = (`-28) = `-BIRTH/YEAR!!!~'

`-DEATH/DAY # `-NUMBER = 7+19+20+14 = 60

`-DEATH/DAY = 7/19 = 7+19 = 26 = RECIPROCAL = 62 = HEIGHT = 6' 2"!!!~'

`-DEATH/DAY = 7/19 = HALF RECIPROCAL = 7/91 = 7+91 = 98 = FLIP 9 to 6 = 68 = RECIPROCAL = (`-86) = `-AGE of `-DEATH for AMERICAN ACTOR JAMES GARNER!!!~'

`-DEATH/DAY = 7/19 = HALF RECIPROCAL = 7/91 = 7(-)91 = 84 = RECIPROCAL = (`-48) = 8x6 = (`-86) = `-AGE of `-DEATH for AMERICAN ACTOR JAMES GARNER!!!~'

58+60 = 118 = 1+1/8 = 28 = RECIPROCAL = 82 = `-DAUGHTER GIGI GARNER'S `-BIRTH/DAY # `-NUMBER is 1+4+19+58 = (`-82)!!!~'

58+60 = 118 = 11x8 = (`-88) = 26 = RECIPROCAL = 62 = `-ADDED `-UP `-TOGETHER = 26+62 = (`-88) = "SEE `-ABOVE for `-LAYOUT on `-DEATH/DAY = (7+19) = 26 = RECIPROCAL = 62"!!!~'

`-BIRTH/MONTH was `-APRIL with 30 DAYS

(30 (-) 7) – DAY of `-BIRTH = 23 = FLIP 3 to 8 = (`-28) = `-BIRTH/YEAR!!!~'

`-DEATH/DAY = 7/19 = 7x19 = 133 = 1(-)3/3 = (`-23) = "SEE `-ABOVE & `-BELOW for `-LINKS"!!!~'

`-DEATH/MONTH was `-JULY with 31 DAYS

(31 (-) 19) – DAY of `-DEATH = 12 = 6x2 = (`-62) = `-HEIGHT = 6' 2"

110

`-DEATH/DAY = 7/19 = 7x19 = 133 = 13x3 = (`-39) = FLIP 3 to 8; FLIP 9 to 6 = (`-86) = `-AGE of `-DEATH for AMERICAN ACTOR JAMES GARNER!!!~'

FRAGMENTED `-BIRTH/DAY # `-NUMBER = 4+7+1+9+ 2+8 = 31

`-BIRTH/DAY # `-NUMBER = 58 (+) 31 = FRAGMENTED `-BIRTH/DAY # `-NUMBER = (`-89) = FLIP 9 to 6 = (`-86) = `-AGE of `-DEATH for AMERICAN ACTOR JAMES GARNER!!!~'

FRAGMENTED `-DEATH/DAY # `-NUMBER = 7+1+9+2+0+ 1+4 = 24

`-DAUGHTER GIGI GARNER'S PARTIAL `-BIRTH/DAY # `-NUMBER = 1+4+19 = (`-24)!!!~'

`-DEATH/DAY # `-NUMBER = 60 (+) 24 = FRAGMENTED `-DEATH/DAY # `-NUMBER = 84 = RECIPROCAL = 48 = 8x6 = (`-86) = `-AGE of `-DEATH for AMERICAN ACTOR JAMES GARNER!!!~'

31+24 = 55 = `-WAS `-MARRIED the `-VERY `-NEXT `-YEAR in (`-56)!!!~'

31+24 = 55 = `-BIRTH/YEAR = 19/28 = 19x28 = 532 = 53+2 = (`-55)!!!~'

FROM `-BIRTH-to-DEATH there are 103 DAYS = 10+3 = (`-13) = 5+8 = (`-58) = `-BIRTH/DAY # `-NUMBER!!!~'

FROM `-BIRTH-to-DEATH there are 103 DAYS = 10+3 = (`-13) = RECIPROCAL = (`-31) = FRAGMENTED `-BIRTH/DAY # `-NUMBER!!!~'

(365 (-) 103) = 262 = 2x62 = 124 = 1x24 = (`-24) = FLIP 2 to 7 = (`-7/4) = RECIPROCAL = (`-4/7) = "SEE `-ABOVE" for `-BIRTH/ DAY `-LINK, ETC...!!!~'

(365 (-) 103) = 262 = 2x62 = 124 = 1x24 = (`-24) = FRAGMENTED `-DEATH/DAY # `-NUMBER!!!~'

(365 (-) 103) = 262 = 2/62 = AMERICAN ACTOR JAMES GARNER'S `-HEIGHT = 6' 2"

(365 (-) 103) = 262 = 26x2 = (`-52) = FLIP 2 to 7 = (`-57) = `-DAUGHTER GIGI GARNER'S `-HEIGHT is 5' 7"!!!~'

`-WAS `-MARRIED to LOIS CLARKE from 1956 to 2014 for (`-58) YEARS = `-BIRTH/DAY # `-NUMBER!!!~'

(`-58) = 5+8 = (`-13) = RECIPROCAL = (`-31) = FRAGMENTED `-BIRTH/DAY # `-NUMBER!!!~'

`-YEARS `-ACTIVE were from 1954 to 2010 = 56 YEARS = `-WAS `-MARRIED in (`-56)!!!~'

AMERICAN ACTOR JAMES GARNER'S `-BIRTH/DAY = 4/7 = 4x7 = 28 = `-BIRTH/YEAR = (`-28)!!!~'

(28+28) = (`-56)!!!~'

`-DAUGHTER GIGI GARNER `-WAS (`-56) `-YEARS of `-AGE at the `-TIME of `-HER `-FATHER'S `-DEATH AMERICAN ACTOR JAMES GARNER!!!~'

`-DAUGHTER GIGI GARNER was `-BORN in (`-58) = `-TOTAL `-YEARS `-MARRIED (`-58); and, `-BIRTH/DAY # `-NUMBER for AMERICAN ACTOR JAMES GARNER `-HER `-FATHER = (`-58)!!!~'

`-DAUGHTER'S `-BIRTH/YEAR = 19/58 = 19(-)58 = 39 = FLIP 3 to 8; FLIP 9 to 6 = (`-86) = `-AGE of `-DEATH for `-FATHER AMERICAN ACTOR JAMES GARNER!!!~'

`-DAUGHTER'S `-BIRTH/DAY # `-NUMBER in `-REVERSE = 58(-)19(-)4(-)1 = (`-34) = X TIMES (`-2) = (`-68) = RECIPROCAL = (`-86) = `-AGE of `-DEATH for `-FATHER AMERICAN ACTOR JAMES GARNER!!!~'

`-MARRIAGE `-ENDED by `-DEATH in 2014 = 20+14 = 34 = X TIMES (`-2) = 68 = RECIPROCAL = (`-86) = `-AGE of `-DEATH for AMERICAN ACTOR JAMES GARNER!!!~'

`-BIRTH/YEAR = 1928 = 1(-)9(-)2/8 = 68 = RECIPROCAL = (`-86) = `-AGE of `-DEATH for AMERICAN ACTOR JAMES GARNER!!!~'

`-DEATH/YEAR = 20/14 = 20x14 = 280 = 28+0 = 28 = `-BIRTH/YEAR!!!~'

AMERICAN PROFESSIONAL GOLFER THOMAS DANIEL WEISKOPF died at the AGE of (`-79)!!!~'

`-BIRTH/DAY = 11/9 = 1+1/9 = 29 = FLIP 2 to 7 = (`-79) = `-AGE of `-DEATH for AMERICAN PROFESSIONAL GOLFER THOMAS DANIEL WEISKOPF!!!~'

`-BIRTH/YEAR = 42 = 20+22 = `-DEATH/YEAR!!!~'

`-BIRTH/DAY # `-NUMBER = 11+9+19+42 = 81

`-PARTIAL `-BIRTH/DAY # `-NUMBER = 11+9+19 = 39 = X TIMES (`-2) = (`-78) = `-DIED the `-VERY `-NEXT `-YEAR of `-AGE at (`-79)!!!~'

`-BIRTH/DAY = 11/9 = 11+9 = 20 = FLIP 2 to 7 = (`-70) = `-DEATH/DAY # `-NUMBER!!!~'

`-DEATH/DAY # `-NUMBER = 8+20+20+22 = 70

`-DEATH/DAY = 8/20 = 8+20 = 28 = FLIP 8 to 3 = (`-23) = `-BIRTH/YEAR = 19(-)42 = (`-23)!!!~'

81+70 = 151 = 1x51 = (`-51) = `-DAUGHTER HEIDI WEISKOPF was (`-51) YEARS of `-AGE at the `-TIME of `-HER `-FATHER'S `-DEATH AMERICAN PROFESSIONAL GOLFER THOMAS DANIEL WEISKOPF!!!~'

`-BIRTH/MONTH was `-NOVEMBER with 30 DAYS

(30 (-) 9) – DAY of `-BIRTH = 21 = 7x3 = (`-73) = `-SON ERIC WEISKOPF was `-BORN in (`-73)!!!~'

`-DEATH/MONTH was `-AUGUST with 31 DAYS

(31 (-) 20) – DAY of `-DEATH = 11 = `-BIRTH/MONTH = (`-11)!!!~'

`-DEATH/DAY = 8/20 = 8+20 = (`-28) = `-TOTAL `-PROFESSIONAL `-WINS = (`-28)!!!~'

FRAGMENTED `-BIRTH/DAY # `-NUMBER = 1+1+9+1+9+4+2 = 27

FRAGMENTED `-DEATH/DAY # `-NUMBER = 8+2+0+2+0+2+2 = 16

FRAGMENTED `-DEATH/DAY # `-NUMBER = 16 = 7+9 = (`-79) = `-AGE of `-DEATH for AMERICAN PROFESSIONAL GOLFER THOMAS DANIEL WEISKOPF!!!~'

FRAGMENTED `-DEATH/DAY # `-NUMBER = 16 = `-WON (`-16) PGA TOUR TITLES from 1968 to 1982 to include the (1973) OPEN CHAMPIONSHIP!!!~'

TOUR TITLE `-VICTORIES `-BEGAN = 1968 = 19+68 = 87 = RECIPROCAL = 78 = `-DIED the `-VERY `-NEXT `-YEAR of `-AGE at (`-79)!!!~'

TOUR TITLE `-VICTORIES `-BEGAN = 1968 = 19(-)68 = (`-49) = `-AGE of `-SON ERIC WEISKOPF at the `-TIME of `-HIS `-FATHER'S `-DEATH AMERICAN PROFESSIONAL GOLFER THOMAS DANIEL WEISKOPF!!!~'

TOUR TITLE `-VICTORIES `-ENDED = 1982 = 19(-)82 = 63 = 7x9 = (`-79) = `-AGE of `-DEATH for AMERICAN PROFESSIONAL GOLFER THOMAS DANIEL WEISKOPF!!!~'

`-1973 OPEN CHAMPIONSHIP = `-SON ERIC WEISKOPF was `-BORN in (`-1973)!!!~'

27+16 = 43 = `-SON ERIC WEISKOPF `-BIRTH/DAY # `-NUMBER in `-REVERSE = 73(-)19(-)10(-)1 = (`-43)!!!~'

FROM `-BIRTH-to-DEATH there are 81 DAYS = `-BIRTH/DAY # `-NUMBER = (`-81)!!!~'

81+81 = 162 = 1+62 = (`-63) = 7x9 = (`-79) = `-AGE of `-DEATH for AMERICAN PROFESSIONAL GOLFER THOMAS DANIEL WEISKOPF!!!~'

FROM `-BIRTH-to-DEATH there are 81 DAYS = `-BIRTH/DAY = 11/9 = 11x9 = 99 = 9x9 = (`-81) = "SEE `-PREVIOUS `-ABOVE; 'for `-LINK"!!!~'

(365 (-) 81) = 284 = 2x84 = 168 = 1(-)8/6 = (`-76) = FLIP 6 to 9 = (`-79) = `-AGE of `-DEATH for AMERICAN PROFESSIONAL GOLFER THOMAS DANIEL WEISKOPF!!!~'

`-SON ERIC WEISKOPF `-BIRTH/YEAR = 19/73 = 19+73 = 92 = RECIPROCAL = 29 = FLIP 2 to 7 = (`-79) = `-AGE of `-DEATH for `-FATHER AMERICAN PROFESSIONAL GOLFER THOMAS DANIEL WEISKOPF!!!~'

`-SON ERIC WEISKOPF `-BIRTH/YEAR = 1973 = 1x9/7(-)3 = 94 = RECIPROCAL = 49 = `-AGE at `-TIME of `-HIS `-FATHER'S `-DEATH AMERICAN PROFESSIONAL GOLFER THOMAS DANIEL WEISKOPF!!!~'

`-DAUGHTER HEIDI WEISKOPF `-PARTIAL `-BIRTH/DAY # `-NUMBER = 3+20+19 = 42 = 20+22 = `-DEATH/YEAR for `-FATHER AMERICAN PROFESSIONAL GOLFER THOMAS DANIEL WEISKOPF!!!~'

`-DAUGHTER HEIDI WEISKOPF `-BIRTH/DAY # `-NUMBER in `-REVERSE = 71(-)19(-)20(-)3 = 29 = FLIP 2 to 7 = (`-79) = `-AGE of `-DEATH for `-FATHER AMERICAN PROFESSIONAL GOLFER THOMAS DANIEL WEISKOPF!!!~'

`-AGE of `-DEATH = 79 = 7x9 = (`-63) = HEIGHT = 6' 3"!!!~'

`-AGE of `-DEATH = 79 = 7x9 = (`-63) = RECIPROCAL = (`-36) = 4x9 = (`-49) = `-SON ERIC WEISKOPF was (`-49) `-YEARS of `-AGE at the `-TIME of `-HIS `-FATHER'S `-DEATH AMERICAN PROFESSIONAL GOLFER THOMAS DANIEL WEISKOPF!!!~'

`-BIRTH/YEAR = 19/42 = 19(-)42 = (`-23) = FLIP 2 to 7; FLIP 3 to 8 = (`-78) = `-DIED the `-VERY `-NEXT `-YEAR of `-AGE at (`-79)!!!~'

`-BIRTH/YEAR = 19/42 = 19(-)42 = (`-23) = `-DAUGHTER HEIDI WEISKOPF `-BIRTH/DAY = 3/20 = 3+20 = (`-23)!!!~'

`-BIRTH/YEAR = 19/42 = 1+4+2/9 = (`-79) = `-AGE of `-DEATH for AMERICAN PROFESSIONAL GOLFER THOMAS DANIEL WEISKOPF!!!~'

`-WAS `-MARRIED to JEANNE WEISKOPF from 1966 to 1999 for (`-33) YEARS!!!~'

(`-66) = FLIP 6 to 9 = (`-99) = `-BIRTH/DAY = 11/9 = 11x9 = (`-99)!!!~'

(`-99) = 9x9 = (`-81) = `-BIRTH/DAY # `-NUMBER = (`-81) & `-TIME from `-BIRTH-to-DEATH = (`-81) DAYS!!!~'

(`-66) = 6x6 = 36 = RECIPROCAL = 63 = 7x9 = (`-79) = `-AGE of `-DEATH for AMERICAN PROFESSIONAL GOLFER THOMAS DANIEL WEISKOPF!!!~'

`-WAS `-BORN in the `-MONTH of (`-11); and, `-DIED in the `-MONTH of (`-8) = (`-11/8) = `-WAS `-BORN the `-VERY `-NEXT `-DAY on (`-11/9)!!!~'

`-WAS `-BORN in the `-MONTH of (`-11); and, `-DIED in the `-MONTH of (`-8) = (`-11/8) = 11x8 = (`-88) = FLIP 8 to 3 = (`-33) = `-WAS `-MARRIED to JEANNE WEISKOPF from 1966 to 1999 for (`-33) YEARS!!!~'

AMERICAN ACTRESS VIRGINIA ANN MARIE PATTON MOSS "IT'S A WONDERFUL LIFE" died at the AGE of (`-97)!!!~'

`-BIRTH/DAY = 6/25 = 6/2+5 = 6/7 = FLIP 6 to 9 = (`-97) = `-AGE of `-DEATH for AMERICAN ACTRESS VIRGINIA ANN MARIE PATTON MOSS "IT'S A WONDERFUL LIFE"!!!~'

`-BIRTH/DAY # `-NUMBER = 6+25+19+25 = 75

`-BIRTH/DAY = 6/25 = 6+25 = (`-31) = FLIP 3 to 8 = (`-8/1) = `-FIRST `-PART of `-DEATH/DAY!!!~'

`-DEATH/DAY # `-NUMBER = 8+18+20+22 = 68

`-DEATH/DAY # `-NUMBER = (`-68) = `-WAS `-BORN in the `-MONTH of (`-6); and, `-DIED in the `-MONTH of (`-8) = (`-68)!!!~'

`-DEATH/DAY # `-NUMBER = (`-68) = FLIP 8 to 3 = (`-63) = 9x7 = (`-97) = `-AGE of `-DEATH for AMERICAN ACTRESS VIRGINIA ANN MARIE PATTON MOSS "IT'S A WONDERFUL LIFE"!!!~'

`-DEATH/DAY # `-NUMBER = (`-68) = FLIP 6 to 9 = (`-98) = `-DIED the `-VERY `-YEAR `-PRIOR at the `-AGE of (`-97)!!!~'

75+68 = 143 = 1+4/3 = (`-53) = RECIPROCAL = (`-35) = 7x5 = (`-75) = `-BIRTH/DAY # `-NUMBER = (`-75)!!!~'

75+68 = 143 = 1x43 = (`-43) = `-YEARS `-ACTIVE from 1943 to 1949!!!~'

1949 = 19+49 = (`-68) = `-DEATH/DAY # `-NUMBER = (`-68)!!!~'

1949 = 19(-)49 = (`-30) = FRAGMENTED `-BIRTH/DAY # `-NUMBER!!!~'

1943 = 19+43 = 62 = FLIP 6 to 9; FLIP 2 to 7 = (`-97) = `-AGE of `-DEATH for AMERICAN ACTRESS VIRGINIA ANN MARIE PATTON MOSS "IT'S A WONDERFUL LIFE"!!!~'

1943 = 19(-)43 = 24 = RECIPROCAL = 42 = 20+22 = `-DEATH/YEAR!!!~'

`-DEATH/DAY = 8/18 = 8+18 = 26 = RECIPROCAL = 62 = FLIP 6 to 9; FLIP 2 to 7 = (`-97) = `-AGE of `-DEATH for AMERICAN ACTRESS VIRGINIA ANN MARIE PATTON MOSS "IT'S A WONDERFUL LIFE"!!!~'

FRAGMENTED `-BIRTH/DAY # `-NUMBER = 6+2+5+1+9+2+5 = 30

FRAGMENTED `-DEATH/DAY # `-NUMBER = 8+1+8+2+0+2+2 = 23

30+23 = (`-53) = RECIPROCAL = (`-35) = 7x5 = (`-75) = `-BIRTH/DAY # `-NUMBER = (`-75)!!!~'

FROM `-BIRTH-to-DEATH there are 54 DAYS = `-DEATH/DAY = 8/18 = 8x18 = 144 = 1+4/4 = (`-54)!!!~'

(365 (-) 54) = 311 = 31+1 = (`-32) = RECIPROCAL = (`-23) = FRAGMENTED `-DEATH/DAY # `-NUMBER!!!~'

`-BIRTH/YEAR = 19/25 = 1x9/2+5 = 9/7 = (`-97) = `-AGE of `-DEATH for AMERICAN ACTRESS VIRGINIA ANN MARIE PATTON MOSS "IT'S A WONDERFUL LIFE"!!!~'

`-DEATH/YEAR = 20/22 = 20+22 = `-42 = 6x7 = (`-67) = FLIP 6 to 9 = (`-97) = `-AGE of `-DEATH for AMERICAN ACTRESS VIRGINIA ANN MARIE PATTON MOSS "IT'S A WONDERFUL LIFE"!!!~'

RUSSIAN JOURNALIST AND POLITICAL ACTIVIST DARYA ALEKSANDROVNA DUGINA died at the AGE of (`-29)!!!~'

`-BIRTH/YEAR = 92 = RECIPROCAL = (`-29) = `-AGE of `-DEATH for RUSSIAN JOURNALIST AND POLITICAL ACTIVIST DARYA ALEKSANDROVNA DUGINA!!!~'

`-BIRTH/DAY # `-NUMBER = 12+15+19+92 = 138

`-BIRTH/DAY # `-NUMBER = 1(38) = 38 / (DIVIDED by) (`-2) = 19 /|\ (1)/19 = 1+1/9 = (`-29) = `-AGE of `-DEATH for RUSSIAN JOURNALIST AND POLITICAL ACTIVIST DARYA ALEKSANDROVNA DUGINA!!!~'

`-BIRTH/DAY # `-NUMBER = 138 = 1(-)3/8 = (`-28) = `-DIED the `-VERY `-NEXT `-YEAR of `-AGE at (`-29)!!!~'

`-PARTIAL `-BIRTH/DAY # `-NUMBER in `-REVERSE = 92(-)19(-)15 = 58 = / (DIVIDED by) (`-2) = (`-29) = `-AGE of `-DEATH for RUSSIAN JOURNALIST AND POLITICAL ACTIVIST DARYA ALEKSANDROVNA DUGINA!!!~'

`-BIRTH/DAY # `-NUMBER = 138 = 1(-)3/8 = (`-28) = `-DEATH/DAY = 8+20 = (`-28)!!!~'

`-DEATH/DAY # `-NUMBER = 8+20+20+22 = 70

`-DEATH/DAY # `-NUMBER = 70 / (DIVIDED by) (`-2) = (`-35) = `-FATHER ALEKSANDR GELYEVICH DUGIN `-BIRTH/ DAY # `-NUMBER in `-REVERSE = 62(-)19(-)7(-)1 = (`-35)!!!~'

138+70 = 208 = 20+8 = (`-28) = `-SEE `-ABOVE for `-LINKS!!!~'

138+70 = 208 = RECIPROCAL = 8/02 = HALF RECIPROCAL = 8/20 = `-DEATH/DAY!!!~'

138(-)70 = (`-68) = SEE `-BELOW for `-LINKAGES!!!~'

FRAGMENTED `-BIRTH/DAY # `-NUMBER = 1+2+1+5+1+9+ 9+2 = 30

FRAGMENTED `-BIRTH/DAY # `-NUMBER = 30 = `-DIED the `-VERY `-YEAR `-PRIOR at the `-AGE of (`-29)!!!~

`-BIRTH/DAY # `-NUMBER = 138 (+) 30 = FRAGMENTED `-BIRTH/DAY # `-NUMBER = (`-168) = 1(-)6/8 = (`-58) = / (`-DIVIDED by) (`-2) = (`-29) = `-AGE of `-DEATH for RUSSIAN JOURNALIST AND POLITICAL ACTIVIST DARYA ALEKSANDROVNA DUGINA!!!~'

`-BIRTH/DAY # `-NUMBER = 138 (+) 30 = FRAGMENTED `-BIRTH/DAY # `-NUMBER = (`-168) = 1x68 = (`-68) = `-BIRTH/ DAY # `-NUMBER (`-138) (-) `-DEATH/DAY # `-NUMBER (`-70) = (`-68)!!!~'

FRAGMENTED `-BIRTH/DAY # `-NUMBER = 30 = X TIMES (`- 2) = (`-60) = `-FATHER ALEKSANDR GELYEVICH DUGIN was (`-60) `-YEARS of `-AGE at the `-TIME of `-HIS `-DAUGHTER'S `-DEATH RUSSIAN JOURNALIST AND POLITICAL ACTIVIST DARYA ALEKSANDROVNA DUGINA!!!~'

FRAGMENTED `-DEATH/DAY # `-NUMBER = 8+2+0+2+0+ 2+2 = 16

`-DEATH/DAY # `-NUMBER = (`-70) (+) (`-16) = FRAGMENTED `-DEATH/DAY # `-NUMBER = (`-86) = RECIPROCAL = (`-68) = "SEE `-ABOVE & `-BELOW"!!!~'

`-BIRTH/MONTH was DECEMBER with 31 DAYS

(31 (-) 15) – DAY of `-BIRTH = 16 = FRAGMENTED `-DEATH/ DAY # `-NUMBER!!!~'

30+16 = 46 = `-BIRTH/DAY # `-NUMBER in `-REVERSE = 92(-)19(-)15(-)12 = (`-46)!!!~'

30+16 = 46 = `-PARTIAL `-BIRTH/DAY # `-NUMBER = 12+15+19 = (`-46)!!!~'

(46+46) = 92 = RECIPROCAL = (`-29) = `-AGE of `-DEATH for RUSSIAN JOURNALIST AND POLITICAL ACTIVIST DARYA ALEKSANDROVNA DUGINA!!!~'

FROM `-BIRTH-to-DEATH there are 117 DAYS = 1+1/7 = (`-27) = `-BIRTH/DAY = 12+15 = (`-27)!!!~'

`-FATHER ALEKSANDR GELYEVICH DUGIN `-PARTIAL `-BIRTH/DAY # `-NUMBER = 1+7+19 = (`-27)!!!~'

`-FATHER ALEKSANDR GELYEVICH DUGIN `-BIRTH/DAY # `-NUMBER = 1+7+19+62 = 89 = 8x9 = (`-72) = RECIPROCAL = (`-27)!!!~'

(365 (-) 117) = 248 = 2+4/8 = (`-68) = `-BIRTH/DAY # `-NUMBER (`-138) (-) `-DEATH/DAY # `-NUMBER (`-70) = (`-68)!!!~'

(365 (-) 117) = 248 = 24(-)8 = 16 = FRAGMENTED `-DEATH/ DAY # `-NUMBER!!!~'

(365 (-) 117) = 248 = RECIPROCAL = 842 = 84 / (DIVIDED by) (`-2) = 42 = 20+22 = `-DEATH/YEAR!!!~'

`-DEATH/MONTH was AUGUST with 31 DAYS

(31 (-) 20) – DAY of `-DEATH = (`-11) = 2+9 = (`-29) = `-AGE of `-DEATH for RUSSIAN JOURNALIST AND POLITICAL ACTIVIST DARYA ALEKSANDROVNA DUGINA!!!~'

`-BIRTH/YEAR = 19/92 = 1+9+9/2 = 19/2 = 1x9/2 = 92 = RECIPROCAL = (`-29) = `-AGE of `-DEATH for RUSSIAN JOURNALIST AND POLITICAL ACTIVIST DARYA ALEKSANDROVNA DUGINA!!!~'

`-DEATH/YEAR = 20/22 = 20+22 = 42 = 6x7 = (`-67) = FLIP 6 to 9; FLIP 7 to 2 = (`-92) = RECIPROCAL = (`-29) = `-AGE of `-DEATH for RUSSIAN JOURNALIST AND POLITICAL ACTIVIST DARYA ALEKSANDROVNA DUGINA!!!~'

`-FATHER ALEKSANDR GELYEVICH DUGIN was `-BORN in (`-62) = RECIPROCAL = (`-26) = FLIP 6 to 9 = (`-29) = `-AGE of `-DEATH of `-DAUGHTER RUSSIAN JOURNALIST AND POLITICAL ACTIVIST DARYA ALEKSANDROVNA DUGINA!!!~'

`-FATHER ALEKSANDR GELYEVICH DUGIN `-BIRTH/ YEAR = 19/62 = 19+62 = 81 = RECIPROCAL = 18 = 2x9 = (`-29) = `-AGE of `-DEATH for `-DAUGHTER RUSSIAN JOURNALIST

DWAYNE W. ANDERSON

AND POLITICAL ACTIVIST DARYA ALEKSANDROVNA DUGINA!!!~'

AMERICAN FOOTBALL QUARTERBACK LEONARD "LEN" RAY DAWSON died at the AGE of (`-87)!!!~'

`-WAS `-BORN in the `-MONTH of (`-6); and, `-DIED in the `-MONTH of (`-8) = (`-6/8) = RECIPROCAL = (`-8/6) = DEATH/DAY = 8/2+4 = 8/24!!!~'

`-BIRTHDAY = 6+20 /|\ `-DEATH/DAY = 8+24 = (6+20+8+24) = 58 = RECIPROCAL = 85 = FLIP 8 to 3 = (`-35) = `-BIRTH/YEAR!!!~'

`-BIRTH/DAY = 6/20 = 6+20 = (`-26) = FRAGMENTED `-BIRTH/DAY # `-NUMBER!!!~'

`-BIRTH/DAY = 6/20 = 6+20 = 26 = FLIP 2 to 7 = 76 = 7x6 = (`-42) = 20+22 = `-DEATH/YEAR!!!~'

`-BIRTH/DAY # `-NUMBER = 6+20+19+35 = 80

`-BIRTH/DAY # `-NUMBER = 80 = 40x2 = 40+2 = (`-42) = 20+22 = `-DEATH/YEAR!!!~'

`-DEATH/DAY # `-NUMBER = 8+24+20+22 = 74

`-AGE of `-DEATH = (`-87) = X TIMES (`-2) = (`-174) = 1x74 = (`-74) = `-DEATH/DAY # `-NUMBER!!!~'

`-DEATH/DAY # `-NUMBER = 74 / (DIVIDED by) (`-2) = (`-37) = FLIP 3 to 8 = (`-87) = `-AGE of `-DEATH for AMERICAN

124

FOOTBALL QUARTERBACK LEONARD "LEN" RAY DAWSON!!!~'

`-DEATH/DAY # `-NUMBER = 74 = 7x4 = 28 = RECIPROCAL = 82 = FLIP 2 to 7 = (`-87) = `-AGE of `-DEATH for AMERICAN FOOTBALL QUARTERBACK LEONARD "LEN" RAY DAWSON!!!~'

`-DEATH/DAY = 8/24 = 8+24 = 32 = FLIP 3 to 8; FLIP 2 to 7 = (`-87) = `-AGE of `-DEATH for AMERICAN FOOTBALL QUARTERBACK LEONARD "LEN" RAY DAWSON!!!~'

`-DEATH/DAY = 8/24 = 8/2x4 = (`-88) = `-DIED the `-VERY `-YEAR `-PRIOR at the `-AGE of (`-87)!!!~'

`-DAY of `-DEATH (`-24th) = RECIPROCAL = (`-42) = 20+22 = `-DEATH/YEAR!!!~'

80+74 = 154 = 1x54 = (`-54) = `-BIRTH/YEAR = 19+35 = (`-54)!!!~'

80+74 = 154 = 1x54 = (`-54) = `-WAS `-MARRIED to JACQUELINE PUZDER in (`-54)!!!~'

FRAGMENTED `-BIRTH/DAY # `-NUMBER = 6+2+0+1+9+3+5 = 26

`-BIRTH/DAY # `-NUMBER = (`-80) (-) (`-26) = FRAGMENTED `-BIRTH/DAY # `-NUMBER = (`-54) = "SEE `-ABOVE & `-BELOW"!!!~'

FRAGMENTED `-DEATH/DAY # `-NUMBER = 8+2+4+2+0+2+2 = 20

`-DEATH/DAY # `-NUMBER = (`-74) (-) (`-20) = FRAGMENTED `-DEATH/DAY # `-NUMBER = (`-54) = "SEE `-ABOVE & BELOW"!!!~'

FRAGMENTED `-DEATH/DAY # `-NUMBER = 20 = 5x4 = `-BIRTH/YEAR = 19+35 = (`-54)!!!~'

26+20 = 46 = 4x6 = (`-24) = RECIPROCAL = (`-42) = 20+22 = `-DEATH/YEAR!!!~'

FROM `-BIRTH-to-DEATH there are 65 DAYS = RECIPROCAL = 56 = 8x7 = (`-87) = `-AGE of `-DEATH for AMERICAN FOOTBALL QUARTERBACK LEONARD "LEN" RAY DAWSON!!!~'

(365 (-) 65) = 300 = 30+0 = 30 = 5x6 = (`-56) = 8x7 = (`-87) = `-AGE of `-DEATH for AMERICAN FOOTBALL QUARTERBACK LEONARD "LEN" RAY DAWSON!!!~'

`-WAS `-MARRIED to JACQUELINE PUZDER from 1954 to 1978 for (`-24) `-YEARS = RECIPROCAL = (`-42) = 20+22 = `-DEATH/YEAR!!!~'

`-MARRIAGE `-BEGAN = 19(-)54 = (`-35) = `-BIRTH/YEAR!!!~'

`-MARRIAGE `-ENDED in 19(-)78 = (`-59) = 5x9 = (`-45) = RECIPROCAL = (`-54) = `-BIRTH/YEAR = 19+35 = (`-54)!!!~'

`-MARRIAGE `-ENDED in (`-78) = RECIPROCAL = (`-87) = `-AGE of `-DEATH for AMERICAN FOOTBALL QUARTERBACK LEONARD "LEN" RAY DAWSON!!!~'

`-BIRTH/YEAR = 19(-)35 = (`-16) = QUARTERBACK # `-NUMBER for KANSAS CITY CHIEFS (`-16), PITTSBURGH STEELERS (`-16); and, CLEVELAND BROWNS (`-16)!!!~'

`-DEATH/DAY = 8/24 = 8(-)24 = (`-16) = QUARTERBACK #
`-NUMBER for KANSAS CITY CHIEFS (`-16), PITTSBURGH
STEELERS (`-16); and, CLEVELAND BROWNS (`-16)!!!~'

`-HALL of `-FAME `-INDUCTION `-YEAR = PRO FOOTBALL
HALL of FAME = IN /|\ (`-87) = `-HIS `-AGE of `-DEATH for
AMERICAN FOOTBALL QUARTERBACK LEONARD "LEN"
RAY DAWSON = (`-87)!!!~'

`-HALL of `-FAME `-INDUCTION `-YEAR = 19(-)87 = (`-68)
= `-WAS `-BORN in the `-MONTH of (`-6); and, `-DIED in the
`-MONTH of (`-8) = (`-6/8)!!!~'

SHINZO ABE got `-MARRIED in (`-87) = RECIPROCAL = (`-
7/8) = `-DEATH/DAY; `-SHOT & `-KILLED!!!~' YOU'RE `-ALL
like `-THIS!!!~'

ACTRESS NAYA RIVERA'S `-BIRTHDAY # `-NUMBER =
(1/12/19/{87}) = (1 + 12 + 19 + {87}) = (`-119)!!!~'

(`-119) = 11x9 = 99 / (DIVIDED by) (`-3) = (`-33) = `-AGE of
`-DEATH for ACTRESS NAYA RIVERA = (`-33)!!!~'

`-ACTRESS NAYA RIVERA was `-BORN in (`-87) =
RECIPROCAL = (`- 78) = `-DIED on (`-7/8) with counting (`-
178) DAYS BETWEEN `-BIRTH; and, `-DEATH & with (`-187)
DAYS BETWEEN `-BIRTH; and, `-DEATH in the `-OTHER
`-DIRECTION by `-WAY of `-COUNTING!!!~'

'-ACTRESS NAYA RIVERA '-PARTIAL '-BIRTH/DAY # '-NUMBER = 1+12+19 = ('-32) = FLIP 3 to 8; FLIP 2 to 7 = ('-87)!!!~'

AMERICAN MUSICIAN JERRY IVAN ALLISON SONGWRITER/DRUMMER for "BUDDY HOLLY & The CRICKETS" died at the AGE of ('-82)!!!~'

'-WAS '-BORN in the '-MONTH of ('-8); and, '-DIED in the '-MONTH of ('-8) = ('-88) = 2(8's) = ('-28) = RECIPROCAL = ('-82) = '-AGE of '-DEATH for AMERICAN MUSICIAN JERRY IVAN ALLISON SONGWRITER/DRUMMER for "The CRICKETS"!!!~'

'-BIRTH/DAY = 8/31 = 83(-)1 = ('-82) = '-AGE of '-DEATH for AMERICAN MUSICIAN JERRY IVAN ALLISON SONGWRITER/DRUMMER for "The CRICKETS"!!!~'

'-BIRTH/DAY = 8/31 = 8(-)31 = ('-23) = RECIPROCAL = ('-32) = FLIP 3 to 8 = ('-82) = '-AGE of '-DEATH for AMERICAN MUSICIAN JERRY IVAN ALLISON SONGWRITER/ DRUMMER for "The CRICKETS"!!!~'

'-BIRTH/DAY # '-NUMBER = 8+31+19+39 = 97

'-BIRTH/DAY # '-NUMBER = 97 = 9+7 = 16 = 2x8 = ('-28) = RECIPROCAL = ('-82) = '-AGE of '-DEATH for AMERICAN MUSICIAN JERRY IVAN ALLISON SONGWRITER/ DRUMMER for "The CRICKETS"!!!~'

'-BIRTH/DAY = 8/31 = 8+31 = 39 = 3x9 = ('-27) = RECIPROCAL = ('-72) = '-DEATH/DAY # '-NUMBER!!!~'

`-BIRTH/YEAR = (`-39) = FLIP 3 to 8 = (`-89) = 8x9 = (`-72) = `-DEATH/DAY # `-NUMBER!!!~'

`-DEATH/DAY # `-NUMBER = 8+22+20+22 = 72

`-DEATH/DAY # `-NUMBER = 72 = FLIP 7 to 2 = (`-22) = `-AGE of `-DEATH for `-BAND `-MATE BUDDY HOLLY!!!~'

`-DEATH/DAY # `-NUMBER = 72 = 7+2 = (`-9) = `-DAYS from `-BIRTH-to-DEATH = (`-9)!!!~'

97+72 = 169 = 1+6/9 = 7/9 = RECIPROCAL = (`-97) = `-BIRTH/DAY # `-NUMBER!!!~'

97(-)72 = 25 = RECIPROCAL = (`-52) = "SEE `-BELOW"!!!~'

`-DEATH/MONTH was AUGUST with 31 DAYS

(31 (-) 22) – DAY of `-DEATH = (`-9) = `-DAYS from `-BIRTH to `-DEATH = (`-9)!!!~'

FRAGMENTED `-BIRTH/DAY # `-NUMBER = 8+3+1+1+9+3+9 = 34

FRAGMENTED `-BIRTH/DAY # `-NUMBER = 34 = X TIMES (`-2) = (`-68) = "SEE `-BELOW"!!!~'

`-BIRTH/DAY # `-NUMBER = 97 (+) 34 = FRAGMENTED `-BIRTH/DAY # `-NUMBER = 131 = FLIP 3 to 8 = 181 = 1+81 = (`-82) = `-AGE of `-DEATH for AMERICAN MUSICIAN JERRY IVAN ALLISON SONGWRITER/DRUMMER for "The CRICKETS"!!!~'

FRAGMENTED `-DEATH/DAY # `-NUMBER = 8+2+2+2+0+2+2 = 18

FRAGMENTED `-DEATH/DAY # `-NUMBER = (`-18) = RECIPROCAL = (`-81) = `-DIED the `-VERY `-NEXT `-YEAR of `-AGE at (`-82)!!!~'

FRAGMENTED `-DEATH/DAY # `-NUMBER = (`-18) = X TIMES (`-2) = (`-36) = RECIPROCAL = (`-63) = 9x7 = (`-97) = `-BIRTH/DAY # `-NUMBER!!!~'

34+18 = 52 = RECIPROCAL = (`-25) = "SEE `-ABOVE"!!!~'

34(-)18 = 16 = 8x2 = (`-82) = `-AGE of `-DEATH for AMERICAN MUSICIAN JERRY IVAN ALLISON SONGWRITER/ DRUMMER for "The CRICKETS"!!!~'

FROM `-BIRTH-to-DEATH there are 9 DAYS = 1+8 = (`-18) = FRAGMENTED `-DEATH/DAY # `-NUMBER!!!~'

(365 (-) 9) = 356 = 3x56 = 168 = 16x8 = 128 = RECIPROCAL = 821 = 82x1 = (`-82) = `-AGE of `-DEATH for AMERICAN MUSICIAN JERRY IVAN ALLISON SONGWRITER/DRUMMER for "The CRICKETS"!!!~'

`-BIRTH/DAY = 8/31 = 8+31 = (`-39) = `-BIRTH/YEAR = (`-39)!!!~'

`-BIRTH/YEAR = 1939 = 19+39 = 58 = 5+8 = 13 = RECIPROCAL = 31 = FLIP 3 to 8 = (`-81) = `-DIED the `-VERY `-NEXT `-YEAR of `-AGE at (`-82)!!!~'

`-BIRTH/YEAR = 19/39 = 1(-)9/3+9 = 8/12 = 82x1 = (`-82) = `-AGE of `-DEATH for AMERICAN MUSICIAN JERRY IVAN ALLISON SONGWRITER/DRUMMER for "BUDDY HOLLY & The CRICKETS"!!!~'

`-BIRTH/YEAR = 1939 = 19+39 = 58 = `-HIS `-ONLY SOLO CHART ENTRY on the "BILLBOARD HOT 100" was "REAL

WILD CHILD" that was ISSUED in 19(58) under the name IVAN....!!!~'

AMERICAN SINGER, GUITARIST; and, PROFESSIONAL BASEBALL PLAYER (COUNTRY MUSIC LEGEND) CHARLEY FRANK PRIDE died at the AGE of (`-86)!!!~'

BIRTH/YEAR = 19/34 = 9/1+3+4 = 9/8 = RECIPROCAL = 8/9 = FLIP 9 to 6 = (`-86) = AGE of DEATH for AMERICAN SINGER, GUITARIST; and, PROFESSIONAL BASEBALL PLAYER (COUNTRY MUSIC LEGEND) CHARLEY FRANK PRIDE!!!~'

EIGHTH & FINAL LEADER of the SOVIET UNION MIKHAIL SERGEYEVICH GORBACHEV died at the AGE of (`-91)!!!~'

`-WAS `-BORN in the `-MONTH of (`-3); and, `-DIED in the `-MONTH of (`-8) = (3/8) = (`-38) = `-DEATH/DAY = 8+30 = (`-38)!!!~'

`-WAS `-BORN in the `-MONTH of (`-3); and, `-DIED in the `-MONTH of (`-8) = (3/8) = 3x8 = 24 = RECIPROCAL = 42 = 20+22 = `-DEATH/YEAR!!!~'

`-PARTIAL `-BIRTH/DAY # `-NUMBER = 3+2+19 = 24 = RECIPROCAL = 42 = 20+22 = `-DEATH/YEAR!!!~'

`-BIRTH/DAY # `-NUMBER = 3+2+19+31 = 55

`-DEATH/DAY # `-NUMBER = 8+30+20+22 = 80

`-DEATH/DAY # `-NUMBER = 80 = WIFE RAISA GORBACHEVA `-DEATH/YEAR = 19(-)99 = (`-80)!!!~'

`-DEATH/DAY # `-NUMBER = 80 = `-GRANDDAUGHTER KSENIA VIRGANSKAYA was `-BORN in (`-80)!!!~'

`-DEATH/YEAR = 20+22 = (`-42) = `-AGE of `-GRANDDAUGHTER KSENIA VIRGANSKAYA at the `-TIME of `-HER `-GRANDFATHER'S `-DEATH EIGHTH & FINAL LEADER of the SOVIET UNION MIKHAIL SERGEYEVICH GORBACHEV!!!~'

55+80 = 135 = 1x35 = (`-35) = `-AGE of `-GRANDDAUGHTER ANASTASIA VIRGANSKAYA at the `-TIME of `-HER `-GRANDFATHER'S `-DEATH EIGHTH & FINAL LEADER of the SOVIET UNION MIKHAIL SERGEYEVICH GORBACHEV!!!~'

55+80 = 135 = 1x35 = (`-35) = FLIP 3 to 8 = (`-85) = MIKHAIL SERGEYEVICH GORBACHEV was the `-GENERAL SECRETARY of the COMMUNIST PARTY of the SOVIET UNION from 19(85) to 19(91)!!!~'

80(-)55 = 25 = WIFE RAISA GORBACHEVA `-PARTIAL `-BIRTH/DAY # `-NUMBER = 1+5+19 = (`-25)!!!~'

80(-)55 = 25 = WIFE RAISA GORBACHEVA `-PARTIAL `-BIRTH/DAY # `-NUMBER = 1+5+19 = (`-25) = 2(5's) = (`-55) = `-BIRTH/DAY # `-NUMBER for FINAL LEADER of the SOVIET UNION MIKHAIL SERGEYEVICH GORBACHEV!!!~'

`-BIRTH/MONTH was MARCH with 31 DAYS

(31 (-) 2) – DAY of BIRTH = 29 = RECIPROCAL = 92 = `-DIED the `-VERY `-YEAR `-PRIOR at the AGE of (`-91)!!!~'

(31 (-) 2) – DAY of BIRTH = 29 = RECIPROCAL = 92 = WIFE RAISA GORBACHEVA `-DEATH/DAY = 9/20 = 9+20 = (`-29) = RECIPROCAL = (`-92) = JUST `-ADD a `-ZERO = (9/20) = `-HER `-DEATH/DAY!!!~'

`-DEATH/DAY = 8/30 = 8x30 = 240 = 24+0 = 24 = RECIPROCAL = 42 = 20+22 = `-DEATH/YEAR!!!~'

FRAGMENTED `-BIRTH/DAY # `-NUMBER = 3+2+1+9+ 3+1 = 19

FRAGMENTED `-BIRTH/DAY # `-NUMBER = 19 = RECIPROCAL = (`-91) = `-AGE of `-DEATH for EIGHTH & FINAL LEADER of the SOVIET UNION MIKHAIL SERGEYEVICH GORBACHEV!!!~'

FRAGMENTED `-DEATH/DAY # `-NUMBER = 8+3+0+2+0+ 2+2 = 17

19x17 = (`-323) = RECIPROCAL-SEQUENCING-NUMEROLOGY-RSN!!!~'

19+17 = 36 = `-GRANDDAUGHTER KSENIA VIRGANSKAYA `-BIRTH/DAY # `-NUMBER in `-REVERSE = 80(-)19(-)21(-)1 = 39 = FLIP 9 to 6 = (`-36)

FROM `-BIRTH-to-DEATH there are 181 DAYS = 1+8/1 = (`-91) = `-AGE of `-DEATH for EIGHTH & FINAL LEADER of the SOVIET UNION MIKHAIL SERGEYEVICH GORBACHEV!!!~'

(365 (-) 181) = 184 = 1x84 = (`-84) = 8x4 = (`-3/2) = `-BIRTH/ DAY!!!~'

`-BIRTH/YEAR = 1931 = 9/1(-)3(-)1 = (`-91) = `-AGE of `-DEATH for EIGHTH & FINAL LEADER of the SOVIET UNION MIKHAIL SERGEYEVICH GORBACHEV!!!~'

`-GRANDDAUGHTER KSENIA VIRGANSKAYA `-BIRTH/ DAY # `-NUMBER = 1+21+19+80 = 1/21 = `-HER `-VERY `-OWN `-BIRTH/DAY!!!~'

19+80 = (`-99) = `-YEAR of `-DEATH of `-GRANDMOTHER RAISA GORBACHEVA!!!~'

19(-)80 = 61 = FLIP 6 to 9 = (`-91) = `-AGE of `-DEATH for `-HER `-GRANDFATHER EIGHTH & FINAL LEADER of the SOVIET UNION MIKHAIL SERGEYEVICH GORBACHEV!!!~'

`-GRANDDAUGHTER ANASTASIA VIRGANSKAYA `-BIRTH/DAY # `-NUMBER in `-REVERSE = 87(-)19(-)27(-)3 = 38 = GRANDFATHER'S `-DEATH/DAY = 8+30 = (`-38) = RECIPROCAL = 8/3 = JUST `-ADD a `-ZERO = (8/30) = `-DEATH/DAY!!!~'

`-GRANDDAUGHTER `-BIRTH/YEAR = 1987 = 19+87 = 106 = 10+6 = 16 = RECIPROCAL = 61 = FLIP 6 to 9 = (`-91) = `-AGE of `-DEATH for `-HER `-GRANDFATHER EIGHTH & FINAL LEADER of the SOVIET UNION MIKHAIL SERGEYEVICH GORBACHEV!!!~'

`-GRANDDAUGHTER `-BIRTH/DAY = 3/27 = 3(-)27 = 24 = RECIPROCAL = 42 = 20+22 = `-DEATH/YEAR for `-HER `-GRANDFATHER EIGHTH & FINAL LEADER of the SOVIET UNION MIKHAIL SERGEYEVICH GORBACHEV!!!~'

`-GRANDAUGHTER `-BIRTH/YEAR = 8/7 = FLIP 8 to 3; FLIP 7 to 2 = (`-3/2) = `-BIRTH/DAY of `-GRANDFATHER EIGHTH

& FINAL LEADER of the SOVIET UNION MIKHAIL SERGEYEVICH GORBACHEV = & = `-BIRTH/YEAR of `-GRANDMOTHER RAISA GORBACHEVA!!!~'

MIKHAIL GORBACHEV'S WIFE RAISA GORBACHEVA was `-BORN in the `-MONTH of (`-1); and, `-DIED in the `-MONTH of (`-9) = 1/9 = RECIPROCAL = 9/1 = `-AGE of `-DEATH for `-HER `-HUSBAND EIGHTH & FINAL LEADER of the SOVIET UNION MIKHAIL SERGEYEVICH GORBACHEV!!!~'

`-THEY were `-MARRIED from 1953 to 1999 for (`-46) YEARS = 4x6 = 24 = RECIPROCAL = 42 = 20+22 = `-DEATH/YEAR for EIGHTH & FINAL LEADER of the SOVIET UNION MIKHAIL SERGEYEVICH GORBACHEV!!!~'

46 / `-DIVIDED by (`-2) = 23 = RECIPROCAL = 3/2 = `-BIRTH/ DAY of `-EIGHTH & FINAL LEADER of the SOVIET UNION MIKHAIL SERGEYEVICH GORBACHEV = & = `-BIRTH/ YEAR of `-WIFE RAISA GORBACHEVA = (`-32) !!!~'

WIFE RAISA GORBACHEVA `-BIRTH/DAY # `-NUMBER = 1+5+19+32 = 57

WIFE RAISA GORBACHEVA `-DEATH/DAY # `-NUMBER = 9+20+19+99 = 147 = 1+4/7 = (`-57) = `-BIRTH/DAY # `-NUMBER!!!~'

WIFE RAISA GORBACHEVA `-DEATH/DAY # `-NUMBER in `-REVERSE = 99(-)19(-)20(-)9 = 51 = RECIPROCAL = 1/5 = `-HER `-VERY `-OWN `-BIRTH/DAY!!!~'

WIFE RAISA GORBACHEVA `-BIRTH/YEAR = 1932 = 19+32 = 51 = RECIPROCAL = 1/5 = `-HER `-VERY `-OWN `-BIRTH/ DAY!!!~'

DWAYNE W. ANDERSON

WIFE RAISA GORBACHEVA `-BIRTH/YEAR = 1932 = 19+32 = (`-51) = WIFE RAISA GORBACHEVA'S `-DEATH/DAY # `-NUMBER in `-REVERSE = 99(-)19(-)20(-)9 = (`-51)!!!~'

`-MARRIAGE in 1953 = The Presidents of `-RUSSIA with the `-NUMBER `-53+ !!!!!~' Russia's Vladimir Lenin died at the `-AGE of `-53; and, Russia's Joseph Stalin died in `-1953 on its `-RECIPROCAL `-DEATH/DAY / 0{3}/0{5}/19{53} / (`-35) = RECIPROCAL = (`-53) = "SEE `-ABOVE"!!!~'

AMERICAN ACTOR WILLIAM de CLERQ REYNOLDS died at the AGE of (`-90)!!!~'

`-BIRTH/DAY = 12/9 = RECIPROCAL = 9/21 = 9/2(-)1 = 91 = `-DIED the `-VERY `-YEAR `-PRIOR at the `-AGE of (`-90)!!!~'

`-DEATH/DAY = 8/24 = 8x24 = 192 = 1(-)92 = (`-91) = `-DIED the `-VERY `-YEAR `-PRIOR at the `-AGE of (`-90)!!!~'

`-BIRTH/YEAR = 1931 = 9/1(-)3(-)1 = (`-91) = `-DIED the `-VERY `-YEAR `-PRIOR at the `-AGE of (`-90)!!!~'

`-BIRTH/DAY # `-NUMBER = 12+9+19+31 = 71

`-BIRTH/DAY = 12+9 = 21 = FLIP 2 to 7 = (`-71) = `-BIRTH/DAY # `-NUMBER!!!~'

`-DEATH/DAY # `-NUMBER = 8+24+20+22 = 74

71+74 = 145 = 1x45 = 45 = X TIMES (`-2) = (`-90) = `-AGE of `-DEATH for AMERICAN ACTOR WILLIAM de CLERQ REYNOLDS!!!~'

`-DEATH/DAY = 8/24 = 8(-)24 = 16 = RECIPROCAL = 61 = FLIP 6 to 9 = (`-91) = `-DIED the `-VERY `-YEAR `-PRIOR at the `-AGE of (`-90)!!!~'

FRAGMENTED `-BIRTH/DAY # `-NUMBER = 1+2+9+1+9+ 3+1 = 26

FRAGMENTED `-BIRTH/DAY # `-NUMBER = 26 = RECIPROCAL = 62

`-BIRTH/YEAR = 31 = X TIMES (`-2) = 62

`-BIRTH/DAY = 12/9 = 12x9 = 108 = 10+8 = 18 = RECIPROCAL = 81 = FLIP 8 to 3 = (`-31) = `-BIRTH/YEAR!!!~'

FRAGMENTED `-DEATH/DAY # `-NUMBER = 8+2+4+2+0+ 2+2 = 20

`-WAS `-BORN in the `-MONTH of (`-12); and, `-DIED in the `-MONTH of (`-8) = (`-12/8) = 12+8 = (`-20) = FRAGMENTED `-DEATH/DAY # `-NUMBER!!!~'

`-WAS `-BORN in the `-MONTH of (`-12); and, `-DIED in the `-MONTH of (`-8) = (`-12/8) = `-BORN the `-VERY `-NEXT `-DAY = 12/9 = `-BIRTH/DAY!!!~'

26+20 = 46 = / (DIVIDED by) (`-2) = (`-23) = RECIPROCAL = (`-32) = `-DEATH/DAY = 8+24 = (`-32)!!!~'

26(-)20 = 6 = FLIP 6 to 9 = (`-9) = JUST `-ADD a `-ZERO = (`-90) = `-AGE of `-DEATH for AMERICAN ACTOR WILLIAM de CLERQ REYNOLDS!!!~'

`-BIRTH/DAY = 12/9 = 12x9 = 108 = `-ONE `-DAY `-BEFORE from `-BIRTH-to-DEATH!!!~'

FROM `-BIRTH-to-DEATH there are 107 DAYS = 10+7 = 17 = RECIPROCAL = 71 = `-BIRTH/DAY # `-NUMBER!!!~'

(365 (-) 107) = 258 = 25x8 = 200 = 20+0 = (`-20) = FRAGMENTED `-DEATH/DAY # `-NUMBER!!!~'

(365 (-) 107) = 258 = 2+58 = 60 = FLIP 6 to 9 = (`-90) = `-AGE of `-DEATH for AMERICAN ACTOR WILLIAM de CLERQ REYNOLDS!!!~'

`-WAS `-MARRIED to MOLLY REYNOLDS from 1950 to 1992 for 42 YEARS = 20+22 = `-DEATH/YEAR for AMERICAN ACTOR WILLIAM de CLERQ REYNOLDS!!!~'

`-DAY of `-DEATH = (24ᵗʰ) = RECIPROCAL = 42 = 20+22 = `-DEATH/YEAR for AMERICAN ACTOR WILLIAM de CLERQ REYNOLDS!!!~'

SOUTH AFRICAN ACTRESS & MODEL CHARLBI DEAN KRIEK died at the AGE of (`-32)!!!~'

`-BIRTH/DAY # `-NUMBER in `-REVERSE = 90(-)19(-)5(-)2 = (`-64) / (DIVIDED by) (`-2) = (`-32) = `-AGE of `-DEATH for SOUTH AFRICAN ACTRESS & MODEL CHARLBI DEAN KRIEK!!!~'

`-BIRTH/DAY # `-NUMBER = 2+5+19+90 = 116

`-BIRTH/DAY # `-NUMBER = 116 = 1x16 = 16 = X TIMES (`-2) = (`-32) = `-AGE of `-DEATH for SOUTH AFRICAN ACTRESS & MODEL CHARLBI DEAN KRIEK!!!~'

`-BIRTH/DAY # `-NUMBER = 116 = 1+16 = 17 = RECIPROCAL = 71 = `-BIRTH/YEAR = 19(-)90 = (`-71)!!!~'

`-DEATH/DAY # `-NUMBER = 8+29+20+22 = 79

`-DEATH/DAY # `-NUMBER = 79 = 7+9 = 16 = X TIMES (`-2) = (`-32) = `-AGE of `-DEATH for SOUTH AFRICAN ACTRESS & MODEL CHARLBI DEAN KRIEK!!!~'

116+79 = 195 = 19+5 = 24 = RECIPROCAL = 42 = 20+22 = `-DEATH/YEAR!!!~'

116(-)79 = 37 = FLIP 7 to 2 = (`-32) = `-AGE of `-DEATH for SOUTH AFRICAN ACTRESS & MODEL CHARLBI DEAN KRIEK!!!~'

FRAGMENTED `-BIRTH/DAY # `-NUMBER = 2+5+1+9+9+0 = 26

`-BIRTH/DAY # `-NUMBER = (`-116) (+) (`-26) = FRAGMENTED `-BIRTH/DAY # -NUMBER = (`-142) = 1(-)4/2 = (`-32) = `-AGE of `-DEATH for SOUTH AFRICAN ACTRESS & MODEL CHARLBI DEAN KRIEK!!!~'

FRAGMENTED `-DEATH/DAY # `-NUMBER = 8+2+9+2+0+2+2 = 25

26+25 = (2+6) (2+5) = 87 = FLIP 8 to 3; FLIP 7 to 2 = (`-32) = `-AGE of `-DEATH for SOUTH AFRICAN ACTRESS & MODEL CHARLBI DEAN KRIEK!!!~'

FROM `-BIRTH-to-DEATH there are 205 DAYS = 20+5 = (`-25) = FRAGMENTED `-DEATH/DAY # `-NUMBER!!!~'

(365 (-) 205) = 160 = 16+0 = 16 = X TIMES (`-2) = (`-32) = `-AGE of `-DEATH for SOUTH AFRICAN ACTRESS & MODEL CHARLBI DEAN KRIEK!!!~'

(365 (-) 205) = 160 = 1x60 = (`-60) = 30x2 = 30+2 = (`-32) = `-AGE of `-DEATH for SOUTH AFRICAN ACTRESS & MODEL CHARLBI DEAN KRIEK!!!~'

`-BIRTH/MONTH was FEBRUARY with 28 DAYS

(28 (-) 5) – DAY of `-BIRTH = 23 = RECIPROCAL = (`-32) = `-AGE of `-DEATH for SOUTH AFRICAN ACTRESS & MODEL CHARLBI DEAN KRIEK!!!~'

`-DEATH/DAY = 8/29 = 8x29 = 232 = Reciprocal-Sequencing-Numerology-RSN!!!~'

`-DEATH/DAY = 8/29 = 8+29 = 37 = FLIP 7 to 2 = (`-32) = `-AGE of `-DEATH for SOUTH AFRICAN ACTRESS & MODEL CHARLBI DEAN KRIEK!!!~'

`-DEATH/DAY = 8/29 = 8(-)29 = 21 = 3x7 = (`-37) = FLIP 7 to 2 = (`-32) = `-AGE of `-DEATH for SOUTH AFRICAN ACTRESS & MODEL CHARLBI DEAN KRIEK!!!~'

`-DEATH/DAY = 8/29 = HALF RECIPROCAL = 8/92 = 8(-)92 = 84 = 8x4 = (`-32) = `-AGE of `-DEATH for SOUTH AFRICAN ACTRESS & MODEL CHARLBI DEAN KRIEK!!!~'

`-WAS `-BORN in the `-MONTH of (`-2); and, `-DIED in the `-MONTH of (`-8) = (`-2/8) = 2x8 = 16 = X TIMES (`-2) = (`-32) = `-AGE of `-DEATH for SOUTH AFRICAN ACTRESS & MODEL CHARLBI DEAN KRIEK!!!~'

AMERICAN COUNTRY MUSIC ARTIST LUKE BELL died at the AGE Of (`-32)!!!~'

`-PARTIAL `-BIRTH/DAY # `-NUMBER = 1+27+19 = 47 = FLIP 7 to 2 = 42 = 20+22 = `-DEATH/YEAR!!!~'

`-BIRTH/MONTH was JANUARY with 31 DAYS

(31 (-) 27) – DAY of `-BIRTH = (`-4)

`-DEATH/MONTH was AUGUST with 31 DAYS

(31 (-) 29) – DAY of `-DEATH = (`-2)

(`-4/2) = 20+22 = `-DEATH/YEAR!!!~'

`-BIRTH/DAY # `-NUMBER = 1+27+19+90 = 137

`-BIRTH/DAY # `-NUMBER = 137 = 1x37 = 37 = FLIP 7 to 2 = (`-32) = `-AGE of `-DEATH for AMERICAN COUNTRY MUSIC ARTIST LUKE BELL!!!~'

`-DEATH/DAY = 8/29 = 8+29 = 37 = `-BIRTH/DAY # `-NUMBER!!!~'

`-DEATH/DAY # `-NUMBER = 8+29+20+22 = 79

`-DEATH/DAY # `-NUMBER = 79 = 7+9 = 16 = X TIMES (`-2) = (`-32) = `-AGE of `-DEATH for AMERICAN COUNTRY MUSIC ARTIST LUKE BELL!!!~'

137+79 = 216 = 2x16 = (`-32) = `-AGE of `-DEATH for AMERICAN COUNTRY MUSIC ARTIST LUKE BELL!!!~'

137(-)79 = 58 = / (DIVIDED by (`-2) = (`-29) = `-DAY of `-DEATH (`-29th)!!!~'

FRAGMENTED `-BIRTH/DAY # `-NUMBER = 1+2+7+1+9+ 9+0 = 29

`-BIRTH/DAY # `-NUMBER = (`-137) (+) (`-29) = FRAGMENTED `-BIRTH/DAY # `-NUMBER = 166 = 16x6 = 96 = / DIVIDED by (`-3) = (`-32) = `-AGE of `-DEATH for AMERICAN COUNTRY MUSIC ARTIST LUKE BELL!!!~'

FRAGMENTED `-BIRTH/DAY # `-NUMBER = 29 = `-DAY of `-DEATH (`-29th)!!!~'

FRAGMENTED `-DEATH/DAY # `-NUMBER = 8+2+9+2+0+ 2+2 = 25

29+25 = 54 = / (DIVIDED by) (`-2) = (`-27) = `-DAY of `-BIRTH (`-27th)!!!~'

29+25 = 54 = `-BIRTH/YEAR = 19(-)90 = 71 = RECIPROCAL = 17 /|\ 71(-)17 = (`-54)!!!~'

(`-29) = RECIPROCAL = (`-92)

92(-)25 = 67 = 6x7 = 42 = 20+22 = `-DEATH/YEAR!!!~'

(`-25) = RECIPROCAL = (`-52)

52(-)29 = 23 = RECIPROCAL = (`-32) = `-AGE of `-DEATH for AMERICAN COUNTRY MUSIC ARTIST LUKE BELL!!!~'

FROM `-BIRTH-to-DEATH there are 214 DAYS = 2x14 = 28 = `-BIRTH/DAY = 1+27 = (`-28)!!!~'

FROM `-BIRTH-to-DEATH there are 214 DAYS = 21+4 = (`-25) = FRAGMENTED `-DEATH/DAY # `-NUMBER!!!~'

FROM `-BIRTH-to-DEATH there are 214 DAYS = 21x4 = 84 = 8x4 = (`-32) = `-AGE of `-DEATH for AMERICAN COUNTRY MUSIC ARTIST LUKE BELL!!!~'

(365 (-) 214) = 151 = 15+1 = 16 = X TIMES (`-2) = (`-32) = `-AGE of `-DEATH for AMERICAN COUNTRY MUSIC ARTIST LUKE BELL!!!~'

`-DEATH/DAY = 8/29 = 8x29 = 232 = Reciprocal-Sequencing-Numerology-RSN!!!~'

`-DEATH/DAY = 8/29 = 8+29 = 37 = FLIP 7 to 2 = (`-32) = `-AGE of `-DEATH for AMERICAN COUNTRY MUSIC ARTIST LUKE BELL!!!~'

`-DEATH/DAY = 8/29 = 8(-)29 = 21 = 3x7 = (`-37) = FLIP 7 to 2 = (`-32) = `-AGE of `-DEATH for AMERICAN COUNTRY MUSIC ARTIST LUKE BELL!!!~'

`-DEATH/DAY = 8/29 = HALF RECIPROCAL = 8/92 = 8(-)92 = 84 = 8x4 = (`-32) = `-AGE of `-DEATH for AMERICAN COUNTRY MUSIC ARTIST LUKE BELL!!!~'

`-BIRTH/DAY = 1/27 = 1+27 = 28 = FLIP 8 to 3 = 23 = RECIPROCAL = (`-32) = `-AGE of `-DEATH for AMERICAN COUNTRY MUSIC ARTIST LUKE BELL!!!~'

`-DEATH/DAY = 8/29 = HALF RECIPROCAL = 8/92 = 8(-)92 = 84 = `-BIRTH/DAY = 1+27 = 28 = X TIMES (`-3) = (`-84) = 8x4 = (`-32) = `-AGE of `-DEATH for AMERICAN COUNTRY MUSIC ARTIST LUKE BELL!!!~'

`-BIRTH/DAY = 1/27 = HALF RECIPROCAL = 1/72 = 1(-)72 = (`-71) = `-BIRTH/YEAR = 19(-)90 = (`-71)!!!~'

`-BIRTH/DAY = 1/27 = HALF RECIPROCAL = 1/72 = 1+72 = 73 = RECIPROCAL = 37 = FLIP 7 to 2 = (`-32) = `-AGE of `-DEATH for AMERICAN COUNTRY MUSIC ARTIST LUKE BELL!!!~'

`-WAS `-BORN in the `-MONTH of (`-1); and, `-DIED in the `-MONTH of (`-8) = (`-1/8) = 6x3 = (`-63) = 7x9 = (`-79) = `-DEATH/DAY # `-NUMBER!!!~'

`-WAS `-BORN in the `-MONTH of (`-1); and, `-DIED in the `-MONTH of (`-8) = (`-1/8) = FLIP 8 to 3 = 1/3 = RECIPROCAL = (`-31) = `-BIRTH/MONTH & `-DEATH/MONTH `-BOTH = (`-31) `-DAYS!!!~'

`-WAS `-BORN in the `-MONTH of (`-1); and, `-DIED in the `-MONTH of (`-8) = (`-1/8) = RECIPROCAL = (`-81) = `-DAY of `-BIRTH (`-27ᵗʰ) X TIMES (`-3) = (`-81)!!!~'

AMERICAN PROFESSIONAL BOXER EARNIE DEE SHAVERS died at the AGE of (`-78)!!!~'

`-BIRTH/DAY = 8/31 = 8(-)31 = (`-23) = FLIP 2 to 7; FLIP 3 to 8 = (`-78) = `-AGE of `-DEATH for AMERICAN PROFESSIONAL BOXER EARNIE DEE SHAVERS!!!~'

`-BIRTH/DAY = 8/31 = 8/3(-)1 = 8/2 = RECIPROCAL = 2/8 = FLIP 2 to 7 = (`-78) = `-AGE of `-DEATH for AMERICAN PROFESSIONAL BOXER EARNIE DEE SHAVERS!!!~'

`-BIRTH/DAY = 8/31 = 8/3+1 = 8/4 = 8x4 = (`-32) = RECIPROCAL = (`-23) = FLIP 2 to 7; FLIP 3 to 8 = (`-78) = `-AGE of `-DEATH for AMERICAN PROFESSIONAL BOXER EARNIE DEE SHAVERS!!!~'

`-BIRTH/DAY # `-NUMBER = 8+31+19+44 = 102

`-BIRTH/DAY # `-NUMBER = 102 / (DIVIDED by) (`-2) = (`-51) = `-DEATH/DAY # `-NUMBER = (`-52)!!!~'

`-DEATH/DAY # `-NUMBER = 9+1+20+22 = 52

`-DEATH/DAY # `-NUMBER = 52 = RECIPROCAL = 25 = `-BIRTH/YEAR = 19(-)44 = (`-25)!!!~'

`-DEATH/DAY # `-NUMBER = 52 = / (DIVIDED by) (`-2) = (`-26) = `-COMPETED `-PROFESSIONALLY as a `-BOXER for (`-26) `-YEARS from 1969 to 1995!!!~'

102+52 = 154 = 1(-)5/4 = (`-44) = `-BIRTH/YEAR!!!~'

102(-)52 = 50 = 25x2 = 25(-)2 = (`-23) = FLIP 2 to 7; FLIP 3 to 8 = (`-78) = `-AGE of `-DEATH for AMERICAN PROFESSIONAL BOXER EARNIE DEE SHAVERS!!!~'

102(-)52 = 50 = `-STARTED `-COMPETING in `-BOXING in 1969 = 19(-)69 = (`-50)!!!~'

FRAGMENTED `-BIRTH/DAY # `-NUMBER = 8+3+1+1+9+4+4 = 30

`-BIRTH/DAY # `-NUMBER = (`-102) (+) (`-30) = FRAGMENTED `-BIRTH/DAY # `-NUMBER = 132 = 1x32 = (`-32) = RECIPROCAL = (`-23) = FLIP 2 to 7; FLIP 3 to 8 = (`-78) = `-AGE of `-DEATH

DWAYNE W. ANDERSON

for AMERICAN PROFESSIONAL BOXER EARNIE DEE SHAVERS!!!~'

FRAGMENTED `-BIRTH/DAY # `-NUMBER = 30 = `-PARTIAL `-DEATH/DAY # `-NUMBER = 9+1+20 = (`-30)!!!~'

FRAGMENTED `-BIRTH/DAY # `-NUMBER = 30 = 5x6 = (`-56) = 7x8 = (`-78) = `-AGE of `-DEATH for AMERICAN PROFESSIONAL BOXER EARNIE DEE SHAVERS!!!~'

FRAGMENTED `-DEATH/DAY # `-NUMBER = 9+1+2+0+2+2 = 16

FRAGMENTED `-DEATH/DAY # `-NUMBER = 16 = 2x8 = (`-28) = FLIP 2 to 7 = (`-78) = `-AGE of `-DEATH for AMERICAN PROFESSIONAL BOXER EARNIE DEE SHAVERS!!!~'

30+16 = 46 = 4x6 = 24 = RECIPROCAL = 42 = 20+22 = `-DEATH/YEAR!!!~'

30+16 = 46 = `-MARRIED to LAVERNE PAYNE in 1965 = 19(-)65 = (`-46)!!!~'

30(-)16 = 14 = 2x7 = 27 = 2(7's) = (`-77) = `-DIED the `-VERY `-NEXT `-YEAR at the `-AGE of (`-78)!!!~'

FROM `-BIRTH-to-DEATH there are 1 DAYS = `-DIED the `-VERY `-NEXT `-DAY `-AFTER `-HIS `-BIRTH/DAY!!!~'

(365 (-) 1) = 364 = 36x4 = 144 = 1x44 = (`-44) = `-BIRTH/YEAR!!!~'

(365 (-) 1) = 364 = 3x64 = 192 = 1(-)9/2 = 8/2 = RECIPROCAL = 2/8 = FLIP 2 to 7 = (`-78) = `-AGE of `-DEATH for AMERICAN PROFESSIONAL BOXER EARNIE DEE SHAVERS!!!~'

(365 (-) 1) = 364 = 36(-)4 = 32 = RECIPROCAL = (`-23) = FLIP 2 to 7; FLIP 3 to 8 = (`-78) = `-AGE of `-DEATH for AMERICAN PROFESSIONAL BOXER EARNIE DEE SHAVERS!!!~'

`-WAS `-MARRIED to LAVERNE PAYNE from 1965 to 1982 for 17 YEARS!!!~'

(`-17) = RECIPROCAL = (`-71)

71+1+7 = (`-79) = `-DIED the `-VERY `-YEAR `-PRIOR at the `-AGE of (`-78)!!!~'

`-MARRIED in (`-65) = FLIP 6 to 9 = (`-95) = `-COMPETITION in `-BOXING `-ENDED in that `-YEAR!!!~'

`-MARRIAGE `-ENDED in 1982 = 19(-)82 = 63 = `-BIRTH/YEAR = 19+44 = (`-63)!!!~'

`-MARRIAGE `-ENDED in (`-82) = RECIPROCAL = 28 = FLIP 2 to 7 = (`-78) = `-AGE of `-DEATH for AMERICAN PROFESSIONAL BOXER EARNIE DEE SHAVERS!!!~'

`-WAS `-BORN in the `-MONTH of (`-8); and, `-DIED in the `-MONTH of (`-9) = (`-89) = `-BIRTH/DAY = 8+31 = 39 = FLIP 3 to 8 = (`-89)!!!~'

`-WAS `-BORN in the `-MONTH of (`-8); and, `-DIED in the `-MONTH of (`-9) = (`-89) = `-BIRTH/DAY = 8+31 /|\ `-DEATH/DAY = 9+1 /|\ 8+31+9+1 = 49 = X TIMES (`-2) = (`-98) = RECIPROCAL = (`-89)!!!~'

`-DEATH/DAY = 9/1 = (`-91) = RECIPROCAL = (`-19)

91(-)19 = (`-72) = 8x9 = (`-89)!!!~'

`-BIRTH/DAY = 8/31 = HALF RECIPROCAL = 8/13 = 8+13 = 21 = 7x3 = (`-73) = FLIP 3 to 8 = (`-78) = `-AGE of `-DEATH for AMERICAN PROFESSIONAL BOXER EARNIE DEE SHAVERS!!!~'

`-BIRTH/YEAR = 1944 = 1+9+4/4 = 14/4 = 14x4 = 56 = 7x8 = (`-78) = `-AGE of `-DEATH for AMERICAN PROFESSIONAL BOXER EARNIE DEE SHAVERS!!!~'

AMERICAN AUTHOR BARBARA EHRENREICH died at the AGE of (`-81)!!!~'

`-BIRTH/DAY # `-NUMBER = 8+26+19+41 = 94

`-BIRTH/DAY # `-NUMBER = 94 = 9+4 = 13 = RECIPROCAL = 31 = FLIP 3 to 8 = (`-81) = `-AGE of `-DEATH for AMERICAN AUTHOR BARBARA EHRENREICH!!!~'

`-DEATH/DAY # `-NUMBER = 9+1+20+22 = 52

(`-52) = RECIPROCAL = (`-25)

52+25 = (`-77) = 7x7 = (`-49) = RECIPROCAL = (`-94) = `-BIRTH/DAY # `-NUMBER!!!~'

94+52 = 146 = 1x46 = (`-46) = 4x6 = 24 = RECIPROCAL = 42 = 20+22 = `-DEATH/YEAR!!!~'

94+52 = 146 = 14x6 = (`-84) = `-BIRTH/DAY # `-NUMBER of `-FORMER `-HUSBAND JOHN EHRENREICH = 2+20+19+43 = (`-84)!!!~'

94(-)52 = 42 = 20+22 = `-DEATH/YEAR!!!~'

FRAGMENTED `-BIRTH/DAY # `-NUMBER = 8+2+6+1+9+ 4+1 = 31

FRAGMENTED `-BIRTH/DAY # `-NUMBER = 31 = FLIP 3 to 8 = (`-81) = `-AGE of `-DEATH for AMERICAN AUTHOR BARBARA EHRENREICH!!!~'

`-BIRTH/DAY # `-NUMBER = (`-94) (-) (`-31) = FRAGMENTED `-BIRTH/DAY # `-NUMBER = 63 = 6x3 = 18 = RECIPROCAL = (`-81) = `-AGE of `-DEATH for AMERICAN AUTHOR BARBARA EHRENREICH!!!~'

FRAGMENTED `-DEATH/DAY # `-NUMBER = 9+1+2+0+ 2+2 = 16

`-DEATH/DAY # `-NUMBER = (`-52) (+) (`-16) = FRAGMENTED `-DEATH/DAY # `-NUMBER = 68 = FLIP 8 to 3 = (`-63) = 6x3 = 18 = RECIPROCAL = (`-81) = `-AGE of `-DEATH for AMERICAN AUTHOR BARBARA EHRENREICH!!!~'

FRAGMENTED `-DEATH/DAY # `-NUMBER = 16 = 8x2 = (`-82) = `-DIED the `-VERY `-YEAR `-PRIOR at the `-AGE of (`-81)!!!~'

FRAGMENTED `-DEATH/DAY # `-NUMBER = 16 = RECIPROCAL = 61 = FLIP 6 to 9 = (`-9/1) = `-DEATH/DAY!!!~'

FRAGMENTED `-DEATH/DAY # `-NUMBER = 16 = 7+9 = (`-79) = `-AGE of `-FORMER `-HUSBAND JOHN EHRENREICH at the `-TIME of `-HIS `-FORMER `-WIFE'S `-DEATH AMERICAN AUTHOR BARBARA EHRENREICH!!!~'

(`-79) = 7x9 = (`-63) = 6x3 = (`-18) = RECIPROCAL = (`-81) = `-AGE of `-DEATH for `-FORMER `-WIFE AMERICAN AUTHOR BARBARA EHRENREICH!!!~'

`-FORMER `-HUSBAND JOHN EHRENREICH `-BIRTH/DAY = 2/20 = 2(-)20 = 18 = RECIPROCAL = (`-81) = `-AGE of `-DEATH for AMERICAN AUTHOR BARBARA EHRENREICH!!!~'

AMERICAN AUTHOR BARBARA EHRENREICH'S `-BIRTH/YEAR = (`-41) = `-FORMER `-HUSBAND JOHN EHRENREICH'S `-PARTIAL `-BIRTH/DAY # `-NUMBER = 2+20+19 = (`-41)!!!~'

41+41 = (`-82) = `-DIED the `-VERY `-YEAR `-PRIOR at the `-AGE of (`-81)!!!~'

`-BIRTH/DAY = 8/26 = 8+26 = (`-34) = FLIP 3 to 8 = (`-84) = `-BIRTH/DAY # `-NUMBER of `-FORMER `-HUSBAND JOHN EHRENREICH = 2+20+19+43 = (`-84)!!!~'

31+16 = 47 = FLIP 7 to 2 = (`-42) = 20+22 = `-DEATH/YEAR!!!~'

31+16 = 47 = `-MARRIED in 1966 = 19(-)66 = (`-47) = 4+7 = (`-11) = `-MARRIED for (`-11) `-YEARS!!!~'

31(-)16 = 15 = 1+5 = (`-6) = `-DAYS from `-BIRTH-to-DEATH!!!~'

FROM `-BIRTH-to-DEATH there are 6 DAYS = FRAGMENTED `-DEATH/DAY # `-NUMBER = 16 = 1x6 = (`-6)!!!~'

`-BIRTH/YEAR = 19/41 = 19+41 = 60 = 6+0 = (`-6) = `-DAYS from `-BIRTH-to-DEATH!!!~'

`-DEATH/DAY = 9/1 = 9x1 = (`-9) = FLIP 9 to 6 = (`-6) = `-DAYS from `-BIRTH-to-DEATH!!!~'

`-MARRIED in (`-66) to JOHN EHRENREICH!!!~'

(365 (-) 6) = 359 = 3+5/9 = (`-89) = `-WAS `-BORN in the `-MONTH of (`-8); and, `-DIED in the `-MONTH of (`-9) = (`-89)!!!~'

`-WAS `-MARRIED to JOHN EHRENREICH from 1966 to 1977 for 11 YEARS = CENTURY = 100(-)11 = (`-89) = `-WAS `-BORN in the `-MONTH of (`-8); and, `-DIED in the `-MONTH of (`-9) = (`-89)!!!~'

`-MARRIED (`-66) /|\ `-DIVORCED (`-77) = (`-67) = 6x7 = 42 = 20+22 = `-DEATH/YEAR!!!~'

`-DIVORCED in 1977 = 19(-)77 = (`-58) = `-BIRTH/YEAR = 1941 = 1(-)9/4+1 = (`-85) = RECIPROCAL = (`-58)!!!~'

(`-89) = 8x9 = 72 = `-SON BEN EHRENREICH was `-BORN in (`-72)!!!~'

`-AGE of `-DEATH for AMERICAN AUTHOR BARBARA EHRENREICH = (`-81) (-) 72 = (`-9) = `-MONTH of `-DEATH!!!~'

`-DEATH/DAY = 9/1 = (`-91) = RECIPROCAL = (`-19)

91(-)19 = 72 = 8x9 = (`-89) = `-WAS `-BORN in the `-MONTH of (`-8); and, `-DIED in the `-MONTH of (`-9) = (`-89)!!!~'

`-BIRTH/DAY = 8/26 = 8+26 = (`-34) = RECIPROCAL = (`-43) = `-FORMER `-HUSBAND JOHN EHRENREICH was `-BORN in (`-43)!!!~'

`-BIRTH/DAY = 8/26 = 8(-)26 = 18 = RECIPROCAL = (`-81) = `-AGE of `-DEATH for AMERICAN AUTHOR BARBARA EHRENREICH!!!~'

AMERICAN JAZZ TRUMPETER JOEY DEFRANCESCO died at the AGE of (`-51)!!!~'

`-BIRTH/DAY = 4/10 = 4(-)10 = 6 = 5+1 = (`-51) = `-AGE of `-DEATH for AMERICAN JAZZ TRUMPETER JOEY DEFRANCESCO!!!~'

`-BIRTH/DAY = 4/10 = 4+1/0 = 5/0 = (`-50) = `-DIED the `-VERY `-NEXT `-YEAR of `-AGE at (`-51)!!!~'

`-BIRTH/YEAR = 1971 = 19(-)71 = 52 = `-DIED the `-VERY `-YEAR `-PRIOR at the `-AGE of (`-51)!!!~'

`-BIRTH/DAY # `-NUMBER = 4+10+19+71 = 104

`-BIRTH/DAY # `-NUMBER = 104 / (DIVIDED by) (`-2) = (`-52) = `-DIED the `-VERY `-YEAR `-PRIOR at the `-AGE of (`-51)!!!~'

`-DEATH/DAY # `-NUMBER = 8+25+20+22 = 75

`-DEATH/DAY # `-NUMBER = 75 = RECIPROCAL = 57 = FLIP 7 to 2 = (`-52) = `-DIED the `-VERY `-YEAR `-PRIOR at the `-AGE of (`-51)!!!~'

`-DAY of `-DEATH = (`-25th) = RECIPROCAL = (`-52) = `-DIED the `-VERY `-YEAR `-PRIOR at the `-AGE of (`-51)!!!~'

`-DEATH/DAY = 8/25 = 8+25 = (`-33) = `-PARTIAL `-BIRTH/DAY # `-NUMBER = 4+10+19 = (`-33)!!!~'

104+75 = 179 = 17+9 = (`-26)

104(-)75 = 29 = FLIP 9 to 6 = (`-26)

26+26 = (`-52) = `-DIED the `-VERY `-YEAR `-PRIOR at the `-AGE of (`-51)!!!~'

FRAGMENTED `-BIRTH/DAY # `-NUMBER = 4+1+0+1+9+ 7+1 = 23

`-WAS `-BORN in the `-MONTH of (`-4); and, `-DIED in the `-MONTH of (`-8) = (`-4/8) = 4x8 = (`-32) = RECIPROCAL = (`- 23) = FRAGMENTED `-BIRTH/DAY # `-NUMBER!!!~'

FRAGMENTED `-DEATH/DAY # `-NUMBER = 8+2+5+2+0+ 2+2 = 21

FRAGMENTED `-DEATH/DAY # `-NUMBER = 21 = X TIMES (`-2) = 42 = 20+22 = `-DEATH/YEAR!!!~'

`-BIRTH/YEAR = 71 = FLIP 7 to 2 = (`-21) = FRAGMENTED `-DEATH/DAY # `-NUMBER!!!~'

23+21 = (2+3) (2(-)1) = (`-51) = `-AGE of `-DEATH for AMERICAN JAZZ TRUMPETER JOEY DEFRANCESCO!!!~'

23+21 = 44 = `-DEATH/DAY = 8/25 = HALF RECIPROCAL = 8/52 = 8(-)52 = (`-44)!!!~'

`-DEATH/DAY = 8/25 = HALF RECIPROCAL = 8/52 = 8+52 = 60 = FLIP 6 to 9 = (`-90) = `-BIRTH/YEAR = 19+71 = (`-90)!!!~'

`-BIRTH/MONTH was APRIL with 30 DAYS

(30 (-) 10) – DAY of `-BIRTH = (`-20) = "SEE `-BELOW"!!!~'

FROM `-BIRTH-to-DEATH there are 137 DAYS = 13+7 = (`-20) = "SEE `-ABOVE"!!!~'

FROM `-BIRTH-to-DEATH there are 137 DAYS = 1x37 = 37 = 3x7 = (`-21) = FRAGMENTED `-DEATH/DAY # `-NUMBER!!!~'

(365 (-) 137) = 228 = 22x8 = 176 = 1x76 = 76 = 7x6 = 42 = 20+22 = `-DEATH/YEAR!!!~'

(365 (-) 137) = 228 = 2(-)28 = 26 = X TIMES (`-2) = (`-52) = `-DIED the `-VERY `-YEAR `-PRIOR at the `-AGE of (`-51)!!!~'

(365 (-) 137) = 228 = 2+28 = 30 = 5x6 = (`-56) = 7x8 = (`-78) = FLIP 7 to 2; FLIP 8 to 3 = (`-23) = FRAGMENTED `-BIRTH/DAY # `-NUMBER!!!~'

`-BIRTH/DAY = 4+10 /|\ `-DEATH/DAY = 8+25 /|\ 4+10+8+25 = 47 = FLIP 7 to 2 = 42 = 20+22 = `-DEATH/YEAR!!!~'

`-BIRTH/YEAR = 1971 = 1/9+7/1 = 1/16/1 = 1(-)16/1 = 15/1 = 15x1 = 15 = RECIPROCAL = (`-51) = `-AGE of `-DEATH for AMERICAN JAZZ TRUMPETER JOEY DEFRANCESCO!!!~'

`-DEATH/MONTH was AUGUST with 31 DAYS

(31 (-) 25) – DAY of `-DEATH = (`-6) = 5+1 = (`-51) = `-AGE of `-DEATH for AMERICAN JAZZ TRUMPETER JOEY DEFRANCESCO!!!~'

`-PARTIAL `-BIRTH/DAY # `-NUMBER in `-REVERSE = 71(-)19(-)10 = 42 = 20+22 = `-DEATH/YEAR!!!~'

`-PARTIAL `-BIRTH/DAY # `-NUMBER in `-REVERSE = 71(-)
19(-)10(-)4 = 38 = 3x8 = 24 = RECIPROCAL = 42 = 20+22 =
`-DEATH/YEAR!!!~'

AMERICAN MUSICIAN (DRUMMER) OLIVER TAYLOR
HAWKINS died at the AGE of (`-50)!!!~'

`-WAS `-MARRIED to ALISON HAWKINS from 2005 to 2022
for 17 YEARS = TAYLOR HAWKINS `-DAY of `-BIRTH =
(`-17ᵗʰ)!!!~'

`-MARRIED in 2005 = 20+05 = 25 = X TIMES (`-2) = (`-50) =
`-AGE of `-DEATH for AMERICAN MUSICIAN (DRUMMER)
OLIVER TAYLOR HAWKINS!!!~'

`-MARRIED in 2005 = 20x05 = 100 / (DIVIDED by) (`-2) = (`-50) =
`-AGE of `-DEATH for AMERICAN MUSICIAN (DRUMMER)
OLIVER TAYLOR HAWKINS!!!~'

`-PARTIAL `-BIRTH/DAY # `-NUMBER = 2+17+19 = (`-38) = 3x8
= 24 = RECIPROCAL = 42 = 20+22 = `-DEATH/YEAR!!!~'

`-BIRTH/DAY = 2/17 = 2(-)17 = 15 = RECIPROCAL = (`-51) =
`-DIED the `-VERY `-YEAR `-PRIOR at the `-AGE of (`-50)!!!~'

`-WAS `-BORN in the `-MONTH of (`-2); and, `-DIED in the
`-MONTH of (`-3) = (`-23) = `-BIRTH/DAY = 2/17 = FLIP 7 to 2
= 2/12 = 2/1+2 = (`-23)!!!~'

`-BIRTH/DAY # `-NUMBER = 2+17+19+72 = 110

155

`-BIRTH/DAY # `-NUMBER = 110 / (DIVIDED by) (`-2) = (`-55) = `-DEATH/DAY = 3/25 = HALF RECIPROCAL = 3/52 = 3+52 = (`-55)!!!~'

(`-55) = 5x5 = 25 = X TIMES (`-2) = (`-50) = `-AGE of `-DEATH for AMERICAN MUSICIAN (DRUMMER) OLIVER TAYLOR HAWKINS!!!~'

`-BIRTH/DAY = 2/17 = 2x17 = (`-34) = `-BIRTH/DAY # `-NUMBER in `-REVERSE = 72(-)19(-)17(-)2 = (`-34)!!!~'

`-DEATH/DAY # `-NUMBER = 3+25+20+22 = 70

`-DEATH/DAY = 3/25 = 3(-)25 = (`-22) = `-YEAR of `-DEATH = (`-22)!!!~'

`-DEATH/DAY = 3/25 = HALF RECIPROCAL = 3/52 = 3(-)52 = (`-49) = `-DIED the `-VERY `-YEAR `-AFTERWARD at the `-AGE of (`-50)!!!~'

(`-49) = RECIPROCAL = (`-94)

`-DEATH/DAY = 3/25 = 3+25 = 28 = `-YEARS `-ACTIVE from 19(94) to 20(22) = (`-28) `-YEARS!!!~'

110+70 = 180 = 18+0 = (`-18) = 3x6 = (`-36) = `-DAYS from `-BIRTH-to-DEATH!!!~'

110(-)70 = 40 = 5x8 = (`-58) = FLIP 8 to 3 = (`-53) = `-BIRTH/YEAR = 19(-)72 = (`-53)!!!~'

FRAGMENTED `-BIRTH/DAY # `-NUMBER = 2+1+7+1+9+ 7+2 = 29

FRAGMENTED `-BIRTH/DAY # `-NUMBER = 29 = `-DAUGHTER ANNABELLE HAWKINS was `-BORN in 2009 = 20+09 = (`-29)!!!~'

FRAGMENTED `-BIRTH/DAY # `-NUMBER = 29 = `-SON OLIVER SHANE HAWKINS was `-BORN in 2006 = 20+06 = (`-26) = FLIP 6 to 9 = (`-29)!!!~'

`-CURRENT `-AGE of `-SON OLIVER SHANE HAWKINS (`-16) & `-DAUGTHER ANNABELLE HAWKINS (`-13) = 16+13 = (`-29)!!!~'

FRAGMENTED `-DEATH/DAY # `-NUMBER = 3+2+5+2+0+2+2 = 16

FRAGMENTED `-DEATH/DAY # `-NUMBER = 16 = `-AGE of `-SON OLIVER SHANE HAWKINS around the `-TIME that `-HIS `-FATHER had `-DIED of which `-HE was `-BORN in 2006!!!~'

FRAGMENTED `-DEATH/DAY # `-NUMBER = 16 = RECIPROCAL = 61 = FLIP 6 to 9 = (`-91) = `-BIRTH/YEAR = 19+72 = (`-91)!!!~'

29+16 = 45 = 4x5 = 20 = FLIP 2 to 7 = (`-70) = `-DEATH/DAY # `-NUMBER!!!~'

29(-)16 = 13 = `-AGE of `-DAUGHTER ANNABELLE HAWKINS around the `-TIME that `-HER `-FATHER had `-DIED of which `-SHE was `-BORN in 2009!!!~'

FROM `-BIRTH-to-DEATH there are 36 DAYS = `-BIRTH/YEAR = (`-72) / (DIVIDED by) (`-2) = (`-36)!!!~'

DWAYNE W. ANDERSON

FROM `-BIRTH-to-DEATH there are 36 DAYS = `-PARTIAL `-BIRTH/DAY # `-NUMBER in `-REVERSE = 72(-)19(-)17 = (`-36)!!!~'

(365 (-) 36) = 329 = 32x9 = 288 = 28+8 = (`-36) = `-DAYS from `-BIRTH-to-DEATH!!!~'

(365 (-) 36) = 329 = 3x29 = 87 = RECIPROCAL = 78 = FLIP 7 to 2; FLIP 8 to 3 = (`-23) = `-WAS `-BORN in the `-MONTH of (`-2); and, `-DIED in the `-MONTH of (`-3) = (`-23)!!!~'

`-PARTIAL `-DEATH/DAY # `-NUMBER = 3+25+20 = 48 = 4x8 = (`-32) = RECIPROCAL = (`-23) = `-WAS `-BORN in the `-MONTH of (`-2); and, `-DIED in the `-MONTH of (`-3) = (`-23)!!!~'

`-BIRTH/YEAR = 1972 = 1+9/7(-)2 = 10/5 = 10x5 = (`-50) = `-AGE of `-DEATH for AMERICAN MUSICIAN (DRUMMER) OLIVER TAYLOR HAWKINS!!!~'

`-HEIGHT of TAYLOR HAWKINS = 5' 10" = 5x10 = (`-50) = `-AGE of `-DEATH for AMERICAN MUSICIAN (DRUMMER) OLIVER TAYLOR HAWKINS!!!~'

`-BIRTH/YEAR = (`-72) = FLIP 7 to 2 = (`-22) = `-DEATH/YEAR!!!~'

`-RECORDED `-EIGHT STUDIO ALBUMS as the DRUMMER for the FOO FIGHTERS between 1999 to 2021 = (`-22) `-YEARS = `-DEATH/YEAR = (`-22)!!!~'

AMERICAN BROADCAST JOURNALIST ANNE LONGWORTH GARRELS died at the AGE of (`-71)!!!~'

`-BIRTH/DAY = 7/2 = `-DIED the `-VERY `-YEAR `-PRIOR at the AGE of (`-71)!!!~'

`-BIRTH/YEAR = 19/51 = 19+51 = (`-70) = `-DIED the `-VERY `-YEAR `-AFTERWARD at the AGE of (`-71)!!!~'

`-BIRTH/DAY # `-NUMBER = 7+2+19+51 = 79

`-WAS `-BORN in the `-MONTH of (`-7); and, `-DIED in the `-MONTH of (`-9) = (`-79) = `-BIRTH/DAY # `-NUMBER = (`-79)!!!~'

`-BIRTH/DAY # `-NUMBER = 79 = RECIPROCAL = (`-9/7) = `-DEATH/DAY!!!~'

`-DEATH/DAY # `-NUMBER = 9+7+20+22 = 58

79+58 = 137 = RECIPROCAL = 731 = 73(-)1 = (`-7/2) = `-BIRTH/DAY!!!~'

79+58 = 137 = RECIPROCAL = 731 = 73(-)1 = (`-72) = `-DIED the `-VERY `-YEAR `-PRIOR at the AGE of (`-71)!!!~'

79(-)58 = 21 = FLIP 2 to 7 = (`-71) = `-AGE of `-DEATH for AMERICAN BROADCAST JOURNALIST ANNE LONGWORTH GARRELS!!!~'

FRAGMENTED `-BIRTH/DAY # `-NUMBER = 7+2+1+9+5+1 = 25

(`-25) = RECIPROCAL = (`-52)

25+52 = (`-77) = `-FORMER `-HUSBAND J. VINTON "VINT" LAWRENCE died this MANY DAYS from `-BIRTH-to-DEATH = (`-77)!!!~'

FRAGMENTED `-DEATH/DAY # `-NUMBER = 9+7+2+0+ 2+2 = 22

FRAGMENTED `-DEATH/DAY # `-NUMBER = 22 = `-DEATH/ YEAR = (`-22)!!!~'

FRAGMENTED `-DEATH/DAY # `-NUMBER = 22 = FLIP 2 to 7 = (`-77) = `-FORMER `-HUSBAND J. VINTON "VINT" LAWRENCE died this MANY DAYS from `-BIRTH-to-DEATH = (`-77)!!!~'

FRAGMENTED `-DEATH/DAY # `-NUMBER = 22 = FLIP 2 to 7 = (`-7/2) = `-BIRTH/DAY!!!~'

25+22 = 47 = FLIP 7 to 2 = 42 = 20+22 = `-DEATH/YEAR!!!~'

FROM `-BIRTH-to-DEATH there are 67 DAYS = 6x7 = 42 = 20+22 = `-DEATH/YEAR!!!~'

(365 (-) 67) = 298 = 2x98 = 196 = 1+96 = (`-9/7) = `-DEATH/ DAY!!!~'

`-BIRTH/MONTH was JULY with 31 DAYS

(31 (-) 2) – DAY of `-BIRTH = 29 = RECIPROCAL = 92 = FLIP 2 to 7 = (`-9/7) = `-DEATH/DAY!!!~'

(31 (-) 2) – DAY of `-BIRTH = 29 = X TIMES (`-2) = (`-58) = `-DEATH/DAY # `-NUMBER!!!~'

`-WAS `-MARRIED to J. VINTON LAWRENCE in 1986!!!~'

(`-1986) = 19(-)86 = 67 = `-DAYS from `-BIRTH-to-DEATH!!!~'

(`-1986) = 19(-)86 = 67 = FLIP 6 to 9 = (`-9/7) = `-DEATH/DAY!!!~'

(`-1986) = 19(-)86 = 67 = 6x7 = 42 = 20+22 = `-DEATH/YEAR!!!~'

`-DEATH/DAY = 9/7 = 9x7 = (`-63) = RECIPROCAL = (`-36) =
FLIP 3 to 8 = (`-86) = `-WAS `-MARRIED in (`-86)!!!~'

`-PARTIAL `-DEATH/DAY # `-NUMBER = 9+7+20 = (`-36) =
FLIP 3 to 8 = (`-86) = `-WAS `-MARRIED in (`-86)!!!~'

`-BIRTH/YEAR = 1951 = 1+9+5/1 = 15/1 = 15+1 = 16 = 7+9 (OR)
9+7 = `-BIRTH/DAY # `-NUMBER (`-79) & `-DEATH/DAY
(`-9/7)!!!~'

`-FORMER `-HUSBAND J. VINTON "VINT" LAWRENCE
`-BIRTH/DAY # `-NUMBER = 6+25+19+39 = 89 = 8x9 = (7/2) =
`-BIRTH/DAY of `-FORMER `-WIFE ANNE LONGWORTH
GARRELS!!!~'

`-FORMER `-HUSBAND J. VINTON "VINT" LAWRENCE
`-BIRTH/DAY # `-NUMBER = 6+25+19+39 = 89 = FLIP 9 to 6 =
(`-86) = `-WAS `-MARRIED in (`-86)!!!~'

`-BIRTH/YEAR = 39 = FLIP 3 to 8; FLIP 9 to 6 = (`-86) = WAS
`-MARRIED in (`-86)!!!~'

`-DEATH/YEAR = 2016 = 20+16 = (`-36) = FLIP 3 to 8 = (`-86) =
WAS `-MARRIED in (`-86)!!!~'

`-FORMER `-HUSBAND J. VINTON "VINT" LAWRENCE
`-DEATH/DAY = 4/9 = 4x9 = (`-36) = FLIP 3 to 8 = (`-86) = WAS
`-MARRIED in (`-86)!!!~'

`-FORMER `-HUSBAND J. VINTON "VINT" LAWRENCE
`-DEATH/DAY # `-NUMBER = 4+9+20+16 = (`-49) = `-DEATH/
DAY = (4/9)!!!~'

`-FORMER `-HUSBAND J. VINTON "VINT" LAWRENCE `-DIED (`-77) DAYS from `-BIRTH-to-DEATH = 7x7 = (`-49) = `-DEATH/DAY!!!~'

`-FORMER `-HUSBAND J. VINTON "VINT" LAWRENCE `-BIRTH/DAY = 6/25 = 6/2+5 = (`-67) = `-DAYS from `-BIRTH-to-DEATH for `-FORMER `-WIFE AMERICAN BROADCAST JOURNALIST ANNE LONGWORTH GARRELS!!!~'

`-FORMER `-HUSBAND J. VINTON "VINT" LAWRENCE `-BIRTH/DAY = 6/25 = 6/2+5 = (`-67) = 6x7 = 42 = 20+22 = `-DEATH/YEAR for `-FORMER `-WIFE AMERICAN BROADCAST JOURNALIST ANNE LONGWORTH GARRELS!!!~'

`-DEATH/MONTH for `-FORMER `-HUSBAND J. VINTON "VINT" LAWRENCE was APRIL with 30 DAYS

(30 (-) 9) = DAY of `-DEATH = 21 = FLIP 2 to 7 = (`-71) = `-AGE of `-DEATH for `-FORMER `-WIFE AMERICAN BROADCAST JOURNALIST ANNE LONGWORTH GARRELS!!!~'

AMERICAN JOURNALIST (CNN) BERNARD SHAW died at the AGE of (`-82)!!!~'

`-DAY of `-BIRTH = (22nd) = `-DEATH/YEAR = (`-22)!!!~'

`-PARTIAL `-BIRTH/DAY # `-NUMBER = 5+22+19 = 46 = 4x6 = 24 = RECIPROCAL = 42 = 20+22 = `-DEATH/YEAR!!!~'

`-BIRTH/DAY # `-NUMBER = 5+22+19+40 = 86

`-BIRTH/DAY # `-NUMBER = 86 = RECIPROCAL = 68 = FLIP 6 to 9 = (`-9/8) = `-DIED the `-VERY `-DAY `-PRIOR on (`-9/7)!!!~'

`-BIRTH/DAY # `-NUMBER = 86 = FLIP 8 to 3 = (`-36) = RECIPROCAL = (`-63) = 9x7 = (`-9/7) = `-DEATH/DAY!!!~'

`-BIRTH/DAY # `-NUMBER = 86 = FLIP 8 to 3 = (`-36) = `-PARTIAL `-DEATH/DAY # `-NUMBER = 9+7+20 = (`-36)!!!~'

36+36 = 72 = FLIP 7 to 2 = (`-22) = `-DEATH/YEAR!!!~'

`-DEATH/DAY # `-NUMBER = 9+7+20+22 = 58

`-DEATH/DAY # `-NUMBER = 58 = 5+8 = 13 = RECIPROCAL = 31 = FLIP 3 to 8 = (`-81) = `-DIED the `-VERY `-NEXT `-YEAR at the `-AGE of (`-82)!!!~'

86+58 = 144 = 14x4 = 56 = 8x7 = (`-87) = FLIP 7 to 2 = (`-82) = `-AGE of `-DEATH for AMERICAN JOURNALIST (CNN) BERNARD SHAW!!!~'

86+58 = 144 = 14+4 = 18 = RECIPROCAL = 81 = `-DIED the `-VERY `-NEXT `-YEAR at the `-AGE of (`-82)!!!~'

86+58 = 144 = 14(-)4 = 10 = 8+2 = (`-82) = `-AGE of `-DEATH for AMERICAN JOURNALIST (CNN) BERNARD SHAW!!!~'

86(-)58 = 28 = RECIPROCAL = (`-82) = `-AGE of `-DEATH for AMERICAN JOURNALIST (CNN) BERNARD SHAW!!!~'

`-DEATH/DAY = 9/7 = 9+7 = 16 = 8x2 = (`-82) = `-AGE of `-DEATH for AMERICAN JOURNALIST (CNN) BERNARD SHAW!!!~'

FRAGMENTED `-BIRTH/DAY # `-NUMBER = 5+2+2+1+9+4+0 = 23

FRAGMENTED `-BIRTH/DAY # `-NUMBER = 23 = -a PROPHETIC # `-NUMBER!!!~'

FRAGMENTED `-BIRTH/DAY # `-NUMBER = 23 = RECIPROCAL = 32 = FLIP 3 to 8 = (`-82) = `-AGE of `-DEATH for AMERICAN JOURNALIST (CNN) BERNARD SHAW!!!~'

`-DEATH/MONTH was SEPTEMBER with 30 DAYS

(30 (-) 7) = DAY of DEATH = (`-23) = FRAGMENTED `-BIRTH/DAY # `-NUMBER!!!~'

FRAGMENTED `-DEATH/DAY # `-NUMBER = 9+7+2+0+2+2 = 22

FRAGMENTED `-DEATH/DAY # `-NUMBER = 22 = `-DAY of `-BIRTH (`-22nd)!!!~'

`-MARRIAGE # `-NUMBER in `-REVERSE = 74(-)19(-)30(-)3 = (`-22) = FRAGMENTED `-DEATH/DAY # `-NUMBER!!!~'

FRAGMENTED `-DEATH/DAY # `-NUMBER = 22 = FLIP 2 to 7 = (`-27) = 5+22 = `-BIRTH/DAY!!!~'

23+22 = 45 = 5x9 = (`-59) = `-BIRTH/YEAR = 19+40 = (`-59)!!!~'

`-WAS `-BORN in the `-MONTH of (`-5); and, `-DIED in the `-MONTH of (`-9) = (`-59)!!!~'

(59+59) = 118 = RECIPROCAL = 811 = 8/1+1 = (`-82) = `-AGE of `-DEATH for AMERICAN JOURNALIST (CNN) BERNARD SHAW!!!~'

23+22 = 45 = RECIPROCAL = 54 = X TIMES (`-2) = 108 = `-DAYS from `-BIRTH-to-DEATH!!!~'

FROM `-BIRTH-to-DEATH there are 108 DAYS = 10+8 = 18 = RECIPROCAL = 81 = `-DIED the `-VERY `-NEXT `-YEAR `-AFTERWARD at the AGE of (`-82)!!!~'

(365 (-) 108) = 257 = 2+57 = 59 = `-BIRTH/YEAR = 19+40 = (`-59)!!!~'

`-WAS `-MARRIED to LINDA ALLSTON in 1974 to 2022 for 48 `-YEARS = 4x8 = (`-32) = RECIPROCAL = (`-23) = FRAGMENTED `-BIRTH/DAY # `-NUMBER!!!~'

`-WAS `-MARRIED to LINDA ALLSTON in 1974 to 2022 for 48 `-YEARS = 8x6 = (`-86) = `-BIRTH/DAY # `-NUMBER!!!~'

`-WAS `-MARRIED to LINDA ALLSTON in 1974 to 2022 for 48 `-YEARS = RECIPROCAL = 84 = DIVIDED by (`-2) = 42 = 20+22 = `-DEATH/YEAR!!!~'

`-MARRIED on 3+30+19+74 = 126 = 1+2/6 = 36 = RECIPROCAL = 63 = 9x7 = (`-9/7) = `-DEATH/DAY!!!~'

`-MARRIED on 3/30 = 3+30 = 33 = FLIP 3 to 8 = (`-88) = 2(8's) = 28 = RECIPROCAL = (`-82) = `-AGE of `-DEATH for AMERICAN JOURNALIST (CNN) BERNARD SHAW!!!~'

`-MARRIED in (`-74) = 7x4 = 28 = RECIPROCAL = (`-82) = `-AGE of `-DEATH for AMERICAN JOURNALIST (CNN) BERNARD SHAW!!!~'

ELIZABETH ALEXANDRA MARY WINDSOR (QUEEN) of the UNITED KINGDOM (ELIZABETH II) died at the AGE of (`-96)!!!~'

QUEEN ELIZABETH II had HER entire LIFE in HER BIRTH/DAY = 4/21/19/26!!!~' MARRIED at 21!!!~' PRINCE PHILIP MARRIED at 26 = RECIPROCAL = 62 = DAYS from DEATH to BIRTHDAY!!!~' WHAT'S LEFT? 4/19 = 49 x 1 = 49 = DAY PRINCE PHILIP DIES = RECIPROCAL = 94 = HER AGE at the TIME of HIS DEATH!!!~'

'-WAS '-MARRIED for ('-73) '-YEARS; and, KING CHARLES III (their SON) takes the '-THRONE at the '-AGE of ('-73)!!!~'

'-PARTIAL '-DEATH/DAY # '-NUMBER = 9+8+20 = 37 = RECIPROCAL = ('-73) = "SEE '-ABOVE"!!!~'

'-DAY of '-BIRTH = ('-21ˢᵗ) = 7x3 = ('-73) = "SEE '-ABOVE"!!!~'

'-DAY of '-BIRTH = ('-21ˢᵗ) = X TIMES ('-2) = 42 = 20+22 = '-DEATH/YEAR!!!~'

'-BIRTH/DAY = 4/21 = FLIP 2 to 7 = 4/71 = 4(-)71 = 67 = 6x7 = 42 = 20+22 = '-DEATH/YEAR!!!~'

'-SON KING CHARLES III '-BIRTH/DAY # '-NUMBER = 11+14+19+48 = ('-92) = FLIP 9 to 6; FLIP 2 to 7 = ('-67) = 6x7 = 42 = 20+22 = '-YEAR '-HE became '-KING!!!~'

'-SON KING CHARLES III '-BIRTH/YEAR = 19+48 = 67 = 6x7 = 42 = 20+22 = '-YEAR '-HE became '-KING!!!~'

'-BIRTH/DAY # '-NUMBER = 4+21+19+26 = 70

QUEEN ELIZABETH II RULED the REALM of the UNITED KINGDOM for ('-70) '-YEARS as QUEEN = ('-70) = '-BIRTH/DAY # '-NUMBER !!!~'

'-BIRTH/DAY = 4(-)21 = ('-17) = 9+8 = '-DEATH/DAY!!!~'

`-ACCESSION as `-QUEEEN in 19/52 = 19+52 = (`-71) = RECIPROCAL = (`-17) = "SEE `-ABOVE"!!!~'

`-DEATH/DAY # `-NUMBER = 9+8+20+22 = 59

`-DEATH/DAY # `-NUMBER = 59 = 5x9 = 45 = `-BIRTH/YEAR = 19+26 = (`-45)!!!~'

`-DEATH/DAY # `-NUMBER = 59 = 5x9 = 45 = RECIPROCAL = 54 = 9x6 = (`-96) = `-AGE of `-DEATH for QUEEN ELIZABETH (II)!!!~'

`-HUSBAND PRINCE PHILIP `-DEATH/DAY # `-NUMBER = 4+9+20+21 = (`-54) = RECIPROCAL = (`-45) = 5x9 = (`-59) = `-DEATH/DAY # `-NUMBER for QUEEN ELIZABETH (II)!!!~'

`-DEATH/DAY # `-NUMBER = 59 = RECIPROCAL = 95 = `-DIED the `-VERY `-NEXT `-YEAR `-AFTERWARD at the AGE of (`-96)!!!~'

70+59 = 129 = RECIPROCAL = 921 = FLIP 2 to 7 = 971 = 9/7+1 = (`-9/8) = `-DEATH/DAY!!!~'

70(-)59 = 11 = 4+7 = (`-47) = `-WAS `-MARRIED in (`-47)!!!~'

FRAGMENTED `-BIRTH/DAY # `-NUMBER = 4+2+1+1+9+2+6 = 25

`-BIRTH/DAY # `-NUMBER = (`-70) (+) (`-25) = FRAGMENTED `-BIRTH/DAY # `-NUMBER = (`-95) = `-DIED the `-VERY `-NEXT `-YEAR `-AFTERWARD at the `-AGE of (`-96)!!!~'

FRAGMENTED `-BIRTH/DAY # `-NUMBER = 25 = QUEEN ELIZABETH II was (`-25) `-YEARS `-OLD for WHEN `-SHE became `-QUEEN of the UNITED KINGDOM in (`-52)!!!~'

(`-52) = RECIPROCAL = (`-25)

FRAGMENTED `-BIRTH/DAY # `-NUMBER = 25 = 4+21 = `-BIRTH/DAY = (`-4/21)!!!~'

FRAGMENTED `-BIRTH/DAY # `-NUMBER = 25 = `-SON KING CHARLES III `-BIRTH/DAY = 11+14 = (`-25)!!!~'

`-SON KING CHARLES III `-BIRTH/DAY = 11/14 = RECIPROCAL = 41/11 = 4/1+1/1 = 4/2/1 = `-BIRTH/DAY of QUEEN ELIZABETH (II)!!!~'

FRAGMENTED `-DEATH/DAY # `-NUMBER = 9+8+2+0+2+2 = 23

FRAGMENTED `-DEATH/DAY # `-NUMBER = 23 = -a PROPHETIC # `-NUMBER!!!~'

FRAGMENTED `-DEATH/DAY # `-NUMBER = 23 = FLIP 3 to 8 = (`-28) = `-MARRIED in 19(-)47 = (`-28)!!!~'

`-HUSBAND PRINCE PHILIP was `-BORN in the `-MONTH of (`-6); and, `-DIED in the `-MONTH of (`-4) = (`-64) = DIVIDED by (`-2) = (`-32) = RECIPROCAL = (`-23) = FRAGMENTED `-DEATH/DAY # `-NUMBER of QUEEN ELIZABETH (II)!!!~'

`-HUSBAND PRINCE PHILIP was `-BORN in the `-MONTH of (`-6); and, `-DIED in the `-MONTH of (`-4) = (`-64) = FLIP 6 to 9 = (`-94) = DIVIDED by (`-2) = (`-47) = `-YEAR `-THEY were `-MARRIED!!!~'

`-HUSBAND PRINCE PHILIP `-BIRTH/DAY # `-NUMBER = 6+10+19+21 = 56 = 7x8 = (`-78) = FLIP 7 to 2; FLIP 8 to 3 = (`-23) = FRAGMENTED `-DEATH/DAY # `-NUMBER of QUEEN ELIZABETH (II)!!!~'

25+23 = 48 = RECIPROCAL = 84 = DIVIDED by (`-2) = 42 = 20+22 = `-DEATH/YEAR!!!~'

25+23 = 48 = RECIPROCAL = 84 = 4x21 = `-BIRTH/DAY = (`-4/21)!!!~'

25+23 = 48 = `-SON KING CHARLES III was `-BORN in (`-48)!!!~'

`-SON KING CHARLES III was `-BORN in 1948 = 19+48 = 67 = 6x7 = 42 = 20+22 = `-YEAR `-HE became `-KING; and, `-YEAR of `-HIS `-MOTHER'S QUEEN ELIZABETH II `-DEATH!!!~'

`-SON KING CHARLES III was `-BORN in 1948 = 19+48 = 67 = FLIP 6 to 9 = (`-9/7) = `-BECAME `-KING the `-VERY `-NEXT `-DAY on (`-9/8)!!!~'

FROM `-BIRTH-to-DEATH there are 140 DAYS = DIVIDED by (`-2) = (`-70) = `-BIRTH/DAY # `-NUMBER!!!~'

(365 (-) 140) = 225 = 2(-)25 = (`-23) = FRAGMENTED `-DEATH/DAY # `-NUMBER!!!~'

`-BIRTH/MONTH was APRIL with 30 DAYS

(30 (-) 21) – DAY of `-BIRTH = (`-9) = `-DEATH/MONTH!!!~'

`-BIRTH/YEAR = 19/26 = 1x9/2+6 = (`-9/8) = `-DEATH/DAY!!!~'

`-PRINCE PHILIP `-DEATH/MONTH was APRIL with 30 DAYS

(30 (-) 9) – DAY of `-DEATH = (`-21) = QUEEN `-ELIZABETH (II) `-DAY of `-BIRTH = (`-21ˢᵗ)!!!~'

`-CAN `-YOU `-SEE that `-THEIR `-DAY of `-BIRTH (WIFE); and, `-DAY of `-DEATH (HUSBAND) are (`-RECIPROCALS-`) of `-EACH `-OTHER (`-HUSBAND & `-WIFE)!!!~'

`-ACCESSION as `-QUEEEN on 2/6/19/52 = 2+6+19+52 = 79 = RECIPROCAL = 9/7 = `-DIED the `-VERY `-NEXT `-DAY `-AFTERWARD for QUEEN ELIZABETH (II) on (`-9/8)!!!~'

26 = X TIMES (`-2) = (`-52)!!!~'

(`-26) = `-BIRTH/YEAR for QUEEN ELIZABETH (II)!!!~'

`-AGE of `-DEATH for `-QUEEN ELIZABETH II = (`-96) = DIVIDED by (`-2) = (`-48) = `-DIED (`-48) HOURS after `-HER `-LAST `-OFFICIAL `-DUTIES with GREAT BRITAIN'S NEW PRIME MINISTER LIZ TRUSS!!!~'

`-WAS `-MARRIED in 1947 = 19+47 = (`-66) = FLIP 6 to 9 = (`-96) = `-AGE of `-DEATH for QUEEN ELIZABETH (II)!!!~'

`-WAS `-MARRIED in 1947 = 19+47 = (`-66) = FLIP 6 to 9 = (`-99) = `-AGE of `-DEATH for `-HUSBAND PRINCE PHILIP, DUKE of EDINBURGH!!!~'

QUEEN ELIZABETH II dies at the AGE of (`-96) = FLIP 6 to 9 = (`-99) = `-AGE of `-DEATH for `-HUSBAND PRINCE PHILIP, DUKE of EDINBURGH!!!~'

QUEEN ELIZABETH II was `-BORN in the `-MONTH of (`-4); and, `-DIED in the `-MONTH of (`-9) = (`-49) = `-DEATH/DAY for `-HUSBAND PRINCE PHILIP, DUKE of EDINBURGH!!!~'

AMERICAN STAND-UP COMEDIAN DAVID A. ARNOLD died at the AGE of (`-54)!!!~'

`-BIRTH/DAY = 3/15 = RECIPROCAL = 51/3 = 51+3 = (`-54) = `-AGE of `-DEATH for AMERICAN STAND-UP COMEDIAN DAVID A. ARNOLD!!!~'

`-BIRTH/DAY # `-NUMBER in `-REVERSE = 68(-)19(-)15(-)3 = 31 = RECIPROCAL = 13 = 6+7 = (`-67) = 6x7 = 42 = 20+22 = `-DEATH/YEAR!!!~'

`-BIRTH/DAY # `-NUMBER = 3+15+19+68 = 105

`-BIRTH/DAY # `-NUMBER = 105 = 10x5 = (`-50) = 25x2 = HALF RECIPROCAL = 52x2 = 52+2 = (`-54) = `-AGE of `-DEATH for AMERICAN STAND-UP COMEDIAN DAVID A. ARNOLD!!!~'

`-BIRTH/YEAR = 1968 = 1(-)6/9+8 = 5/17 = 5/1+7 = (`-58) = `-DEATH/DAY # `-NUMBER!!!~'

`-DEATH/DAY # `-NUMBER = 9+7+20+22 = 58

`-DEATH/DAY # `-NUMBER = 58 = 5x8 = 40 = / DIVIDED by (`-2) = 20 = 5x4 = (`-54) = `-AGE of `-DEATH for AMERICAN STAND-UP COMEDIAN DAVID A. ARNOLD!!!~'

105+58 = 163 = 1x63 = (`-63) = 9x7 = (`-9/7) = `-DEATH/DAY!!!~'

105/58 = 10(-)5 /|\ 5+8 = 5/13 = 5/1+3 = (`-54) = `-AGE of `-DEATH for AMERICAN STAND-UP COMEDIAN DAVID A. ARNOLD!!!~'

FRAGMENTED `-BIRTH/DAY # `-NUMBER = 3+1+5+1+9+ 6+8 = 33

`-BIRTH/DAY # `-NUMBER = (`-105) (-) (`-33) = FRAGMENTED `-BIRTH/DAY # `-NUMBER = 72 = 8x9 = (`-89) = / DIVIDED by (`-2) = 44.5 = RECIPROCAL = (54.4) = `-AGE of `-DEATH for AMERICAN STAND-UP COMEDIAN DAVID A. ARNOLD!!!~'

FRAGMENTED `-DEATH/DAY # `-NUMBER = 9+7+2+0+ 2+2 = 22

33+22 = 55 = `-DIED the `-VERY `-YEAR `-PRIOR at the `-AGE of (`-54)!!!~'

33/22 = (`-32) = `-BIRTH/DAY = 3/15 = 31.5 = ROUNDED UP = (`-32)!!!~'

`-BIRTH/DAY = 3/15 = HALF RECIPROCAL = 3/51 = 3+51 = (`-54) = `-AGE of `-DEATH for AMERICAN STAND-UP COMEDIAN DAVID A. ARNOLD!!!~'

33/22 = (`-32) = `-BIRTH/DAY = 3/15 = HALF RECIPROCAL = 3/51 = 3(-)51 = (`-48) = 4x8 = (`-32)

FROM `-BIRTH-to-DEATH there are 176 DAYS = 1x76 = (`-76) = 7x6 = 42 = 20+22 = `-DEATH/YEAR!!!~'

(365 (-) 176) = 189 = 18+9 = 27 = X TIMES (`-2) = (`-54) = `-AGE of `-DEATH for AMERICAN STAND-UP COMEDIAN DAVID A. ARNOLD!!!~'

(365 (-) 176) = 189 = 1x89 = (`-89) = FLIP 8 to 3 = (`-39) = `-WAS `-BORN in the `-MONTH of (`-3); and, `-DIED in the `-MONTH of (`-9) = (`-39)!!!~'

`-PARTIAL `-DEATH/DAY # `-NUMBER = 9+7+20 = 36 = RECIPROCAL = 63 = FLIP 3 to 8 = (`-68) = `-BIRTH/YEAR!!!~'

`-PARTIAL `-DEATH/DAY # `-NUMBER = 9+7+20 = 36 = `-BIRTH/DAY = 3/15 = 3/1+5 = (`-36)!!!~'

`-PARTIAL `-DEATH/DAY # `-NUMBER = 9+7+20 = 36 = `-BIRTH/YEAR = 19(-)68 = 49 = 4x9 = (`-36)!!!~'

`-WAS `-BORN in the `-MONTH of (`-3); and, `-DIED in the `-MONTH of (`-9) = (`-39) = 3x9 = (`-27) = X TIMES (`-2) = (`-54) = `-AGE of `-DEATH for AMERICAN STAND-UP COMEDIAN DAVID A. ARNOLD!!!~'

`-BIRTH/YEAR = 1968 = 1+9/6+8 = 10/14 = 10+14 = 24 = RECIPROCAL = 42 = 20+22 = `-DEATH/YEAR!!!~'

`-BIRTH/YEAR = (`-68) = RECIPROCAL = (`-86) = FLIP 6 to 9 = (`-89) = / DIVIDED by (`-2) = 44.5 = RECIPROCAL = 54.4 = `-AGE of `-DEATH for AMERICAN STAND-UP COMEDIAN DAVID A. ARNOLD!!!~'

`-DEATH/MONTH was `-SEPTEMBER with 30 DAYS

(30 (-) 7) – DAY of `-DEATH = (`-23) = 17+6 = (`-176) = DAYS from `-BIRTH-to-DEATH!!!~'

(30 (-) 7) – DAY of `-DEATH = (`-23) = RECIPROCAL = (`-32) = 4x8 = (`-48) = 6x8 = (`-68) = `-BIRTH/YEAR!!!~'

(30 (-) 7) – DAY of `-DEATH = (`-23) = RECIPROCAL = (`-32) = FLIP 3 to 8; FLIP 2 to 7 = (`-87) = `-BIRTH/YEAR = 19+68 = (`-87)!!!~'

AMERICAN ACTRESS/MODEL/ACTIVIST MARSHA VIRGINIA HUNT died at the AGE of (`-104)!!!~'

`-BIRTH/DAY # `-NUMBER = 10+17+19+17 = 63

`-BIRTH/DAY # `-NUMBER = 63 = 9x7 = (`-9/7) = `-DEATH/DAY!!!~'

`-DEATH/DAY # `-NUMBER = 9+7+20+22 = 58

`-DEATH/DAY # `-NUMBER = 58 = 5x8 = (`-40) = 10x4 = (`-104) = `-AGE of `-DEATH for AMERICAN ACTRESS/MODEL/ACTIVIST MARSHA VIRGINIA HUNT!!!~'

63+58 = 121 = 38+83 = `-WAS `-MARRIED to JERRY HOPPER in (`-38)!!!~'

(`-38) = RECIPROCAL = (`-83)

63+58 = 121 = 1+21 = (`-22) = FRAGMENTED `-DEATH/DAY # `-NUMBER!!!~'

63(-)58 = 5 = 1+0+4 = (`-104) = `-AGE of `-DEATH for AMERICAN ACTRESS/MODEL/ACTIVIST MARSHA VIRGINIA HUNT!!!~'

FRAGMENTED `-BIRTH/DAY # `-NUMBER = 1+0+1+7+1+9+1+7 = 27

FRAGMENTED `-BIRTH/DAY # `-NUMBER = 27 = FLIP 7 to 2 = (`-22) = `-DEATH/YEAR!!!~'

FRAGMENTED `-BIRTH/DAY # `-NUMBER = 27 = `-BIRTH/DAY = 10+17 = (`-27)!!!~'

FRAGMENTED `-DEATH/DAY # `-NUMBER = 9+7+2+0+
2+2 = 22

FRAGMENTED `-DEATH/DAY # `-NUMBER = 22 = `-DEATH/
YEAR!!!~'

27+22 = 49 = 4x9 = 36 = RECIPROCAL = 63 = `-BIRTH/DAY #
`-NUMBER!!!~'

27+22 = 49 = 4+9 = 13 = 5+8 = (`-58) = `-DEATH/DAY #
`-NUMBER!!!~'

27(-)22 = 5 = 1+0+4 = (`-104) = `-AGE of `-DEATH for AMERICAN
ACTRESS/MODEL/ACTIVIST   MARSHA   VIRGINIA
HUNT!!!~'

FROM `-BIRTH-to-DEATH there are 40 DAYS = 5x8 = (`-58) =
`-DEATH/DAY # `-NUMBER!!!~'

(365 (-) 40) = 325 = 32(-)5 = (`-27) = FRAGMENTED `-BIRTH/
DAY # `-NUMBER!!!~'

`-BIRTH/YEAR = 1917 = 19+17 = 36 = RECIPROCAL = 63
= `-BIRTH/DAY # `-NUMBER = (`-63) = & = 9x7 = (`-9/7) =
`-DEATH/DAY!!!~'

`-PARTIAL `-DEATH/DAY # `-NUMBER = 9+7+20 = 36 =
RECIPROCAL = (`-63) = "SEE `-ABOVE"!!!~'

`-YEARS `-ACTIVE from 1935 to 2014 for (`-79) YEARS =
RECIPROCAL = (`-9/7) = `-DEATH/DAY!!!~'

`-WAS `-BORN in the `-MONTH of (`-10); and, `-DIED in the
`-MONTH of (`-9) = (`-10/9) = 10+9 = (`-19) = FLIP 9 to 6 = (`-16)

= STARTED `-BEING `-ACTIVE in 19(-)35 = (`-16) = 9+7 = (`-9/7) = `-DEATH/DAY!!!~'

`-PARTIAL `-BIRTH/DAY # `-NUMBER = 10+17+19 = (`-46) = `-WAS `-MARRIED to ROBERT PRESNELL JR. in (`-46)!!!~'

`-WAS `-MARRIED to ROBERT PRESNELL JR. from 1946 to 1986 for (`-40) YEARS = 5x8 = (`-58) = `-DEATH/DAY # `-NUMBER!!!~'

`-MARRIED in 1946 = 19(-)46 = 27 = FRAGMENTED `-BIRTH/ DAY # `-NUMBER!!!~'

`-MARRIAGE `-ENDED in 1986 = 19(-)86 = 67 = 6x7 = 42 = 20+22 = `-DEATH/YEAR!!!~'

`-MARRIAGE `-ENDED in 1986 = 19+86 = 105 = `-DIED the `-VERY `-YEAR `-PRIOR at the `-AGE of (`-104) for AMERICAN ACTRESS/MODEL/ACTIVIST MARSHA VIRGINIA HUNT!!!~'

`-WAS `-MARRIED to JERRY HOPPER from 1938 to 1945 for (7) YEARS!!!~'

(`-7) = X TIMES (`-2) = 14 = `-JUST `-INSERT a `-ZERO = (`-104) = `-AGE of `-DEATH for AMERICAN ACTRESS/MODEL/ ACTIVIST MARSHA VIRGINIA HUNT!!!~'

`-MARRIAGE `-ENDED in 1945 = 19+45 = 64 = RECIPROCAL = 46 = `-MARRIED `-AGAIN in (`-46)!!!~'

`-DEATH/MONTH was SEPTEMBER with 30 DAYS

(30 (-) 7) – DAY of `-DEATH = (`-23) = FLIP 2 to 7; FLIP 3 to 8 = (`-78) = `-ADD `-BIRTH/YEAR & `-DEATH/YEAR `-TOGETHER = 19+17+20+22 = (`-78)!!!~'

`-BIRTH/MONTH was OCTOBER with 31 DAYS

(31 (-) 17) – DAY of `-BIRTH = 14 = `-JUST `-INSERT a `-ZERO = (`-104) = `-AGE of `-DEATH for AMERICAN ACTRESS/MODEL/ACTIVIST MARSHA VIRGINIA HUNT!!!~'

AMERICAN PROFESSIONAL BASEBALL PITCHER ANTHONY MICHAEL VARVARO died at the AGE of (`-37)!!!~'

`-DAY of `-BIRTH - (31st) + `-DAY of `-DEATH - (`-11th) = 42 = 20+22 = `-DEATH/YEAR!!!~'

`-WAS `-BORN in the `-MONTH of (`-10); and, `-DIED in the `-MONTH of (`-9) = (`-10/9) = 10+9 = 19 = X TIMES (`-2) = (`-38) = `-DIED the `-VERY `-YEAR `-PRIOR at the `-AGE of (`-37)!!!~'

`-BIRTH/DAY = 10/31 = 10(-)31 = (`-21) = 3x7 = (`-37) = `-AGE of `-DEATH for AMERICAN PROFESSIONAL BASEBALL PITCHER ANTHONY MICHAEL VARVARO!!!~'

`-BIRTH/DAY = 10/31 = HALF RECIPROCAL = 10/13 = 10+13 = (`-23) = RECIPROCAL = (`-32) = FLIP 2 to 7 = (`-37) = `-AGE of `-DEATH for AMERICAN PROFESSIONAL BASEBALL PITCHER ANTHONY MICHAEL VARVARO!!!~'

`-BIRTH/DAY # `-NUMBER = 10+31+19+84 = 144

`-BIRTH/DAY # `-NUMBER = 144 = 14(-)4 = (`-10) = 3+7 = (`-37) = `-AGE of `-DEATH for AMERICAN PROFESSIONAL BASEBALL PITCHER ANTHONY MICHAEL VARVARO!!!~'

`-BIRTH/DAY = 10/31 = FLIP 3 to 8 = 10/81 = 10+81 = 91 = `-DEATH/DAY = 9/11!!!~'

`-DEATH/DAY # `-NUMBER = 9+11+20+22 = 62

`-DEATH/DAY # `-NUMBER = 62 = X TIMES (`-2) = 124 = 12x4 = (`-48) = RECIPROCAL = (`-84) = `-BIRTH/YEAR!!!~'

144+62 = 206 = 20+6 = 26 = RECIPROCAL = 62 = `-DEATH/DAY # `-NUMBER!!!~'

144(-)62 = 82 = FLIP 8 to 3; FLIP 2 to 7 = (`-37) = `-AGE of `-DEATH for AMERICAN PROFESSIONAL BASEBALL PITCHER ANTHONY MICHAEL VARVARO!!!~'

FRAGMENTED `-BIRTH/DAY # `-NUMBER = 1+0+3+1+1+9+8+4 = 27

FRAGMENTED `-DEATH/DAY # `-NUMBER = 9+1+1+2+0+2+2 = 17

27+17 = 44 = `-BIRTH/DAY # `-NUMBER = 144 = 1x44 = (`-44)!!!~'

27(-)17 = 10 = 3+7 = (`-37) = `-AGE of `-DEATH for AMERICAN PROFESSIONAL BASEBALL PITCHER ANTHONY MICHAEL VARVARO!!!~'

FROM `-BIRTH-to-DEATH there are 50 DAYS = 30+20 = (3+0) (2+0) = (`-32) = FLIP 2 to 7 = (`-37) = `-AGE of `-DEATH for AMERICAN PROFESSIONAL BASEBALL PITCHER ANTHONY MICHAEL VARVARO!!!~'

(365 (-) 50) = 315 = 31+5 = (`-36) = `-DIED the `-VERY `-YEAR `-AFTERWARD at the `-AGE of (`-37)!!!~'

`-DEATH/MONTH was SEPTEMBER with 30 DAYS

(30 (-) 11) - DAY of `-DEATH = 19 = `-WAS `-BORN in the `-MONTH of (`-10); and, `-DIED in the `-MONTH of (`-9) = (`-10/9) = 10+9 = (`-19) = "SEE `-ABOVE"!!!~'

`-BIRTH/YEAR = 19(-)84 = 65 = / DIVIDED by (`-2) = (`-32.5) = FLIP 2 to 7 = (`-37.5) = `-AGE of `-DEATH for AMERICAN PROFESSIONAL BASEBALL PITCHER ANTHONY MICHAEL VARVARO!!!~'

`-BIRTH/YEAR = 19(-)84 = 65 = 6+5 = (`-11) = `-DAY of `-DEATH (`-11th)!!!~'

`-WAS `-MARRIED to KERRY ANN THOMSON in 2011 = 20+11 = (`-31) = `-DAY of `-BIRTH (`-31st)!!!~'

`-BIRTH/YEAR = 84 = 8x4 = (`-32) = FLIP 2 to 7 = (`-37) = `-AGE of `-DEATH for AMERICAN PROFESSIONAL BASEBALL PITCHER ANTHONY MICHAEL VARVARO!!!~'

`-PROFESSIONAL `-PITCHING # `-NUMBER = (`-38) ATLANTA BRAVES PITCHER = 3x8 = 24 = RECIPROCAL = 42 = 20+22 = `-DEATH/YEAR!!!~'

`-PROFESSIONAL `-PITCHING # `-NUMBER = (`-46) BOSTON RED SOX PITCHER = 4x6 = 24 = RECIPROCAL = 42 = 20+22 = `-DEATH/YEAR!!!~'

`-PROFESSIONAL `-PITCHING # `-NUMBER = (`-48) CHICAGO CUBS PITCHER = (`-48) = RECIPROCAL = (`-84) = `-BIRTH/YEAR!!!~'

`-PROFESSIONAL `-PITCHING # `-NUMBER = (`-48) CHICAGO CUBS PITCHER = 4x8 = 32 = FLIP 2 to 7 = (`-37) = `-AGE of `-DEATH for AMERICAN PROFESSIONAL BASEBALL PITCHER ANTHONY MICHAEL VARVARO!!!-'

`-BIRTH/YEAR = 1984 = 1+9+8+4 = (`-22) = `-DEATH/YEAR!!!-'

AMERICAN ACTOR-COMEDIAN-WRITER JAKIM MAULANA "JAK KNIGHT" died at the AGE of (`-28)!!!-'

`-BIRTH/DAY = 11/6 = 11x6 = 66 = 6x6 = (`-36) = RECIPROCAL = (`-63) = `-DEATH/DAY = 7/14 = 7x14 = 98 = FLIP 9 to 6; FLIP 8 to 3 = (`-63)!!!-'

`-BIRTH/DAY = 11/6 = 11x6 = 66 = 6x6 = (`-36) = RECIPROCAL = (`-63) = `-DEATH/DAY # `-NUMBER = (`-63)!!!-'

`-PARTIAL `-BIRTH/DAY # `-NUMBER = 11+6+19 = (`-36) = RECIPROCAL = (`-63) = `-DEATH/DAY = 7/14 = 7x14 = 98 = FLIP 9 to 6; FLIP 8 to 3 = (`-63)!!!-'

`-PARTIAL `-BIRTH/DAY # `-NUMBER = 11+6+19 = (`-36) = RECIPROCAL = (`-63) = `-DEATH/DAY # `-NUMBER = (`-63)!!!-'

`-BIRTH/DAY # `-NUMBER = 11+6+19+93 = 129

`-BIRTH/DAY # `-NUMBER = 129 = 1(-)29 = (`-28) = `-AGE of `-DEATH for AMERICAN ACTOR-COMEDIAN-WRITER JAKIM MAULANA "JAK KNIGHT"!!!-'

`-BIRTH/DAY # `-NUMBER = 129 = 12x9 = 108 = 10+8 = (`-18) = FRAGMENTED `-DEATH/DAY # `-NUMBER!!!-'

`-BIRTH/YEAR = 1993 = 19(-)93 = 74 = / DIVIDED by (`-2) = 37 = 3x7 = (`-21)!!!~'

`-BIRTH/DAY # `-NUMBER = 129 = 12+9 = (`-21) = `-DEATH/DAY = 7+14 = (`-21)!!!~'

(21+21) = 42 = 20+22 = `-DEATH/YEAR!!!~'

(21+21+21) = (`-63) = `-DEATH/DAY # `-NUMBER!!!~'

`-BIRTH/DAY # `-NUMBER = 129 = RECIPROCAL = 921 = 92+1 = (`-93) = `-BIRTH/YEAR!!!~'

`-PARTIAL `-BIRTH/DAY # `-NUMBER in `-REVERSE = 93(-)19(-)6 = 68 = FLIP 8 to 3 = (`-63) = `-DEATH/DAY # `-NUMBER!!!~'

`-DEATH/DAY # `-NUMBER = 7+14+20+22 = 63

`-DEATH/DAY # `-NUMBER = 63 = FLIP 6 to 9 = (`-93) = `-BIRTH/YEAR!!!~'

129+63 = 192 = 1+92 = (`-93) = `-BIRTH/YEAR!!!~'

129(-)63 = 66 = 6x6 = 36 = RECIPROCAL = 63 = `-DEATH/DAY # `-NUMBER!!!~'

129(-)63 = 66 = 11x6 = (`-11/6) = `-BIRTH/DAY!!!~'

FRAGMENTED `-BIRTH/DAY # `-NUMBER = 1+1+6+1+9+9+3 = 30

FRAGMENTED `-BIRTH/DAY # `-NUMBER = 30 = 5x6 = (`-56) = / DIVIDED by (`-2) = (`-28) = `-AGE of `-DEATH for AMERICAN ACTOR-COMEDIAN-WRITER JAKIM MAULANA "JAK KNIGHT"!!!~'

`-BIRTH/DAY # `-NUMBER = (`-129) (+) (`-30) = FRAGMENTED `-BIRTH/DAY # `-NUMBER = 159 = FLIP 9 to 6 = 156 = 1x56 = (`-56) = / DIVIDED by (`-2) = (`-28) = `-AGE of `-DEATH for AMERICAN ACTOR-COMEDIAN-WRITER JAKIM MAULANA "JAK KNIGHT"!!!~'

FRAGMENTED `-DEATH/DAY # `-NUMBER = 7+1+4+2+0+ 2+2 = 18

30+18 = 48 = 4x8 = 32 = RECIPROCAL = 23 = FLIP 3 to 8 = (`-28) = `-AGE of `-DEATH for AMERICAN ACTOR-COMEDIAN-WRITER JAKIM MAULANA "JAK KNIGHT"!!!~'

30+18 = 48 = 4+8 = (`-12) = `-BIRTH/YEAR = 19+93 = 112 = 1x12 = (`-12)!!!~'

30(-)18 = 12 = `-BIRTH/YEAR = 19+93 = 112 = 1x12 = (`-12)!!!~'

FROM `-BIRTH-to-DEATH there are 115 DAYS = 11/5 = `-WAS `-BORN the `-VERY `-NEXT `-DAY on (`-11/6)!!!~'

FROM `-BIRTH-to-DEATH there are 115 DAYS = 11+5 = 16 = 2x8 = (`-28) = `-AGE of `-DEATH for AMERICAN ACTOR-COMEDIAN-WRITER JAKIM MAULANA "JAK KNIGHT"!!!~'

(365 (-) 115) = 250 = 2(-)50 = 48 = 4x8 = 32 = RECIPROCAL = 23 = FLIP 3 to 8 = (`-28) = `-AGE of `-DEATH for AMERICAN ACTOR-COMEDIAN-WRITER JAKIM MAULANA "JAK KNIGHT"!!!~'

`-WAS `-BORN in the `-MONTH of (`-11); and, `-DIED in the `-MONTH of (`-7) = (`-11/7) = 11+7 = (`-18) = FRAGMENTED `-DEATH/DAY # `-NUMBER!!!~'

`-DEATH/MONTH was JULY with 31 DAYS

(31 (-) 14) – DAY of `-DEATH = 17 = 1x17 = (`-11/7) = `-WAS `-BORN in the `-MONTH of (`-11); and, `-DIED in the `-MONTH of (`-7) = (`-11/7)!!!~'

`-DEATH/DAY = 7/14 = 7x14 = 98 = FLIP 8 to 3 = (`-93) = `-BIRTH/YEAR!!!~'

`-BIRTH/YEAR = 1993 = 1(-)3/9+9 = 2/18 = 2x18 = 36 = RECIPROCAL = 63 = `-DEATH/DAY # `-NUMBER!!!~'

`-BIRTH/YEAR = 1993 = 1(-)3/9+9 = 2/18 = 28x1 = (`-28) = `-AGE of `-DEATH for AMERICAN ACTOR-COMEDIAN-WRITER JAKIM MAULANA "JAK KNIGHT"!!!~'

`-BIRTH/YEAR = 1993 = 19(-)93 = 74 = 7x4 = (`-28) = `-AGE of `-DEATH for AMERICAN ACTOR-COMEDIAN-WRITER JAKIM MAULANA "JAK KNIGHT"!!!~'

AMERICAN ACTOR DWAYNE BERNARD HICKMAN died at the AGE of (`-87)!!!~'

`-BIRTH/DAY = 5/18 = 5/1x8 = (`-58) = HEIGHT = 5' 8"!!!~'

`-BIRTH/DAY = 5/18 = 5+18 = (`-23) = RECIPROCAL = (`-32) = FLIP 3 to 8; FLIP 2 to 7 = (`-87) = `-AGE of `-DEATH for AMERICAN ACTOR DWAYNE BERNARD HICKMAN!!!~'

`-BIRTH/DAY = 5/18 = 5x18 = 90 = 9+0 = (`-9) = `-DEATH/DAY = 1/9 = 1x9 = (`-9)!!!~'

`-BIRTH/DAY # `-NUMBER = 5+18+19+34 = 76

`-BIRTH/DAY # `-NUMBER = 76 = 7x6 = 42 = 20+22 = `-DEATH/YEAR!!!~'

`-PARTIAL `-BIRTH/DAY # `-NUMBER = 5+18+19 = 42 = 20+22 = `-DEATH/YEAR!!!~'

`-BIRTH/DAY = 5/18 = FLIP 8 to 3 = 5/13 = 5/1(-)3 = (`-52) = `-DEATH/DAY # `-NUMBER!!!~'

`-BIRTH/YEAR = 1934 = 19+34 = (`-53) = 5x3 = 15 = 8+7 = (`-87) = `-AGE of `-DEATH for AMERICAN ACTOR DWAYNE BERNARD HICKMAN!!!~'

`-DEATH/DAY # `-NUMBER = 1+9+20+22 = 52

`-PARTIAL `-DEATH/DAY # `-NUMBER = 1+9+20 = 30 = 5x6 = (`-56) = 8x7 = (`-87) = `-AGE of `-DEATH for AMERICAN ACTOR DWAYNE BERNARD HICKMAN!!!~'

76+52 = 128 = RECIPROCAL = 821 = 82x1 = 82 = FLIP 2 to 7 = (`-87) = `-AGE of `-DEATH for AMERICAN ACTOR DWAYNE BERNARD HICKMAN!!!~'

76(-)52 = 24 = RECIPROCAL = 42 = 20+22 = `-DEATH/YEAR!!!~'

FRAGMENTED `-BIRTH/DAY # `-NUMBER = 5+1+8+1+9+3+4 = 31

FRAGMENTED `-BIRTH/DAY # `-NUMBER = 31 = RECIPROCAL = 13 = 5(-)18 = `-BIRTH/DAY!!!~'

FRAGMENTED `-DEATH/DAY # `-NUMBER = 1+9+2+0+ 2+2 = 16

`-DEATH/DAY # `-NUMBER = (`-52) (+) (`-16) = FRAGMENTED `-DEATH/DAY # `-NUMBER = (`-68) = RECIPROCAL = (`-86) = `-DIED the `-VERY `-YEAR `-AFTERWARD at the `-AGE of (`-87)!!!~'

FRAGMENTED `-DEATH/DAY # `-NUMBER = 16 = FLIP 6 to 9 = (`-1/9) = `-DEATH/DAY!!!~'

FRAGMENTED `-DEATH/DAY # `-NUMBER = 16 = X TIMES (`-2) = (`-32) = FLIP 3 to 8; FLIP 2 to 7 = (`-87) = `-AGE of `-DEATH for AMERICAN ACTOR DWAYNE BERNARD HICKMAN!!!~'

31+16 = 3x1/1+6 = 3/7 = FLIP 3 to 8 = (`-87) = `-AGE of `-DEATH for AMERICAN ACTOR DWAYNE BERNARD HICKMAN!!!~'

31(-)16 = 15 = 8+7 = (`-87) = `-AGE of `-DEATH for AMERICAN ACTOR DWAYNE BERNARD HICKMAN!!!~'

31(-)16 = 15 = RECIPROCAL = 51 = `-WAS `-BORN in the `-MONTH of (`-5); and, `-DIED in the `-MONTH of (`-1) = (`-51)!!!~'

31(-)16 = 15 = `-BIRTH/YEAR = 19(-)34 = (`-15)!!!~'

FROM `-BIRTH-to-DEATH there are 129 DAYS = 12+9 = 21 = 3x7 = (`-37) = FLIP 3 to 8 = (`-87) = `-AGE of `-DEATH for AMERICAN ACTOR DWAYNE BERNARD HICKMAN!!!~'

(365 (-) 129) = 236 = 23+6 = 29 = X TIMES (`-2) = (`-58) = HEIGHT = 5' 8" = & = `-BIRTH/DAY = 5/18!!!~'

`-YEARS `-ACTIVE from 1942 to 2005 for (`-63) `-YEARS = RECIPROCAL = (`-36) = FLIP 6 to 9 = (`-39) = "SEE `-BELOW for `-YEARS `-MARRIED to JOAN ROBERTS"!!!~'

1942 = 19(-)42 = 23 = RECIPROCAL = (`-32) = FLIP 3 to 8; FLIP 2 to 7 = (`-87) = `-AGE of `-DEATH for AMERICAN ACTOR DWAYNE BERNARD HICKMAN!!!~'

`-WAS `-MARRIED to JOAN ROBERTS from 1983 to 2022 for (`-39) YEARS!!!~'

`-IF `-THEY were `-MARRIED for (`-38) `-YEARS; THEN, = RECIPROCAL = (`-83) = `-YEAR THEY were `-MARRIED!!!~'

`-WIFE'S `-BIRTH/DAY # `-NUMBER = 2+19+19+52 = 92 = RECIPROCAL = 29 = FLIP 2 to 7; FLIP 9 to 6 = (`-76) = `-BIRTH/DAY # `-NUMBER of `-HUSBAND AMERICAN ACTOR DWAYNE BERNARD HICKMAN!!!~'

`-MARRIED in (`-83) = FLIP 3 to 8 = (`-88) = `-HUSBAND AMERICAN ACTOR DWAYNE BERNARD HICKMAN died within `-HIS (`-88th) YEAR of `-EXISTENCE!!!~'

`-MARRIED in 1983 = 19(-)83 = 64 = 8x8 = (`-88) = `-HUSBAND AMERICAN ACTOR DWAYNE BERNARD HICKMAN died within `-HIS (`-88th) YEAR of `-EXISTENCE!!!~'

`-WIFE was `-BORN in (`-52) = `-DEATH/DAY # `-NUMBER = (`-52) = of `-HUSBAND AMERICAN ACTOR DWAYNE BERNARD HICKMAN!!!~'

`-WIFE'S `-BIRTH/YEAR = 19/52 = 19(-)52 = (`-33) = FLIP 3 to 8 = (`-88) = `-HUSBAND AMERICAN ACTOR DWAYNE

BERNARD HICKMAN died within `-HIS (`-88th) YEAR of `-EXISTENCE!!!~'

`-WIFE'S `-BIRTH/YEAR = 19/52 = 19(-)52 = (`-33) = FLIP 3 to 8 = (`-83) = `-YEAR of `-MARRIAGE to `-HUSBAND AMERICAN ACTOR DWAYNE BERNARD HICKMAN!!!~'

`-WIFE was `-BORN in (`-52) = `-TOTAL `-YEARS of `-ALL `-YEARS `-MARRIED = (`-52) = `-DEATH/DAY # `-NUMBER = for `-HUSBAND AMERICAN ACTOR DWAYNE BERNARD HICKMAN!!!~'

39+4+9 = (`-52)!!!~'

`-WAS `-MARRIED to JOANNE PAPILE from 1977 to 1981 for (`-4) `-YEARS!!!~'

`-MARRIED in = 1977 = 19(-)77 = 58 = FLIP 8 to 3 = (`-53) = `-BIRTH/YEAR = 19+34 = (`-53)!!!~'

`-MARRIED in = 1977 = 19+77 = 96 = RECIPROCAL = (`-69) = `-AGE of AMERICAN ACTOR DWAYNE BERNARD HICKMAN'S `-WIFE (JOAN ROBERTS) at the `-TIME of `-HER `-HUSBAND'S `-DEATH!!!~'

`-DIVORCED in = 1981 = 19(-)81 = 62 = / DIVIDED by (`-2) = (`-31) = FRAGMENTED `-BIRTH/DAY # `-NUMBER for `-FORMER `-HUSBAND AMERICAN ACTOR DWAYNE BERNARD HICKMAN!!!~'

`-WAS `-MARRIED to AMERICAN ACTRESS/FORMER MODEL CAROL CHRISTENSEN from 1963 to 1972 for (`-9) `-YEARS!!!~'

`-MARRIED in = 1963 = 19+63 = 82 = FLIP 2 to 7 = (`-87) = `-AGE of `-DEATH for `-FORMER `-HUSBAND AMERICAN ACTOR DWAYNE BERNARD HICKMAN!!!~'

`-DIVORCED in = 1972 = 19+72 = 91 = RECIPROCAL = 1/9 = `-DEATH/DAY for `-FORMER `-HUSBAND AMERICAN ACTOR DWAYNE BERNARD HICKMAN!!!~'

`-DIVORCED in = 1972 = 19(-)72 = (`-53) = `-BIRTH/YEAR (19+34) = (`-53) = for `-FORMER `-HUSBAND AMERICAN ACTOR DWAYNE BERNARD HICKMAN!!!~'

`-FORMER `-WIFE AMERICAN ACTRESS/FORMER MODEL CAROL CHRISTENSEN `-BIRTH/DAY = 9/14 = 9+14 = (`-23) = RECIPROCAL = (`-32) = FLIP 3 to 8; FLIP 2 to 7 = (`-87) = `-AGE of `-DEATH for `-FORMER `-HUSBAND AMERICAN ACTOR DWAYNE BERNARD HICKMAN!!!~'

`-FORMER `-WIFE AMERICAN ACTRESS/FORMER MODEL CAROL CHRISTENSEN `-BIRTH/YEAR = 19/37 = 19+37 = 56 = 8x7 = (`-87) = `-AGE of `-DEATH for `-FORMER `-HUSBAND AMERICAN ACTOR DWAYNE BERNARD HICKMAN!!!~'

`-FORMER `-WIFE AMERICAN ACTRESS/FORMER MODEL CAROL CHRISTENSEN `-PARTIAL`-BIRTH/DAY # `-NUMBER = 9+14+19 = 42 = 20+22 = `-DEATH/YEAR for `-FORMER `-HUSBAND AMERICAN ACTOR DWAYNE BERNARD HICKMAN!!!~'

`-FORMER `-WIFE AMERICAN ACTRESS/FORMER MODEL CAROL CHRISTENSEN `-BIRTH/DAY # `-NUMBER = 9+14+19+37 = 79 = FLIP 9 to 6 = (`-76) = `-BIRTH/DAY # `-NUMBER for `-FORMER `-HUSBAND AMERICAN ACTOR DWAYNE BERNARD HICKMAN!!!~'

`-FORMER `-WIFE AMERICAN ACTRESS/FORMER MODEL CAROL CHRISTENSEN `-DEATH/DAY # `-NUMBER = 6+4+20+05 = 35 = RECIPROCAL = 53 = `-BIRTH/YEAR = 19+34 = (`-53) = for `-FORMER `-HUSBAND AMERICAN ACTOR DWAYNE BERNARD HICKMAN!!!~'

`-FORMER `-WIFE AMERICAN ACTRESS/FORMER MODEL CAROL CHRISTENSEN was `-BORN in the `-MONTH of (`-9); and, `-DIED in the `-MONTH of (`-6) = (`-96) = RECIPROCAL = (`-69) = `-AGE of AMERICAN ACTOR DWAYNE BERNARD HICKMAN'S `-WIFE (JOAN ROBERTS) at the `-TIME of `-HER `-HUSBAND'S `-DEATH!!!~'

`-BIRTH/YEAR = 19/34 = 1(-)9/3+4 = (`-87) = `-AGE of `-DEATH for AMERICAN ACTOR DWAYNE BERNARD HICKMAN!!!~'

`-DEATH/MONTH was JANUARY with 31 DAYS

(31 (-) 9) – DAY of `-DEATH = 22 = `-DEATH/YEAR!!!~'

AMERICAN LAWYER (FORMER SOLICITOR GENERAL of the UNITED STATES) KENNETH WINSTON STAR died at the AGE of (`-76)!!!~'

`-AGE of `-DEATH = (`-76) = 7x6 = 42 = 20+22 = `-DEATH/YEAR!!!~'

`-BIRTH/YEAR = 46 = 4x6 = 24 = RECIPROCAL = 42 = 20+22 = `-DEATH/YEAR!!!~'

`-PARTIAL `-DEATH/DAY # `-NUMBER = 9+13+20 = 42 = 20+22 = `-DEATH/YEAR!!!~'

`-WAS `-BORN in the `-MONTH of (`-7); and, `-DIED in the `-MONTH of (`-9) = (`-79) = FLIP 9 to 6 = (`-76) = `-AGE of `-DEATH for AMERICAN LAWYER KENNETH WINSTON STAR!!!~'

`-BIRTH/DAY = 7/21 = FLIP 2 to 7 = 7/71 = 7/7(-)1 = (`-76) = `-AGE of `-DEATH for AMERICAN LAWYER KENNETH WINSTON STAR!!!~'

`-BIRTH/DAY = 7/21 = 7+2/1 = 9/1 = `-FIRST `-PART of `-DEATH/DAY!!!~'

`-BIRTH/DAY # `-NUMBER = 7+21+19+46 = 93

`-BIRTH/DAY # `-NUMBER = 93 = `-DEATH/DAY = 9/13 = 93x1 = (`-93)!!!~'

`-BIRTH/DAY # `-NUMBER = 93 = `-DEATH/DAY = 9/13 = 9/1x3 = (`-93)!!!~'

`-DEATH/DAY = 9/13 = 9+13 = 22 = `-BIRTH/DAY = 7/21 = FLIP 7 to 2 = 2/21 = 22x1 = (`-22) = `-DEATH/YEAR!!!~'

`-DEATH/DAY = 9/13 = 9+13 = 22 = `-BIRTH/DAY = 7/21 = FLIP 7 to 2 = 2/21 = 2x21 = (`-42) = 20+22 = `-DEATH/YEAR!!!~'

`-DEATH/DAY # `-NUMBER = 9+13+20+22 = 64

`-DEATH/DAY # `-NUMBER = 64 = RECIPROCAL = 46 = `-BIRTH/YEAR!!!~'

93+64 = 157 = 1+5/7 = 67 = RECIPROCAL = (`-76) = `-AGE of `-DEATH for AMERICAN LAWYER KENNETH WINSTON STAR!!!~'

93(-)64 = 29 = FLIP 2 to 7; FLIP 9 to 6 = (`-76) = `-AGE of `-DEATH for AMERICAN LAWYER KENNETH WINSTON STAR!!!~'

FRAGMENTED `-BIRTH/DAY # `-NUMBER = 7+2+1+1+9+ 4+6 = 30

FRAGMENTED `-BIRTH/DAY # `-NUMBER = 30 = 15x2 = 1+5/2 = 6/2 = FLIP 2 to 7 = (`-67) = RECIPROCAL = (`-76) = `-AGE of `-DEATH for AMERICAN LAWYER KENNETH WINSTON STAR!!!~'

FRAGMENTED `-BIRTH/DAY # `-NUMBER = 30 = 6x5 = (`-65) = `-BIRTH/YEAR = 19+46 = (`-65)!!!~'

FRAGMENTED `-DEATH/DAY # `-NUMBER = 9+1+3+2+0+ 2+2 = 19

FRAGMENTED `-DEATH/DAY # `-NUMBER = 19 = X TIMES (`-4) = (`-76) = `-AGE of `-DEATH for AMERICAN LAWYER KENNETH WINSTON STAR!!!~'

30+19 = 49 = 4x9 = 36 = RECIPROCAL = 63 = `-WAS `-BORN in the `-MONTH of (`-7); and, `-DIED in the `-MONTH of (`-9) = (`-79) = 7x9 = (`-63)!!!~'

30(-)19 = 11 = 6+5 = (`-65) = `-BIRTH/YEAR = 19+46 = (`-65)!!!~'

FROM `-BIRTH-to-DEATH there are 54 DAYS = / DIVIDED by (`-2) = (`-27) = 9x3 = (`-93) = `-BIRTH/DAY # `-NUMBER!!!~'

FROM `-BIRTH-to-DEATH there are 54 DAYS = / DIVIDED by (`-2) = (`-27) = `-BIRTH/YEAR = 19(-)46 = (`-27)!!!~'

(365 (-) 54) = 311 = 3x11 = 33 = FLIP 3 to 8 = (`-88) = 8x8 = (`-64) = `-DEATH/DAY # `-NUMBER!!!~'

(365 (-) 54) = 311 = RECIPROCAL = 113 = 19+94 = `-IN 1994 `-HE `-HEADED the `-INVESTIGATION of MEMBERS of the CLINTON ADMINISTRATION; otherwise known as, The WHITEWATER CONTROVERSY!!!~'

19(-)94 = 75 = `-DIED the `-VERY `-NEXT `-YEAR -AFTERWARD at the `-AGE of (`-76)!!!~'

`-WHITEWATER `-INVESTIGATION `-ENDED in 1998 = 19(-)98 = (`-79) = `-WAS `-BORN in the `-MONTH of (`-7); and, `-DIED in the `-MONTH of (`-9) = (`-79)!!!~'

FROM `-BIRTH-to-DEATH there are 54 DAYS = 5x4 = 20 = FLIP 2 to 7 = (`-70) = `-WAS `-MARRIED in (`-70)!!!~'

`-WAS `-MARRIED to ALICE MENDELL from 1970 to 2022 for (`-52) YEARS!!!~'

(`-52) = FLIP 2 to 7 = (`-57) = RECIPROCAL = (`-75) = `-DIED the `-VERY `-NEXT `-YEAR -AFTERWARD at the `-AGE of (`-76)!!!~'

`-MARRIED in = 19+70 = (`-89) = RECIPROCAL = (`-98) = FLIP 8 to 3 = (`-93) = `-BIRTH/DAY # `-NUMBER for AMERICAN LAWYER KENNETH WINSTON STAR!!!~'

`-MARRIED in = 19+70 = (`-89) = RECIPROCAL = (`-98) = FLIP 8 to 3 = (`-93) = `-DEATH/DAY = 9/13 = for AMERICAN LAWYER KENNETH WINSTON STAR!!!~'

AMERICAN ACTOR ROGER EARL MOSLEY "MAGNUM P.I." died at the AGE of (`-83)!!!~'

`-AGE of `-DEATH = 83 = 8x3 = 24 = RECIPROCAL = 42 = 20+22 = `-DEATH/YEAR!!!~'

`-BIRTH/YEAR = (`-38) = RECIPROCAL = (`-83) = `-AGE of `-DEATH for AMERICAN ACTOR ROGER EARL MOSLEY!!!~'

`-BIRTH/DAY = 12/18 = RECIPROCAL = 81/21 = 8x1/2+1 = (`-83) = `-AGE of `-DEATH for AMERICAN ACTOR ROGER EARL MOSLEY!!!~'

`-BIRTH/DAY # `-NUMBER = 12+18+19+38 = 87

`-BIRTH/DAY # `-NUMBER = 87 = `-DEATH/DAY = (`-8/7)!!!~'

`-BIRTH/DAY # `-NUMBER = 87 = FLIP 7 to 2 = (`-82) = `-DIED the `-VERY `-NEXT `-YEAR `-AFTERWARD at the `-AGE of (`-83)!!!~'

`-BIRTH/YEAR = 1938 = 19+38 = (`-57) = `-DEATH/DAY # `-NUMBER!!!~'

`-DEATH/DAY # `-NUMBER = 8+7+20+22 = 57

`-DEATH/DAY # `-NUMBER = 57 = 5x7 = 35 = `-PARTIAL `-DEATH/DAY # `-NUMBER = 8+7+20 = (`-35)

`-DEATH/DAY # `-NUMBER = 57 = 5+7 = (`-12) = 6x2 = 6' 2" = `-HEIGHT!!!~'

87+57 = 144 = 14x4 = (`-56) = 8x7 = (`-87) = `-BIRTH/DAY # `-NUMBER = (`-87) = & = `-DEATH/DAY = (`-8/7)!!!~'

87(-)57 = 30 = `-BIRTH/DAY = 12+18 = (`-30)

FRAGMENTED `-BIRTH/DAY # `-NUMBER = 1+2+1+8+1+9+ 3+8 = 33

FRAGMENTED `-BIRTH/DAY # `-NUMBER = 33 = FLIP 3 to 8 = (`-83) = `-AGE of `-DEATH for AMERICAN ACTOR ROGER EARL MOSLEY!!!~'

FRAGMENTED `-DEATH/DAY # `-NUMBER = 8+7+2+0+ 2+2 = 21

FRAGMENTED `-DEATH/DAY # `-NUMBER = 21 = X TIMES (`-4) = (`-84) = `-DIED the `-VERY `-YEAR `-PRIOR at the AGE of (`-83)!!!~'

`-BIRTH/YEAR = 1938 = 1+9+3/8 = 13/8 = 13+8 = (`-21) = FRAGMENTED `-DEATH/DAY # `-NUMBER!!!~'

33+21 = 54 = 6x9 = (`-69) = "MAGNUM P.I. finished in 1988 = 19(-)88 = (`-69)!!!~'

33+21 = 54 = 6x9 = (`-69) = FLIP 6 to 9 – (`-99) = "MAGNUM P.I." began in 1980 = 19+80 = (`-99)!!!~'

33+21 = 54 = 6x9 = (`-69) = `-BIRTH/DAY = 12/18 = HALF RECIPROCAL = 12/81 = 12(-)81 = (`-69)!!!~'

33+21 = 54 = 6x9 = (`-69) = 69 = X TIMES (`-2) = 138 = 1x38 = 38 = BIRTH/YEAR = & = RECIPROCAL = (`-83) = `-AGE of `-DEATH for AMERICAN ACTOR ROGER EARL MOSLEY!!!~'

33(-)21 = 12 = RECIPROCAL = 21 = FRAGMENTED `-DEATH/ DAY # `-NUMBER!!!~'

FROM `-BIRTH-to-DEATH there are 133 DAYS = 1x33 = (`-33) = FRAGMENTED `-BIRTH/DAY # `-NUMBER!!!~'

FROM `-BIRTH-to-DEATH there are 133 DAYS = 1x33 = (`-33) = FLIP 3 to 8 = (`-83) = `-AGE of `-DEATH for AMERICAN ACTOR ROGER EARL MOSLEY!!!~'

(365 (-) 133) = 232 = Reciprocal-Sequencing-Numerology-RSN!!!~'

(365 (-) 133) = 232 = 2+3/2 = 52 = FLIP 2 to 7 = (`-57) = `-DEATH/DAY # `-NUMBER!!!~'

(365 (-) 133) = 232 = 2(-)32 = (`-30) = `-BIRTH/DAY = 12+18 = (`-30)

`-DEATH/MONTH was AUGUST with 31 DAYS

(31 (-) 7) – DAY of `-DEATH = 24 = RECIPROCAL = 42 = 20+22 = `-DEATH/YEAR!!!~'

`-WAS `-BORN in the `-MONTH of (`-12); and, `-DIED in the `-MONTH of (`-8) = (`-12/8) = RECIPROCAL = (`-8/21) = 8/2+1 = (`-83) = `-AGE of `-DEATH for AMERICAN ACTOR ROGER EARL MOSLEY!!!~'

`-BIRTH/YEAR = 1938 = 1+9+3/8 = 13/8 = 1x3/8 = (`-38) = RECIPROCAL = (`-83) = `-AGE of `-DEATH for AMERICAN ACTOR ROGER EARL MOSLEY "MAGNUM P.I." !!!~'

HEIGHT = 6' 2" = 6x2 = (`-12) = `-BIRTH/MONTH!!!~'

HEIGHT = 6' 2" = (`-62) = / DIVIDED by (`-2) = 31 = RECIPROCAL = 13 = FLIP 3 to 8 = (`-18) = `-DAY of `-BIRTH = (`-18th)!!!~'

FRENCH-SWISS FILM DIRECTOR JEAN-LUC GODARD died at the AGE of (`-91)!!!~'

`-WAS `-BORN in the `-MONTH of (`-12); and, `-DIED in the `-MONTH of (`-9) = (`-12/9) = RECIPROCAL = (`-9/12) = `-DIED the `-VERY `-NEXT `-DAY on (`-9/13)!!!~'

`-DEATH/DAY = 9/13 = 9/1(-)3 = (`-92) = `-DIED the `-VERY `-YEAR `-PRIOR at the AGE of (`-91)!!!~'

`-BIRTH/YEAR = 1930 = 1x9/3+0 = (`-93) = `-DEATH/DAY = 9/13 = 9/1x3 = (`-93)!!!~'

`-BIRTH/DAY # `-NUMBER = 12+3+19+30 = 64

`-BIRTH/DAY # `-NUMBER = (`-64) = `-DEATH/DAY # `-NUMBER = (`-64)!!!~'

`-DEATH/DAY # `-NUMBER = 9+13+20+22 = 64

64+64 = 128 = RECIPROCAL = 821 = 8+1/2 = (`-92) = `-DIED the `-VERY `-YEAR `-PRIOR at the AGE of (`-91)!!!~'

FRAGMENTED `-BIRTH/DAY # `-NUMBER = 1+2+3+1+9+3+0 = 19

FRAGMENTED `-BIRTH/DAY # `-NUMBER = 19 = RECIPROCAL = (`-91) = `-AGE of `-DEATH for FRENCH-SWISS FILM DIRECTOR JEAN-LUC GODARD!!!~'

`-BIRTH/DAY # `-NUMBER = (`-64) (-) (`-19) = FRAGMENTED `-BIRTH/DAY # `-NUMBER = (`-45) = X TIMES (`-2) = (`-90) = `-DIED the `-VERY `-YEAR `-AFTERWARD at the `-AGE of (`-91)!!!~'

`-SEE this `-PATTERN of `-SUBTRACTION = (45/54) (36/63) = in `-ALL of the `-CADENCES!!!~' For `-YOU to `-ENJOY!!!~'

FRAGMENTED `-DEATH/DAY # `-NUMBER = 9+1+3+2+0+2+2 = 19

FRAGMENTED `-DEATH/DAY # `-NUMBER = 19 = RECIPROCAL = (`-91) = `-AGE of `-DEATH for FRENCH-SWISS FILM DIRECTOR JEAN-LUC GODARD!!!~'

`-DEATH/DAY # `-NUMBER = (`-64) (-) (`-19) = FRAGMENTED `-DEATH/DAY # `-NUMBER = (`-45) = X TIMES (`-2) = (`-90) = `-DIED the `-VERY `-YEAR `-AFTERWARD at the `-AGE of (`-91)!!!~'

`-SEE this `-PATTERN of `-SUBTRACTION = (45/54) (36/63) = in `-ALL of the `-CADENCES!!!~' For `-YOU to `-ENJOY!!!~'

19+19 = (`-38) = 3x8 = 24 = RECIPROCAL = 42 = 20+22 = `-DEATH/YEAR!!!~'

FROM `-BIRTH-to-DEATH there are 81 DAYS = `-RECIPROCAL = 18 = `-MARRIED for a `-TOTAL of (`-18) `-YEARS = `-MARRIED to ANNE WIAZEMSKY (FRENCH ACTRESS/NOVELIST) from 1967 to 1979 for (`-12) YEARS = (+) = `-MARRIED to ANNA KARINA (DANISH-FRENCH FILM ACTRESS) from 1961 to 1967 for (`-6) `-YEARS!!!~'

`-YEARS `-MARRIED = (`-12/6) = FLIP 6 to 9 = (`-12/9) = `-WAS `-BORN in the `-MONTH of (`-12); and, `-DIED in the `-MONTH of (`-9) = (`-12/9)!!!~'

`-WAS `-BORN in the `-MONTH of (`-12); and, `-DIED in the `-MONTH of (`-9) = (`-12/9) = 12x9 = (`-108) = 10+8 = 18 = RECIPROCAL = (`-81) = `-DAYS FROM `-BIRTH-to-DEATH!!!~'

`-DEATH/DAY = 9/13 = 9x13 = 117 = 1+17 = (`-18) = RECIPROCAL = (`-81) = `-DAYS FROM `-BIRTH-to-DEATH!!!~'

(365 (-) 81) = 284 = 28(-)4 = 24 = RECIPROCAL = 42 = 20+22 = `-DEATH/YEAR!!!~'

`-BIRTH/YEAR = 1930 = 9/1(-)3(-)0 = (`-92) = `-DIED the `-VERY `-YEAR `-PRIOR at the AGE of (`-91)!!!~'

`-PARTIAL `-DEATH/DAY # `-NUMBER = 9+13+20 = 42 = 20+22 = `-DEATH/YEAR!!!~'

`-FORMER `-WIFE ANNE WIAZEMSKY (FRENCH ACTRESS/NOVELIST) `-BIRTH/DAY = 5/14 = 5+14 = (`-19) = FRAGMENTED `-BIRTH/DAY # `-NUMBER (`-19) & FRAGMENTED `-DEATH/DAY # `-NUMBER (`-19) = of `-FORMER `-HUSBAND FRENCH-SWISS FILM DIRECTOR JEAN-LUC GODARD = RECIPROCAL = (`-91) = `-HIS `-VERY `-OWN `-AGE of `-DEATH = (`-91)!!!~'

`-WAS `-MARRIED to ANNE WIAZEMSKY (FRENCH ACTRESS/NOVELIST) from 1967 to 1979 for (`-12) YEARS!!!~'

`-MARRIED in = (`-67) = 6x7 = 42 = 20+22 = `-DEATH/YEAR for FRENCH-SWISS FILM DIRECTOR JEAN-LUC GODARD!!!~'

`-DIVORCED in = (`-79) = 7x9 = 63 = RECIPROCAL = 36 = 12x3 = (`-12/3) = `-BIRTH/DAY of FRENCH-SWISS FILM DIRECTOR JEAN-LUC GODARD!!!~'

`-DIVORCE in = (`-79) = `-FORMER `-PREVIOUS `-WIFE ANNA KARINA (DANISH-FRENCH FILM ACTRESS) died at the `-AGE of (`-79)!!!~'

`-WAS `-MARRIED to `-FORMER `-WIFE ANNA KARINA (DANISH-FRENCH FILM ACTRESS) from 1961 to 1967 for (`-6) `-YEARS!!!~'

`-FORMER `-WIFE ANNA KARINA (DANISH-FRENCH FILM ACTRESS) `-WAS `-BORN in the `-MONTH of (`-9); and, `-DIED in the `-MONTH of (`-12) = (`-9/12) = RECIPROCAL to = FORMER `-HUSBAND FRENCH-SWISS FILM DIRECTOR JEAN-LUC GODARD!!!~'

`-FORMER `-HUSBAND FRENCH-SWISS FILM DIRECTOR JEAN-LUC GODARD `-WAS `-BORN in the `-MONTH of (`-12); and, `-DIED in the `-MONTH of (`-9) = (`-12/9) = RECIPROCAL = 9/12 = `-DIED the `-VERY `-NEXT `-DAY on (`-9/13)!!!~'

`-FORMER `-WIFE ANNA KARINA (DANISH-FRENCH FILM ACTRESS) `-BIRTH/DAY # `-NUMBER = 9+22+19+40 = 90 = `-FORMER `-HUSBAND FRENCH-SWISS FILM DIRECTOR JEAN-LUC GODARD died the `-VERY `-NEXT `-YEAR `-AFTERWARD at the `-AGE of (`-91)!!!~'

`-FORMER `-WIFE ANNA KARINA (DANISH-FRENCH FILM ACTRESS) `-PARTIAL `-DEATH/DAY # `-NUMBER = 12+14+20 = 46 = RECIPROCAL = (`-64) = `-BIRTH/DAY # `-NUMBER (`-64) & `-DEATH/DAY # `-NUMBER (`-64) = of `-FORMER `-HUSBAND FRENCH-SWISS FILM DIRECTOR JEAN-LUC GODARD!!!~'

`-FORMER `-WIFE ANNA KARINA (DANISH-FRENCH FILM ACTRESS) `-DEATH/YEAR = 2019 = 20+19 = (`-39) =

RECIPROCAL = (`-93) = `-FORMER `-HUSBAND FRENCH-SWISS FILM DIRECTOR JEAN-LUC GODARD `-DEATH/DAY = (`-9/13)!!!~'

`-FORMER `-WIFE ANNA KARINA (DANISH-FRENCH FILM ACTRESS) `-DEATH/YEAR = (`-19) = FRAGMENTED `-BIRTH/DAY # `-NUMBER (`-19) & FRAGMENTED `-DEATH/DAY # `-NUMBER (`-19) = of `-FORMER `-HUSBAND FRENCH-SWISS FILM DIRECTOR JEAN-LUC GODARD = RECIPROCAL = (`-91) = `-HIS `-VERY `-OWN `-AGE of `-DEATH = (`-91)!!!~'

JAPANESE ACTRESS YOKO SHIMADA "SHOGUN" died at the AGE of (`-69)!!!~'

`-WAS `-BORN in the `-MONTH of (`-5); and, `-DIED in the `-MONTH of (`-7) = (`-5/7) = HEIGHT = 5' 7"!!!~'

`-DAY of `-DEATH = (25ᵗʰ) = RECIPROCAL = 52 = FLIP 2 to 7 = (`-57) = HEIGHT = 5' 7"!!!~'

`-BIRTH/DAY = 5/17 = 5/1x7 = (`-57) = HEIGHT = 5' 7"!!!~'

`-BIRTH/DAY # `-NUMBER = 5+17+19+53 = 94

`-BIRTH/DAY # `-NUMBER = 94 = / DIVIDED by (`-2) = (`-47) = RECIPROCAL = (`-74) = `-DEATH/DAY # `-NUMBER!!!~'

`-DEATH/DAY # `-NUMBER = 7+25+20+22 = 74

94+74 = 168 = 1+68 = (`-69) = `-AGE of `-DEATH for JAPANESE ACTRESS YOKO SHIMADA "SHOGUN"!!!~'

94(-)74 = 20 = FRAGMENTED `-DEATH/DAY # `-NUMBER!!!~'

94(-)74 = 20 = 5x4 = (`-54) = RECIPROCAL = (`-45)

54+45 = (`-99) = FLIP 9 to 6 = (`-69) = `-AGE of `-DEATH for JAPANESE ACTRESS YOKO SHIMADA "SHOGUN"!!!~'

94(-)74 = 20 = 5x4 = (`-54) = 6x9 = (`-69) = `-AGE of `-DEATH for JAPANESE ACTRESS YOKO SHIMADA "SHOGUN"!!!~'

FRAGMENTED `-BIRTH/DAY # `-NUMBER = 5+1+7+1+9+ 5+3 = 31

FRAGMENTED `-DEATH/DAY # `-NUMBER = 7+2+5+2+0+ 2+2 = 20

31+20 = 51 = `-FIRST `-PART of `-BIRTH/DAY!!!~'

31(-)20) = 11 = 7+4 = (`-74) = `-DEATH/DAY # `-NUMBER!!!~'

FROM `-BIRTH-to-DEATH there are 69 DAYS = (`-69) = `-AGE of `-DEATH for JAPANESE ACTRESS YOKO SHIMADA "SHOGUN"!!!~'

(365 (-) 69) = 296 = 29x6 = 174 = 1x74 = (`-74) = `-DEATH/DAY # `-NUMBER!!!~'

(365 (-) 69) = 296 = 2x96 = 192 = FLIP 2 to 7 = 197 = 1(-)7/9 = (`-69) = `-AGE of `-DEATH for JAPANESE ACTRESS YOKO SHIMADA "SHOGUN"!!!~'

(365 (-) 69) = 296 = 2x96 = 192 = FLIP 2 to 7 = 197 = 1(-)97 = (`-96) = RECIPROCAL = (`-69) = `-AGE of `-DEATH for JAPANESE ACTRESS YOKO SHIMADA "SHOGUN"!!!~'

'-BIRTH/YEAR = 1953 = 9/1+5+3 = ('-99) = FLIP 9 to 6 = ('-69) = '-AGE of '-DEATH for JAPANESE ACTRESS YOKO SHIMADA "SHOGUN"!!!~'

'-DEATH/DAY = 7/25 = 7+25 = 32 = X TIMES ('-3) = ('-96) = RECIPROCAL = ('-69) = '-AGE of '-DEATH for JAPANESE ACTRESS YOKO SHIMADA "SHOGUN"!!!~'

'-WAS the '-PORTRAYAL of "MARIKO" in the 1980 MINISERIES "SHOGUN" = 19+80 = ('-99) = FLIP 9 to 6 = ('-69) = '-AGE of '-DEATH for JAPANESE ACTRESS YOKO SHIMADA "SHOGUN"!!!~'

ENGLISH ACTOR DAVID HATTERSLEY WARNER died at the AGE of ('-80)!!!~

'-BIRTH/DAY # '-NUMBER = 7+29+19+41 = 96

'-DEATH/DAY # '-NUMBER = 7+24+20+22 = 73

96+73 = 169 = 1x69 = ('-69) = RECIPROCAL = ('-96) = '-BIRTH/DAY # '-NUMBER!!!~'

96(-)73 = 23 = FLIP 2 to 7 = ('-73) = '-DEATH/DAY # '-NUMBER!!!~'

FRAGMENTED '-BIRTH/DAY # '-NUMBER = 7+2+9+1+9+4+1 = 33

FRAGMENTED '-BIRTH/DAY # '-NUMBER = 33 = FLIP 3 to 8 = ('-88) = '-WAS '-MARRIED to HARRIET LINDGREN in 1969 = 19+69 = ('-88)!!!~'

FRAGMENTED `-DEATH/DAY # `-NUMBER = 7+2+4+2+0+ 2+2 = 19

33+19 = 52 = 5x2 = (`-10) = 7+3 = (`-73) = `-DEATH/DAY # `-NUMBER!!!~'

33(-)19 = 14 = 7+7 = `-WAS `-BORN in the `-MONTH of (`-7); and, `-DIED in the `-MONTH of (`-7)!!!~'

`-DEATH/DAY = 7/24 = HALF RECIPROCAL = 7/42 = 7+42 = (`-49) = 7x7 = `-WAS `-BORN in the `-MONTH of (`-7); and, `-DIED in the `-MONTH of (`-7)!!!~'

`-DAY of `-DEATH = (24th) = RECIPROCAL = (`-42) = 20+22 = `-DEATH/DAY!!!~'

FROM `-BIRTH-to-DEATH there are 5 DAYS = "The `-HAND of `-GOD"!!!~'

(365 (-) 5) = 360 = 3x60 = 180 = 1x80 = (`-80) = `-AGE of `-DEATH for ENGLISH ACTOR DAVID HATTERSLEY WARNER!!!~'

`-YEARS `-ACTIVE from 1962 to 2022 for 60 `-YEARS = `-BIRTH/ YEAR = 19+41 = (`-60)!!!~'

`-YEAR `-BEGAN = (`-62) = HEIGHT = 6' 2"!!!~

1962 = 19+62 = (`-81) = `-WAS `-MARRIED to SHEILAH KENT in (`-81)!!!~'

1981 = EMMY AWARD for MOST OUTSTANDING SUPPORTING ACTOR!!!~'

ENGLISH ACTOR DAVID HATTERSLEY WARNER `-died within `-HIS (`-81st) `-YEAR of `-EXISTENCE!!!~'

'-AGE of '-DEATH = ('-80) = 8x10 = 8+10 = ('-18) = RECIPROCAL = ('-81)!!!~'

'-BIRTH/DAY = 7/29 = 7+29 = 36 = 3x6 = ('-18) = RECIPROCAL = ('-81) = "SEE '-ABOVE"!!!~'

'-WAS '-MARRIED to HARRIET LINDGREN in ('-69) = RECIPROCAL = ('-96) = '-BIRTH/DAY # '-NUMBER!!!~'

'-DIVORCED HARRIET LINDGREN in 1972 = 19+72 = ('-91) = RECIPROCAL = ('-19) = FRAGMENTED '-DEATH/DAY # '-NUMBER for ENGLISH ACTOR DAVID HATTERSLEY WARNER!!!~'

AMERICAN ACTOR WILLIAM GARSON PASZAMANT died at the AGE of ('-57)!!!~'

'-BIRTH/DAY # '-NUMBER = 2+20+19+64 = 105

'-BIRTH/DAY # '-NUMBER = 105 = / DIVIDED by ('-2) = 52.5 = FLIP 2 to 7 = ('-57.5) = '-AGE of '-DEATH for AMERICAN ACTOR WILLIAM GARSON PASZAMANT!!!~'

'-DEATH/DAY # '-NUMBER = 9+21+20+21 = 71

'-DEATH/DAY # '-NUMBER = 71 = FLIP 7 to 2 = ('-21) = '-DEATH/YEAR!!!~'

'-DEATH/DAY # '-NUMBER = 71 = / DIVIDED by ('-2) = 35.5 = 5.05x7.03 = ('-57) = '-AGE of '-DEATH for AMERICAN ACTOR WILLIAM GARSON PASZAMANT!!!~'

105+71 = 176 = 1(-)76 = 75 = RECIPROCAL = (`-57) = `-AGE of `-DEATH for AMERICAN ACTOR WILLIAM GARSON PASZAMANT!!!~'

FRAGMENTED `-BIRTH/DAY # `-NUMBER = 2+2+0+1+9+6+4 = 24

FRAGMENTED `-DEATH/DAY # `-NUMBER = 9+2+1+2+0+2+1 = 17

FRAGMENTED `-DEATH/DAY # `-NUMBER = 17 = RECIPROCAL = 71 = `-DEATH/DAY # `-NUMBER!!!~'

`-BIRTH/MONTH was FEBRUARY with 28 DAYS

(28 (-) 20) – DAY of `-BIRTH = (`-8)

`-DEATH/MONTH was SEPTEMBER with 30 DAYS

(30 (-) 21) – DAY of `-DEATH = (`-9)

(8+9) = (`-17) = FRAGMENTED `-DEATH/DAY # `-NUMBER!!!~'

24+17 = 41 = 20+21 = `-DEATH/YEAR!!!~'

FROM `-BIRTH-to-DEATH there are 213 DAYS = 21+3 = (`-24) = FRAGMENTED `-BIRTH/DAY # `-NUMBER!!!~'

(365 (-) 213) = 152 = 1x52 = 52 = FLIP 2 to 7 = (`-57) = `-AGE of `-DEATH for AMERICAN ACTOR WILLIAM GARSON PASZAMANT!!!~'

`-PARTIAL `-BIRTH/DAY # `-NUMBER = 2+20+19 = 41 = 20+21 = `-DEATH/YEAR!!!~'

`-PARTIAL `-DEATH/DAY # `-NUMBER with HALF RECIPROCAL = 9+12+20 = 41 = 20+21 = `-DEATH/YEAR!!!~'

`-BIRTH/YEAR = 1964 = 9(-)4/1+6 = (`-57) = `-AGE of `-DEATH for AMERICAN ACTOR WILLIAM GARSON PASZAMANT!!!~'

`-WAS `-BORN in the `-MONTH of (`-2); and, `-DIED in the `-MONTH of (`-9) = (`-29) = X TIMES (`-2) = (`-58) = HEIGHT = 5' 8"!!!~'

`-BIRTH/DAY = 2+20 (+) `-DEATH/DAY = 9+21 /|\ 2+20+9+21 = (`-52) = FLIP 2 to 7 = (`-57) = `-AGE of `-DEATH for AMERICAN ACTOR WILLIAM GARSON PASZAMANT!!!~'

AMERICAN ACTOR ROBERT ALAN MORSE died at the AGE of (`-90)!!!~'

`-BIRTH/DAY = 5/18 = 5/1x8 = (`-58) = `-DAUGHTER/ACTRESS ROBIN MORSE was (`-58) `-YEARS of `-AGE at the `-TIME of `-HER `-FATHER'S (AMERICAN ACTOR ROBERT ALAN MORSE) `-DEATH!!!~'

`-BIRTH/DAY = 5/18 = HALF RECIPROCAL = 5/81 = 5(-)81 = 76 = 7x6 = 42 = 20+22 = `-DEATH/YEAR!!!~'

`-BIRTH/DAY # `-NUMBER = 5+18+19+31 = 73

`-BIRTH/DAY # `-NUMBER = 73 = RECIPROCAL = 37 = `-FORMER `-WIFE CAROLE D' ANDREA was `-BORN in the `-YEAR of (`-37)!!!~'

`-DEATH/DAY # `-NUMBER = 4+20+20+22 = 66

`-DEATH/DAY # `-NUMBER = 66 = 6+6 = (`-12) = FRAGMENTED `-DEATH/DAY # `-NUMBER!!~'

`-DEATH/DAY # `-NUMBER = 66 = 6x6 = (`-36) = RECIPROCAL = (`-63) = `-DAUGHTER/ACTRESS ROBIN MORSE was `-BORN in (`-63)!!!~'

73+66 = 139 = RECIPROCAL = 931 = 93x1 = 93 = FLIP 9 to 6 = (`-63) = "SEE `-ABOVE & `-BELOW"!!!~'

73(-)66 = (`-7) = `-BIRTH/MONTH of `-DAUGHTER/ACTRESS ROBIN MORSE (`-7)!!!~'

FRAGMENTED `-BIRTH/DAY # `-NUMBER = 5+1+8+1+9+3+1 = 28

`-BIRTH/DAY # `-NUMBER = (`-73) (-) (`-28) = FRAGMENTED `-BIRTH/DAY # `-NUMBER = (`-45) = X TIMES (`-2) = (`-90) = `-AGE of `-DEATH for AMERICAN ACTOR ROBERT ALAN MORSE!!!~'

FRAGMENTED `-BIRTH/DAY # `-NUMBER = 28 = `-DAYS from `-BIRTH-to-DEATH!!!~'

FRAGMENTED `-BIRTH/DAY # `-NUMBER = 28 = `-DAUGHTER/ACTRESS ROBIN MORSE `-BIRTH/YEAR = 19+63 = 82 = RECIPROCAL = (`-28)!!!~'

FRAGMENTED `-DEATH/DAY # `-NUMBER = 4+2+0+2+0+2+2 = 12

`-DEATH/DAY # `-NUMBER = (`-66) (-) (`-12) = FRAGMENTED `-DEATH/DAY # `-NUMBER = (`-54) = RECIPROCAL = (`-45) = X TIMES (`-2) = (`-90) = `-AGE of `-DEATH for AMERICAN ACTOR ROBERT ALAN MORSE!!!~'

FRAGMENTED `-DEATH/DAY # `-NUMBER = 12 = `-BIRTH/YEAR = 19(-)31 = (`-12)!!!~'

28+12 = 40 = 5x8 = (`-58) = `-DAUGHTER/ACTRESS ROBIN MORSE was (`-58) `-YEARS of `-AGE at the `-TIME of `-HER `-FATHER'S (AMERICAN ACTOR ROBERT ALAN MORSE) `-DEATH!!!~'

28(-)12 = 16 = 2x8 = (`-28) = FRAGMENTED `-BIRTH/DAY # `-NUMBER (`-28) = & = `-DAYS from `-BIRTH-to-DEATH = (`-28)!!!~'

FROM `-BIRTH-to-DEATH there are 28 DAYS = FRAGMENTED `-BIRTH/DAY # `-NUMBER!!!~'

(365 (-) 28) = 337 = 33x7 = 231 = 23x1 = 23 = FLIP 3 to 8 = (`-28) = `-DAYS from `-BIRTH-to-DEATH!!!~'

(365 (-) 28) = 337 = 33x7 = 231 = 23x1 = (`-23) = `-BIRTH/DAY = 5+18 = (`-23)

`-PARTIAL `-BIRTH/DAY # `-NUMBER = 5+18+19 = 42 = 20+22 = `-DEATH/YEAR!!!~'

`-DEATH/DAY = 4/20 = 4+20 = (`-24) = RECIPROCAL = (`-42) = 20+22 = `-DEATH/YEAR!!!~'

`-WAS `-BORN in the `-MONTH of (`-5); and, `-DIED in the `-MONTH of (`-4) = (`-54) = 5+4 = (`-9) = "JUST `-ADD a `-ZERO" = (`-90) = `-AGE of `-DEATH for AMERICAN ACTOR ROBERT ALAN MORSE!!!~'

`-WAS `-BORN in the `-MONTH of (`-5); and, `-DIED in the `-MONTH of (`-4) = (`-54) = RECIPROCAL = (`-45) = X TIMES

(`-2) = (`-90) = `-AGE of `-DEATH for AMERICAN ACTOR ROBERT ALAN MORSE!!!~'

`-WAS `-MARRIED to ELIZABETH ROBERTS from 1989 to 2022 for (`-33) YEARS!!!~'

`-MARRIED in = 1989 = 19+89 = 108 = 1+8/0 = (`-90) = `-AGE of `-DEATH for AMERICAN ACTOR ROBERT ALAN MORSE!!!~'

`-MARRIED in = 1989 = 19+89 = 108 = 10+8 = (`-18) = `-DAY of `-BIRTH = (`-18th)!!!~'

`-WAS `-MARRIED to CAROLE D' ANDREA from 1961 to 1981 for (`-20) YEARS!!!~'

`-MARRIED in = 1961 = 19(-)61 = 42 = 20+22 = `-DEATH/ YEAR!!!~'

`-DIVORCED in = (`-81) = RECIPROCAL = (`-18) = `-DAY of `-BIRTH = (`-18th)!!!~'

`-FORMER `-WIFE CAROLE D' ANDREA `-PARTIAL `-BIRTH/DAY # `-NUMBER = 8+28+19 = (`-55) = HEIGHT = 5' 5" for `-FORMER `-HUSBAND AMERICAN ACTOR ROBERT ALAN MORSE!!!~'

`-FORMER `-WIFE CAROLE D' ANDREA `-BIRTH/DAY # `-NUMBER = 8+28+19+37 = 92 = RECIPROCAL = 29 = X TIMES (`-2) = (`-58) = `-AGE of `-DAUGHTER/ACTRESS ROBIN MORSE at the TIME of `-HER `-FATHER'S `-DEATH AMERICAN ACTOR ROBERT ALAN MORSE!!!~'

`-FORMER `-WIFE CAROLE D' ANDREA `-BIRTH/DAY = 8/28 = 8+28 = (`-36) = RECIPROCAL = (`-63) = `-DAUGHTER/ ACTRESS ROBIN MORSE was `-BORN in (`-63)!!!~'

`-DAUGHTER/ACTRESS ROBIN MORSE `-BIRTH/YEAR = 1963 = 9/1+6+3 = 9/10 = 9x10 = (`-90) = `-AGE of `-DEATH for `-HER `-FATHER AMERICAN ACTOR ROBERT ALAN MORSE!!!~'

`-DAUGHTER/ACTRESS ROBIN MORSE `-CURRENT `-AGE = (`-59) = 5x9 = (`-45) = X TIMES (`-2) = (`-90) = `-AGE of `-DEATH for `-HER `-FATHER AMERICAN ACTOR ROBERT ALAN MORSE!!!~'

`-DAUGHTER/ACTRESS ROBIN MORSE `-BIRTH/DAY # `-NUMBER in `-REVERSE = 63(-)19(-)8(-)7 = 29 = X TIMES (`-2) = (`-58) = was (`-58) `-YEARS of `-AGE at the `-TIME of `-HER `-FATHER'S (AMERICAN ACTOR ROBERT ALAN MORSE) `-DEATH!!!~'

`-DAUGHTER/ACTRESS ROBIN MORSE `-BIRTH/DAY # `-NUMBER = 7+8+19+63 = 97 = FLIP 7 to 2 = 92 = RECIPROCAL = 29 = X TIMES (`-2) = (`-58) = was (`-58) `-YEARS of `-AGE at the `-TIME of `-HER `-FATHER'S (AMERICAN ACTOR ROBERT ALAN MORSE) `-DEATH!!!~'

`-TOTAL `-YEARS `-MARRIED = (`-33) + (`-20) = (`-53) = FLIP 3 to 8 = (`-58) = `-DAUGHTER/ACTRESS ROBIN MORSE was (`-58) `-YEARS of `-AGE at the `-TIME of `-HER `-FATHER'S AMERICAN ACTOR ROBERT ALAN MORSE `-DEATH!!!~'

AMERICAN ACTOR ROBERT DEAN STOCKWELL died at the AGE of (`-85)!!!~'

`-BIRTH/DAY = 3/5 = FLIP 3 to 8 = (`-85) = `-AGE of `-DEATH for AMERICAN ACTOR ROBERT DEAN STOCKWELL!!!~'

`-DAUGHTER SOPHIA STOCKWELL `-BIRTH/DAY = 8/5 = (`-85) = `-AGE of `-DEATH for `-HER `-FATHER AMERICAN ACTOR ROBERT DEAN STOCKWELL!!!~'

`-DAUGHTER SOPHIA STOCKWELL = `-BIRTH/YEAR = (`-85) = `-AGE of `-DEATH for `-HER `-FATHER AMERICAN ACTOR ROBERT DEAN STOCKWELL!!!~'

`-BIRTH/DAY # `-NUMBER = 3+5+19+36 = 63

`-BIRTH/DAY # `-NUMBER = 63 = RECIPROCAL = 36 = `-DAUGHTER SOPHIA STOCKWELL was (`-36) `-YEARS of `-AGE at the `-TIME of `-HER `-FATHER'S `-DEATH / AMERICAN ACTOR ROBERT DEAN STOCKWELL!!!~'

`-FORMER `-WIFE AMERICAN FILM ACTRESS MILLIE PERKINS `-PARTIAL `-BIRTH/DAY # `-NUMBER = 5+12+19 = (`-36) = RECIPROCAL = (`-63) = `-BIRTH/DAY # `-NUMBER of `-FORMER `-HUSBAND AMERICAN ACTOR ROBERT DEAN STOCKWELL!!!~'

`-BIRTH/DAY # `-NUMBER = 63 = RECIPROCAL = 36 = `-BIRTH/YEAR!!!~'

`-DEATH/DAY # `-NUMBER = 11+7+20+21 = 59

`-SON AUSTIN STOCKWELL'S `-PARTIAL `-BIRTH/DAY # `-NUMBER in `-REVERSE = 83(-)19(-)5 = (`-59) = `-DEATH/DAY # `-NUMBER of `-FATHER AMERICAN ACTOR ROBERT DEAN STOCKWELL = (`-59)!!!~'

63+59 = 122 = 1x22 = (`-22) = FLIP 2 to 7 = (`-77) = `-DEATH/DAY = 11/7 = 11x7 = (`-77)!!!~'

63(-)59 = 4 = 11(-)7 = (`-11/7) = `-DEATH/DAY!!!~'

FRAGMENTED `-BIRTH/DAY # `-NUMBER = 3+5+1+9+ 3+6 = 27

FRAGMENTED `-BIRTH/DAY # `-NUMBER = 27 = `-DEATH/ DAY = 11/7 = 1+1/7 = (`-27)

FRAGMENTED `-DEATH/DAY # `-NUMBER = 1+1+7+2+0+ 2+1 = 14

FRAGMENTED `-DEATH/DAY # `-NUMBER = 14 = RECIPROCAL = 41 = 20+21 = `-DEATH/YEAR!!!~'

27+14 = 41 = 20+21 = `-DEATH/YEAR!!!~'

27(-)14 = 13 = 8+5 = (`-85) = `-AGE of `-DEATH for `-HER `-FATHER AMERICAN ACTOR ROBERT DEAN STOCKWELL!!!~'

27(-)14 = 13 = FLIP 3 to 8 = (`-18) = "SEE `-BELOW for `-DAYS from `-BIRTH-to-DEATH = (`-118)!!!~'

FROM `-BIRTH-to-DEATH there are 118 DAYS = `-SON AUSTIN STOCKWELL'S `-BIRTH/DAY # `-NUMBER = 11+5+19+83 = 118!!!~'

(365 (-) 118) = 247 = 24x7 = 168 = RECIPROCAL = 861 = 86(-)1) = (`-85) = `-AGE of `-DEATH for AMERICAN ACTOR ROBERT DEAN STOCKWELL!!!~'

`-DEATH/MONTH was NOVEMBER with 30 DAYS

(30 (-) 7) – DAY of `-DEATH = (`-23) = FLIP 2 to 7; FLIP 3 to 8 = (`-78) = 7x8 = (`-56) = HEIGHT = 5' 6"!!!~'

AMERICAN ACTOR ROBERT DEAN STOCKWELL `-PARTIAL `-DEATH/DAY # `-NUMBER = 11+7+20 = (`-38) = "SEE the `-FOLLOWING `-BELOW"!!!~'

`-SON AUSTIN STOCKWELL was (`-38) `-YEARS of `-AGE at the `-TIME of `-HIS `-FATHER'S `-DEATH AMERICAN ACTOR ROBERT DEAN STOCKWELL!!!~'

`-SON AUSTIN STOCKWELL'S `-BIRTH/YEAR = (`-83) = RECIPROCAL = (`-38) = `-AGE `-AT the `-TIME of `-HIS `-FATHER'S `-DEATH AMERICAN ACTOR ROBERT DEAN STOCKWELL!!!~'

`-SON AUSTIN STOCKWELL'S `-PARTIAL `-BIRTH/DAY # `-NUMBER = 11+5+19 = (`-35) = `-FATHER'S `-BIRTHDAY = FLIP 3 to 8 = (`-85) = `-FATHER'S `-AGE of `-DEATH / AMERICAN ACTOR ROBERT DEAN STOCKWELL!!!~'

`-SON AUSTIN STOCKWELL'S `-BIRTH/DAY # `-NUMBER = 11+5+19+83 = 118 = `-FATHER'S `-DAYS in `-TIME from `-BIRTH-to-DEATH!!!~'

`-SON AUSTIN STOCKWELL'S `-BIRTH/DAY # `-NUMBER in `-REVERSE = 83(-)19(-)5(-)11 = 48 = RECIPROCAL = 84 = `-HIS `-FATHER `-DIED the `-VERY `-NEXT `-YEAR `-AFTERWARD at the `-AGE of (`-85)!!!~'

`-WAS `-MARRIED to JOY MARCHENKO from 1981 to 2004 for (`-23) `-YEARS!!!~'

`-DEATH/MONTH was NOVEMBER with 30 DAYS

(30 (-) 7) – DAY of `-DEATH = (`-23)!!!~'

`-MARRIED in = 1981 = 19(-)81 = 62 = / DIVIDED by (`-2) = (`-31) = `-WAS `-BORN in the `-MONTH of (`-3); and, `-DIED in the `-MONTH of (`-11) = (`-3/11)!!!-'

`-WAS `-MARRIED to MILLIE PERKINS from 1960 to 1962 for (`-2) `-YEARS!!!-'

`-MARRIED in = 1960 = 19+60 = 79 = 7x9 = (`-63) = `-BIRTH/DAY # `-NUMBER for AMERICAN ACTOR ROBERT DEAN STOCKWELL!!!-'

`-MARRIED in = 1960 = 19+60 = 79 = 7x9 = (`-63) = RECIPROCAL = (`-36) = `-BIRTH/YEAR for AMERICAN ACTOR ROBERT DEAN STOCKWELL!!!-'

`-MARRIED in = 1960 = 19(-)60 = 41 = 20+21 = `-DEATH/YEAR!!!-'

`-DIVORCED in = 1962 = 19+62 = (`-81) = RECIPROCAL = (`-18) = `-DEATH/DAY = 11/7 = 11+7 = (`-18) = & = "SEE `-ABOVE for the `-OTHER `-DESCRIPTIVE `-LINKS"!!!-'

`-DIVORCED in = (`-62) = (`-OTHER) `-MARRIAGE BEGAN in 19(-)81 = (`-62)!!!-'

AMERICAN ACTOR ROBERT DEAN STOCKWELL `-PARTIAL `-DEATH/DAY # `-NUMBER = 11+7+20 = (`-38) = "SEE the `-FOLLOWING `-BELOW & `-ABOVE with `-HIS `-SON from `-ANOTHER `-MARRIAGE"!!!-'

`-FORMER `-WIFE AMERICAN FILM ACTRESS MILLIE PERKINS was `-BORN in (`-38) = & = RECIPROCAL = `-WAS (`-83) at the `-TIME of `-HER `-FORMER `-HUSBAND'S `-DEATH AMERICAN ACTOR ROBERT DEAN STOCKWELL = THIS;

is the `-RECIPROCAL of `-HIS `-SON from `-ANOTHER `-MARRIAGE, AUSTIN STOCKWELL!!!~'

AMERICAN ACTOR RAYMOND ALLEN LIOTTA died at the AGE of (`-67)!!!~'

`-DEATH/DAY = 5/26 = 5+2/6 = (`-76) = RECIPROCAL = (`-67) = `-AGE of `-DEATH for AMERICAN ACTOR RAYMOND ALLEN LIOTTA!!!~'

`-DEATH/DAY = 5/26 = HALF RECIPROCAL = 5/62 = 5+62 = (`-67) = `-AGE of `-DEATH for AMERICAN ACTOR RAYMOND ALLEN LIOTTA!!!~'

`-BIRTH/DAY # `-NUMBER = 12+18+19+54 = 103

`-BIRTH/DAY # `-NUMBER = 103 = 10+3 = 13 = 6+7 = (`-67) = `-AGE of `-DEATH for AMERICAN ACTOR RAYMOND ALLEN LIOTTA!!!~'

`-DEATH/DAY = 5/26 = 5(-)26 = (`-21) = 7x3 = (`-73) = `-DEATH/DAY # `-NUMBER!!!~'

`-DEATH/DAY # `-NUMBER = 5+26+20+22 = 73

`-DEATH/DAY # `-NUMBER = 73 = `-BIRTH/YEAR = 19+54 = (`-73)!!!~'

`-DEATH/DAY # `-NUMBER = 73 = FLIP 7 to 2 = (`-23) = `-DAUGHTER KARSEN LIOTTA was (`-23) `-YEARS of `-AGE at the `-TIME of `-HER `-FATHER'S `-DEATH AMERICAN ACTOR RAYMOND ALLEN LIOTTA!!!~'

RAY LIOTTA'S DAUGHTER KARSEN LIOTTA `-BIRTH/YEAR = 1998 = 19(-)98 = 79 = FLIP 9 to 6 = 76 = RECIPROCAL = (`-67) = `-AGE of `-DEATH for `-HER `-FATHER AMERICAN ACTOR RAYMOND ALLEN LIOTTA!!!~'

103+73 = 176 = 1x76 = 76 = 7x6 = 42 = 20+22 = `-DEATH/YEAR!!!~'

103+73 = 176 = 1x76 = 76 = RECIPROCAL = (`-67) = `-AGE of `-DEATH for AMERICAN ACTOR RAYMOND ALLEN LIOTTA!!!~'

103(-)73 = 30 = `-BIRTH/DAY = 12+18 = (`-30)

FRAGMENTED `-BIRTH/DAY # `-NUMBER = 1+2+1+8+1+9+5+4 = 31

`-BIRTH/DAY # `-NUMBER = (`-103) (+) (`-31) = FRAGMENTED `-BIRTH/DAY # `-NUMBER = 134 =1x34 = 34 = X TIMES (`-2) = (`-68) = AMERICAN ACTOR RAYMOND ALLEN LIOTTA died within `-HIS (`-68th) YEAR of `-EXISTENCE!!!~'

FRAGMENTED `-BIRTH/DAY # `-NUMBER = 31 = RECIPROCAL = 13 = 6+7 = (`-67) = `-AGE of `-DEATH for AMERICAN ACTOR RAYMOND ALLEN LIOTTA!!!~'

FRAGMENTED `-BIRTH/DAY # `-NUMBER = 31 = `-DEATH/DAY = 5+26 = (`-31)!!!~'

`-BIRTH/MONTH was DECEMBER with 31 DAYS

(31 (-) 18) – DAY of `-BIRTH = (`-13) = RECIPROCAL = (`-31) = FRAGMENTED `-BIRTH/DAY # `-NUMBER!!!~'

FRAGMENTED `-DEATH/DAY # `-NUMBER = 5+2+6+2+0+2+2 = 19

`-DEATH/DAY # `-NUMBER = (`-73) (+) (`-19) = FRAGMENTED `-DEATH/DAY # `-NUMBER = 92 = FLIP 9 to 6; FLIP 2 to 7 = (`-67) = `-AGE of `-DEATH for AMERICAN ACTOR RAYMOND ALLEN LIOTTA!!!~'

31+19 = 50 = 25x2 = HALF RECIPROCAL = 52x2 = 52+2 = (`-54) = `-BIRTH/YEAR!!!~'

31(-)19 = 12 = 6x2 = (`-62) = FLIP 2 to 7 = (`-67) = `-AGE of `-DEATH for AMERICAN ACTOR RAYMOND ALLEN LIOTTA!!!~'

31(-)19 = 12 = `-FATHER (RAYMOND ALLEN LIOTTA), `-MOTHER (MICHELLE GRACE), & `-DAUGHTER (KARSEN LIOTTA) were `-ALL `-BORN in the `-MONTH of (`-12)!!!~'

FROM `-BIRTH-to-DEATH there are 159 DAYS = 15+9 = 24 = RECIPROCAL = 42 = 20+22 = `-DEATH/YEAR!!!~'

FROM `-BIRTH-to-DEATH there are 159 DAYS = 1+5/9 = (`-69) = 6x9 = (`-54) = `-BIRTH/YEAR for AMERICAN ACTOR RAYMOND ALLEN LIOTTA!!!~'

(365 (-) 159) = 206 = 20+6 = 26 = RECIPROCAL = 62 = FLIP 2 to 7 = (`-67) = `-AGE of `-DEATH for AMERICAN ACTOR RAYMOND ALLEN LIOTTA!!!~'

`-WAS `-MARRIED to MICHELLE GRACE from 1997 to 2004 for (`-7) `-YEARS!!!~'

`-MARRIED in (`-97) = FLIP 9 to 6 = (`-67) = `-AGE of `-DEATH for AMERICAN ACTOR RAYMOND ALLEN LIOTTA!!!~'

`-DIVORCED in = 2004 = 20+04 = 24 = RECIPROCAL = 42 = 20+22 = `-DEATH/YEAR!!!~'

`-FORMER `-WIFE MICHELLE GRACE `-BIRTH/DAY # `-NUMBER = 12+4+19+68 = 103 = `-EXACT `-SAME `-BIRTH/ DAY # `-NUMBER as `-HER `-FORMER `-HUSBAND AMERICAN ACTOR RAYMOND ALLEN LIOTTA = (`-103)!!!~'

(103+103) = 206 = 20+6 = 26 = RECIPROCAL = 62 = FLIP 2 to 7 = (`-67) = `-AGE of `-DEATH for AMERICAN ACTOR RAYMOND ALLEN LIOTTA!!!~'

(103+103) = 206 = `-DAYS from `-BIRTH-to-DEATH in the `-OTHER `-DIRECTION for AMERICAN ACTOR RAYMOND ALLEN LIOTTA!!!~'

`-FORMER `-WIFE MICHELLE GRACE `-PARTIAL `-BIRTH/ DAY # `-NUMBER = 12+4+19 = 35 = RECIPROCAL = (`-53) = `-HER `-AGE at the `-TIME of `-DEATH of `-HER `-FORMER `-HUSBAND AMERICAN ACTOR RAYMOND ALLEN LIOTTA!!!~'

HER `-FORMER `-HUSBAND AMERICAN ACTOR RAYMOND ALLEN LIOTTA `-BIRTH/YEAR = 19(-)54 = (`-35) = "SEE `-IMMEDIATELY `-ABOVE"!!!~'

`-FORMER `-WIFE MICHELLE GRACE `-BIRTH/YEAR = (`-68) = `-FORMER `-HUSBAND AMERICAN ACTOR RAYMOND ALLEN LIOTTA died within `-HIS (`-68th) YEAR of `-EXISTENCE!!!~'

`-WAS `-BORN in the `-MONTH of (`-12); and, `-DIED in the `-MONTH of (`-5) = (`-12/5) = 12x5 = (`-60) = HEIGHT = 6' 0" = for AMERICAN ACTOR RAYMOND ALLEN LIOTTA!!!~'

RAPPER RAKIM HASHEEM ALLEN "PnB ROCK" died at the AGE of (`-30)!!!~'

`-BIRTH/DAY = 12/9 = *RECIPROCAL* = `-DEATH/DAY = 9/12

(12+9) = (`-21) = (9+12) = (`-21)

21+21 = 42 = 20+22 = `-DEATH/YEAR!!!~'

`-BIRTH/DAY # `-NUMBER = 12+9+19+91 = 131

`-BIRTH/DAY # `-NUMBER = 131 = 1(-)31 = (`-30) = `-AGE of `-DEATH for RAPPER RAKIM HASHEEM ALLEN "PnB ROCK"!!!~'

`-BIRTH/DAY # `-NUMBER = 131 = 1+31 = (`-32) = FRAGMENTED `-BIRTH/DAY # `-NUMBER!!!~'

`-DEATH/DAY # `-NUMBER = 9+12+20+22 = 63

`-DEATH/DAY # `-NUMBER = 63 = 6x3 = (`-18) = FRAGMENTED `-DEATH/DAY # `-NUMBER!!!~'

`-PARTIAL `-BIRTH/DAY # `-NUMBER in `-REVERSE = 91(-)19(-)9 = (`-63) = `-DEATH/DAY # `-NUMBER!!!~'

`-BIRTH/DAY # `-NUMBER in `-REVERSE = 91(-)19(-)9(-)12 = (`-51) = 51x1 = HEIGHT = 5' 11"!!!~'

`-PARTIAL DEATH/DAY # `-NUMBER = 9+12+20 = 41 = RECIPROCAL = 14 = 2x7 = (`-27) = RECIPROCAL = (`-72) = `-BIRTH/YEAR = 19(-)91!!!~'

131+63 = 194 = 19x4 = 76 = 7x6 = 42 = 20+22 = `-DEATH/YEAR!!!~'

131+63 = 194 = 1x94 = 94 = 9x4 = 36 = RECIPROCAL = 63 = `-DEATH/DAY # `-NUMBER!!!~'

131(-)63 = 68 = FLIP 8 to 3 = 63 = DEATH/DAY # `-NUMBER!!!~'

FRAGMENTED `-BIRTH/DAY # `-NUMBER = 1+2+9+1+9+ 9+1 = 32

`-BIRTH/DAY # `-NUMBER = (`-131) (+) (`-32) = FRAGMENTED `-BIRTH/DAY # `-NUMBER = 163 = 1x63 = (`-63) = `-DEATH/ DAY # `-NUMBER!!!~'

FRAGMENTED `-DEATH/DAY # `-NUMBER = 9+1+2+2+0+ 2+2 = 18

FRAGMENTED `-DEATH/DAY # `-NUMBER = 18 = 6x3 = (`-63) = `-DEATH/DAY # `-NUMBER!!!~'

`-DEATH/MONTH was SEPTEMBER with 30 DAYS

(30 (-) 12) – DAY of `-DEATH = (`-18) = FRAGMENTED `-DEATH/DAY # `-NUMBER!!!~'

`-DEATH/DAY # `-NUMBER = (`-63) (+) (`-18) = FRAGMENTED `-DEATH/DAY # `-NUMBER = 81 = FLIP 8 to 3 = (`-31) = `-BIRTH/DAY # `-NUMBER = 131 = 1x31 = (`-31)!!!~'

32+18 = 50 = 30+20 = (3+0) (2+0) = (`-32) = FRAGMENTED `-BIRTH/DAY # `-NUMBER!!!~'

32(-)18 = 14 = 6+8 = (`-68) = FLIP 8 to 3 = (`-63) = `-DEATH/DAY # `-NUMBER!!!~'

FROM `-BIRTH-to-DEATH there are 88 DAYS = 8x8 = 64 = / DIVIDED by (`-2) = (`-32) = FRAGMENTED `-BIRTH/DAY # `-NUMBER!!!~'

FROM `-BIRTH-to-DEATH there are 88 DAYS = 8+8 = 16 = X TIMES (`-2) = (`-32) = FRAGMENTED `-BIRTH/DAY # `-NUMBER!!!~'

FROM `-BIRTH-to-DEATH there are 88 DAYS = 8+8 = 16 = 5+11 = (`-5/11) = HEIGHT = 5' 11"!!!~'

(365 (-) 88) = 277 = 2+77 = 79 = 7x9 = (`-63) = `-DEATH/DAY # `-NUMBER!!!~'

`-WAS `-BORN in the `-MONTH of (`-12); and, `-DIED in the `-MONTH of (`-9) = (`-12/9) = 12x9 = 108 = 10+8 = (`-18) = FRAGMENTED `-DEATH/DAY # `-NUMBER!!!~'

`-WAS `-BORN in the `-MONTH of (`-12); and, `-DIED in the `-MONTH of (`-9) = (`-12/9) = 12x9 = 108 = / DIVIDED by (`-3) = 36 = RECIPROCAL = (`-63) = `-DEATH/DAY # `-NUMBER!!!~'

`-BIRTH/DAY = 12/9 = HALF RECIPROCAL = 21/9 = 21+9 = (`-30) = `-AGE of `-DEATH for RAPPER RAKIM HASHEEM ALLEN "PnB ROCK"!!!~'

`-DEATH/DAY = 9/12 = HALF RECIPROCAL = 9/21 = 9+21 = (`-30) = `-AGE of `-DEATH for RAPPER RAKIM HASHEEM ALLEN "PnB ROCK"!!!~'

/|\ `-WAS `-BORN in the `-MONTH of (`-**12**); and, `-DIED in the `-MONTH of (`-**9**) = (`-**12/9**) = {`-**BIRTH/DAY**} = *RECIPROCAL* = (`-**9/12**) = {`-**DEATH/DAY**}!!!~' /|\ {`-**TAKE** `-**SPECIAL** `-**NOTE** `-**HERE!!!~'**}

CLOSURE of `-BOOK: -

WE'RE `-ALL in a `-LITTLE `-FAMILY `-HERE!!!~'

AMERICAN ACTRESS BLOSSOM ROCK (EDITH MARIE BLOSSOM MACDONALD) (THE ADDAMS FAMILY) died at the AGE of (`-82)!!!~

`-BIRTH/DAY # `-NUMBER = 8/21/18/95 = 8+21+18+95 = 142

`-BIRTH/DAY # `-NUMBER = 142 = 14x2 = (`-28) = RECIPROCAL = (`-82) = `-AGE of `-DEATH for AMERICAN ACTRESS BLOSSOM ROCK (EDITH MARIE BLOSSOM MACDONALD) (THE ADDAMS FAMILY)!!!~'

ACTOR JAY SILVERHEELS (TONTO from the LONE RANGER) was `-BORN in the `-MONTH of (`-**5**); and, `-DIED within the `-MONTH of (`-**3**) = (`-**5/3**) = RECIPROCAL = (`-**3/5**) = `-HIS `-VERY `-OWN `-DEATH/DAY!!!~'

ACTOR JAY SILVERHEELS (TONTO from the LONE RANGER) **DEATH/DAY # `-NUMBER in `-REVERSE** = (80 (-) 19 (-) 5 (-) 3) = (`-**53**) = RECIPROCAL = (`-**3/5**) = **DEATH/ DAY!!!~'**

"- The ELVIS AARON PRESLEY `-FAMILY –"

AMERICAN SINGER & ACTOR <u>ELVIS AARON PRESLEY</u> (`- **42**) (`-**AGE of `-DEATH**) (BIRTH: **JANUARY 8, <u>1935</u>**) (DEATH: **AUGUST 16**, 1977)!!!~'

`-**<u>BIRTH/YEAR</u>** = (`-**<u>1935</u>**) = (19 + 35) = (`-**<u>54</u>**) = RECIPROCAL (MIRROR) = (`-**<u>45</u>**) = **"<u>DIED</u> (`-<u>145</u>** *DAYS AWAY* **from** `-HIS `-**<u>BIRTHDAY</u>"!!!~'**

FORMER WIFE (PRISCILLA ANN PRESLEY) was `-BORN in (`-45), HER `-BIRTH/DAY = (5/24) = (5-to-4), SHE'S 5' 4" in `-HEIGHT, `-HER CURRENT `-AGE at the `-TIME of `-HER `-DAUGHTER'S `-DEATH = (`-77); `-EQUATION (77 x TIMES (2)) = (`-154)!!!~'

FORMER WIFE (PRISCILLA ANN PRESLEY) `-BIRTH/ YEAR = 1945 = (19 + 45) = (`-64) = RECIPROCAL = (`-46) = `-AGE of `-DEATH of `-MOTHER-IN-LAW GLADYS LOVE PRESLEY!!!~'

`-MARRIED to `-ELVIS AARON PRESLEY from 1967 to 1973 = (`-EQUATIONS)-':

1967 = 19 + 67 = (`-86) = RECIPROCAL = (`-68) = `-YEAR that `-DAUGHTER (LISA MARIE PRESLEY) would be `-BORN!!!~'

1967 = 19 (-) 67 = (`-48) = `-MOTHER GLADYS LOVE PRESLEY was `-BORN in the MONTH (`-4); and, `-DIED in the `-MONTH of (`-8)!!!~'

1973 = 19 (-) 73 = (`-54)!!!~'

1973 = 19 + 73 = (`-92) = `-EQUATION = (92 / `-DIVIDED by (2)) = (`-46) = `-AGE of `-DEATH of "ELVIS AARON PRESLEY'S" `-MOTHER (GLADYS LOVE PRESLEY)!!!~'

(ELVIS AARON PRESLEY) `-BIRTHDAY # `-NUMBER = (1 + 8 + 19 + 35) = (`-63) = `-AGE of `-DEATH of `-HIS `-FATHER VERNON PRESLEY!!!~'

`-FATHER VERNON PRESLEY `-BIRTH/YEAR = 1916 = (19 + 16) = (`-35) = `-BIRTH/YEAR of `-SON "ELVIS AARON PRESLEY"!!!~'

'-FATHER VERNON PRESLEY was '-**BORN** in the '-**MONTH** of ('-**4**); and, '-**DIED** in the '-**MONTH** of ('-**6**) = ('-**46**) = '-AGE of '-DEATH of '-WIFE GLADYS LOVE PRESLEY!!!~'

'-DAUGHTER (LISA MARIE PRESLEY) '-BIRTH/DAY # '-NUMBER in '-REVERSE = (68 (-) 19 (-) 1 (-) 2) = ('-**46**) = '-AGE of '-DEATH of '-GRANDMOTHER GLADYS LOVE PRESLEY!!!~'

'-DAUGHTER'S '-BIRTH/DAY (LISA MARIE PRESLEY) = (2/1) = (7 x 3) = ('-YEAR that '-HER '-PARENTS would get '-DIVORCED)!!!~'

The '-**WEDDING** '-**DAY** SHOWED the '-**BIRTH** of THEIR '-**CHILD**!!!~' The '-**CHILD'S** '-**BIRTH/DAY** SHOWED the '-**YEAR** of '-**DIVORCE** of '-HER '-TWO '-PARENTS!!!~'

DAUGHTER (LISA MARIE PRESLEY) '-**DIED** at the '-AGE of ('-**54**)!!!~' '-BIRTH/YEAR was ('-**68**) = RECIPROCAL = ('-**86**) = '-FATHER (ELVIS AARON PRESLEY'S) '-DEATH/DAY = (8/16)!!!~' '-HER '-BIRTH/DAY # '-NUMBER = (2 + 1 + 19 + 68) = ('-**90**); '-EQUATION (90 / '-DIVIDED by (2)) = ('-**45**) = RECIPROCAL = ('-**54**)!!!~'

DAUGHTER (LISA MARIE PRESLEY) '-BIRTH/DAY # '-NUMBER = ('-**90**) = FLIP 9 to 6 = ('-**60**) = GRANDMOTHER'S GLADYS LOVE PRESLEY'S '-BIRTH/DAY # '-NUMBER = ('-**60**)!!!~'

DAUGHTER (LISA MARIE PRESLEY) '-BIRTH/DAY = (2/1) = RECIPROCAL = '-DAY of '-DEATH = ('-**12**)!!!~'

'-BIRTH/DAY = 2/1 /|\ RECIPROCALS /|\ '-DEATH/DAY = 1/12

`-WAS `-<u>BORN</u> in the `-<u>MONTH</u> of (`-<u>2</u>); and, `-<u>DIED</u> in the `-<u>MONTH</u> of (`-<u>1</u>) = (`-<u>2/1</u>) = `-HER `-VERY `-OWN `-BIRTH/ DAY (LISA MARIE PRESLEY)!!!~' JUST LIKE `-HER `-FATHER `-BELOW!!!~'

DAUGHTER (LISA MARIE PRESLEY) `-<u>DIED</u> (`-<u>20</u>) DAYS BEFORE `-HER `-NEXT `-BIRTH/DAY = (`-<u>20</u>) = (5 x 4) = "<u>SEE</u> the `-<u>LINKAGES</u>"!!!~'

`-<u>CALENDAR</u> `-<u>YEAR</u> = (365 (-) 20) = (`-<u>345</u>) = PROPHETIC-<u>L</u>INEAR-<u>P</u>ROGRESSION-<u>PLP</u>!!!~'

`-YEARS ACTIVE as a SINGER/SONGWRITER (LISA MARIE PRESLEY) = 1997 to 2023 = (`-26 YEARS TOTAL) = "FLIP 2 to 7; FLIP 6 to 9" = (`-<u>79</u>) = RECIPROCAL = (`-<u>97</u>) = "YEAR `-SHE `-GOT `-STARTED"!!!~'

`-GRANDFATHER VERNON PRESLEY `-DIED in (`-<u>79</u>) = (7 x 9) = (`-<u>63</u>) = `-HIS VERY OWN `-AGE of `-DEATH!!!~'

"-ELVIS AARON PRESLEY-"

`-<u>BIRTHDAY</u> = JANUARY 8$^{th}$ = (<u>1/8</u>) = RECIPROCAL (MIRROR) = (<u>8/1</u>) = "<u>PART</u> of `-<u>DEATH/DAY</u> (<u>81</u>/6)"!!!~'

`-<u>DEATH/DAY</u> = AUGUST 16$^{th}$ = (<u>8/16</u>) = (86 x 1) = (`-<u>86</u>) = "The `-<u>MARK</u>"!!!~'

`-BIRTHDAY # `-NUMBER = (1 + 8 + 19 + 35) = (`-<u>63</u>) = RECIPROCAL (MIRROR) = (`-<u>36</u>) = <u>3</u>(<u>6's</u>) = (`-<u>666</u>) = "The `-<u>MARK</u>"!!!~'

`-<u>DEATH/DAY</u> # `-NUMBER = (8 + 16 + 19 + 77) = (`-<u>120</u>) = `-<u>EQUATION</u> = (1 x 20) = (`-<u>20</u>) = (5 x 4) = (`-<u>54</u>)!!!~'

FORMER WIFE (PRISCILLA ANN PRESLEY) `-BIRTH/DAY = 5/24 = (5 x 24) = (`-120) = `-DEATH/DAY # `-NUMBER of `-FORMER HUSBAND (ELVIS AARON PRESLEY)!!!-'

FORMER WIFE (PRISCILLA ANN PRESLEY) `-DAY of `-BIRTH = (`-24ᵗʰ) = RECIPROCAL = (`-42) = `-AGE of `-DEATH of `-FORMER `-HUSBAND (ELVIS AARON PRESLEY)!!!-'

(ELVIS AARON PRESLEY) `-**DEATH/DAY** = 8/16 = (8 + 16) = (`-**24**) = RECIPROCAL = (`-**42**) = `-HIS `-VERY `-OWN `-**AGE** of `-**DEATH!!!-'**

`-DEATH/DAY # `-NUMBER in `-**REVERSE** = (77 (-) 19 (-) 1**6** (-) **8**) = (`-**34**) = FLIP 3 to 8 = (`-**84**) = `-**MOTHER** GLADYS LOVE PRESLEY `-**DIED** in the `-**MONTH** of (`-**8**); and, was `-**BORN** in the `-**MONTH** of (`-**4**)!!!-'

`-HE `-**DIED** (`-**145**) DAYS before `-HIS `-**NEXT** `-**BIRTHDAY!!!-'**
(365 (-) **145**) = (`-**220**) = (2 x 20) = (`-**40**) = (8x5) = RECIPROCAL = (`-**58**) = `-HIS `-**MOTHER** `-GLADYS PRESLEY `-DIED in (`-**58**)!!!-'

GLADYS PRESLEY `-DEATH/YEAR = 1958 = 19 + 58 = (`-77) = `-AGE of `-DAUGHTER-IN-LAW at the `-TIME of `-HER `-GRANDDAUGHTER'S `-DEATH!!!-'

GLADYS LOVE PRESLEY `-DEATH/DAY = 8/14 = (8) (1+4) = (`-85) = RECIPROCAL = (`-58)!!!-'

GLADYS LOVE PRESLEY `-DIED in the `-MONTH of (`-8); and, was `-BORN in the `-MONTH of (`-4) = (`-8/4) = `-DEATH/DAY = (8/14)!!!- JUST LIKE `-HER `-SON (ELVIS

AARON PRESLEY) & `-HER `-GRANDDAUGHTER (LISA MARIE PRESLEY)!!!~'

GLADYS PRESLEY `-DEATH/DAY # `-NUMBER = (8 + 14 + 19 + 58) = (`-99) = `-EQUATION = (9 x 9) = (`-81) = `-HER `-SON'S (DEATH/BIRTH) & = RECIPROCAL = (1/8) = `-SON'S `-BIRTH/DAY!!!~'

GLADYS PRESLEY `-BIRTH/DAY # `-NUMBER = (4 + 25 + 19 + 12) = (`-60) = FLIP 6 TO 9 = (`-90) = `-EQUATION = (90 / `-DIVIDED by (`-2)) = (`-45) = RECIPROCAL = (`-54) = "SEE the `-LINKAGES from `-ABOVE"!!!~'

GLADYS PRESLEY `-DIED (`-254) DAYS from `-BIRTH-to-DEATH!!!~'

254 = (2 x 54) = 108 = (10 + 8) = (`-18) = 1/8 = "SON'S `-BIRTH/DAY" & SON'S `-BIRTH/DEATH `-MONTHS!!!~'

VERNON PRESLEY `-DIED (`-77) DAYS from `-BIRTH-to-DEATH!!!~'

`-EQUATION = (77 x TIMES (`-2)) = (`-154) = "SEE the `-LINKAGES"!!!~'

VERNON PRESLEY (`-77) from `-BIRTH-to-DEATH = "AGE of `-DAUGHTER-IN-LAW at the `-TIME of WHEN `-HIS `-GRANDDAUGHTER `-DIED"!!!~'

`-CALENDAR `-YEAR = (365 (-) 77) = (`-288) = (28 + 8) = (`-36) = RECIPROCAL = (`-63) = `-ACTUAL `-AGE of `-DEATH for VERNON PRESLEY!!!~'

HUSBAND VERNON PRESLEY `-DEATH/YEAR = 1979 = (19 (-) 79) = (`-60) = `-WIFE'S `-BIRTH/DAY # `-NUMBER &

= FLIP 6 to 9 = (`-90) = GRANDDAUGHTER'S (LISA MARIE PRESLEY'S) `-BIRTH/DAY # `-NUMBER!!!~'

HUSBAND VERNON PRESLEY = 1979 = (19 + 79) = (`-98) = FLIP 9 to 6; FLIP 8 to 3 = (`-63) = `-AGE of `-DEATH of `-HUSBAND!!!~'

`-FATHER VERNON PRESLEY `-BIRTH/DAY # `-NUMBER = (4 + 10 + 19 + 16) = (`-49)!!!~'

`-FATHER VERNON PRESLEY `-DEATH/DAY # `-NUMBER = (6 + 26 + 19 + 79) = (`-130)!!!~'

`-FATHER VERNON PRESLEY `-DEATH/DAY/`-BIRTH/ DAY # `-NUMBERS = (130 (-) 49) = (`-81) = `-HIS `-SON'S (**DEATH/BIRTH**) & = RECIPROCAL = (1/8) = `-SON'S `-**BIRTH/DAY**!!!~'

`-FATHER VERNON PRESLEY `-DEATH/DAY = 6/26 = (6) (2 + 6) = (`-68) = `-**BIRTH/YEAR** of `-GRANDDAUGHTER (LISA MARIE PRESLEY)!!!~'

`-FATHER VERNON PRESLEY `-DEATH/DAY = 6/26 = (6) (2 (-) 6) = (`-64) = RECIPROCAL = (`-46) = `-AGE of `-DEATH of `-WIFE (GLADYS LOVE PRESLEY)!!!~'

ELVIS AARON PRESLEY `-**DEATH/DAY** = (8/16) = (8) (1(-)6) = (`-85) = RECIPROCAL = (`-58) = **MOTHER** GLADYS LOVE PRESLEY `-**DIED** in (`-58)!!!~'

ELVIS AARON PRESLEY `-**DEATH/YEAR** = 1977 = (19 (-) 77) = (`-58) = "**SEE** the `-**PREVIOUS**"!!!~'

ELVIS AARON PRESLEY `-PARTIAL `-DEATH/DAY # `-NUMBER in `-REVERSE = (77 (-) 19 (-) 16) = (`-**42**) = `-AGE of `-DEATH for (ELVIS ARRON PRESLEY)!!!~'

HE DIED AT THE `-AGE of (`-**42**)!!!~'
`-BIRTHDAY = JANUARY 8 = (1 x 8) = (`-**8**)!!!~'
`-DEATH/DAY = AUGUST 16 = (8 x 16) = (`-**128**) = `-EQUATION = (12 x 8) = (`-**96**) = `-EQUATION = (9 x 6) = (`-**54**) = "SEE the `-MANY `-LINKAGES `-ABOVE"!!!~'
(128 + 8) = (`-**136**) = (36 x 1) = (`-**36**) = RECIPROCAL = (`-**63**) = "SEE `-ABOVE & `-BELOW"!!!~'

(128 (-) 8) = (`-**120**) = `-DEATH/DAY # `-NUMBER for "ELVIS AARON PRESLEY"!!!~'
(136 + 120) = (`-**256**) = `-EQUATION = (2 (-) 56) = (`-**54**) = "SEE the `-LINKAGES"!!!~'
(136 (-) 120) = (`-**16**)!!!~'
(256 + 16) = (`-**272**) = "**RECIPROCAL-SEQUENCING-NUMEROLOGY-RSN**"!!!~'

(ELVIS AARON PRESLEY) FRAGMENTED BIRTHDAY # `-NUMBER** = JANUARY 8, 1935 = (1 + 8 + 1 + 9 + 3 + 5) = (`-27**) = `-EQUATION = (27 x TIMES (`-2)) = (`-**54**) = `-SEE the `-LINKAGES!!!~'

GRANDSON BENJAMIN KEOUGH `-**DIED** at the `-**AGE** of (`-**27**) x TIMES (`-**2**) = (`-**54**)!!!~'

(ELVIS AARON PRESLEY) FRAGMENTED DEATH/DAY # `-NUMBER** = AUGUST 16, 1977 = (8 + 1 + 6 + 1 + 9 + 7 + 7) = (`-39**) = `-EQUATION = (3 x 9) = (`-**27**) = "SEE the `-PRECEDING `-LINKAGES from `-ABOVE & `-BELOW"!!!~'

(ELVIS AARON PRESLEY) FRAGMENTED `-DEATH/DAY # `-NUMBER = (`-39) = RECIPROCAL = (`-93) = `-**EQUATION** = (93 / (DIVIDED by) (2)) = (`-46.5) = `-AGE of `-DEATH of HIS `-MOTHER GLADYS LOVE PRESLEY!!!~'

`-MOTHER GLADYS PRESLEY `-DEATH/YEAR = 1958 = (19 (-) 58) = (`-39) = `-SON'S (ELVIS AARON PRESLEY'S) FRAGMENTED `-DEATH/DAY # `-NUMBER!!!~'

(39 (-) 27) = (`-12) = `-DAY of `-DEATH of `-DAUGHTER (LISA MARIE PRESLEY); and, (=) RECIPROCAL = (2/1) = `-BIRTH/DAY of `-DAUGHTER (LISA MARIE PRESLEY)!!!~'

`-DIFFERENCE in `-AGES of `-DEATH between `-FATHER (ELVIS AARON PRESLEY) & `-DAUGHTER (LISA MARIE PRESLEY) = (42 (-) 54 = (`-12) = RECIPROCAL = (`-21) = (LISA MARIE PRESLEY'S) `-BIRTH/DAY = (2/1)!!!~'

`-DIFFERENCE in `-AGES of `-DEATH between `-FATHER (VERNON PRESLEY) & `-SON (ELVIS AARON PRESLEY) = (63 (-) 42 = (`-21) = (LISA MARIE PRESLEY'S) `-BIRTH/DAY = (2/1)!!!~'

`-DIFFERENCE in `-AGES of `-DEATH between `-HUSBAND (VERNON PRESLEY) & `-WIFE (GLADYS LOVE PRESLEY) = (63 (-) 46 = (`-17) = RECIPROCAL = (`-71)!!!~'

`-EQUATION = (71 (-) 17) = (`-54) = "SEE the LINKAGES"!!!~'

(39 + 27) = (`-66) = `-FRAGMENTED `-BIRTHDAY # `-NUMBER & `-FRAGMENTED `-DEATH/DAY # `-NUMBER `-ADDED `-UP `-TOGETHER!!!~'

(`-**66**) = `-**EQUATION** = (6 x 6) = (`-**36**) = RECIPROCAL = (`-**63**) = `-**AGE of `-DEATH of `-FATHER VERNON PRESLEY!!!~'**

(66 (-) 12) = (`-**54**) = `-**BIRTH/YEAR** = (`-**1935**) = (19 + 35) = (`-**54**) = RECIPROCAL (MIRROR) = (`-**45**) = **"DIED** (`-**145**) *DAYS AWAY* from `-HIS `-**BIRTHDAY"**; and, `-**PLEASE** `-**REVIEW** to `-**SEE** the `-**MANY** `-**LINKAGES** as LISTED `-**BEFORE!!!~'**

`-**BIRTHDAY**; and, `-**DEATH/DAY!!!~'**:
(**816** + **18**) = (`-**834**)!!!~'
(**816** (-) **18**) = (`-**798**)!!!~'
(834 (-) 798) = (`-**36**) = **3**(**6**'s) = (`-**666**) = **"The `-MARK"!!!~'**

JANUARY 8 (**BIRTH/DAY**) + AUGUST 16 (**DEATH/DAY**) = (**1** + **8** + **8** + **16**) = (`-**33**) = `-**HALF** of FRAGMENTED `-**DEATH/ DAY** # & FRAGMENTED `-**BIRTHDAY** # `-**NUMBERS** `-ADDED `-UP `-**TOGETHER!!!~'**

(`-**33** x 2) = (`-**66**) = `-FRAGMENTED `-BIRTHDAY # `-NUMBER & `-FRAGMENTED `-DEATH/DAY # `-NUMBER; `-ADDED `-UP `-**TOGETHER!!!~'**

`-**DIED** in the `-MONTH of (`-**8**) & was `-**BORN** in the `-MONTH of (`-**1**) = (`-**8/1**) = RECIPROCAL (MIRROR) = (`-**1/8**) = `-**BIRTHDAY** = **"(JANUARY 8**th**) for ELVIS AARON PRESLEY"** = `-**PLEASE** `-**REVIEW** the `-**MANY** `-**LINKAGES**-'!!!~'

"YOUR `-DAYS of `-LIVING are `-NUMBERED!!!~'"

`-THROUGHOUT the `-EXPANSE of `-all `-TIME; everything, has been `-ALLOTTED by `-KISMET!!!~' The CEMENTED

`-DESTINY of `-IT `-all, to be `-pantingly; AND, `-PERFECTLY `-SCRIPTED with the`-PRECISION of a `-GOD to `-his VERY OWN ASSIGNED `-PURPOSES; and, `-DIRECTION of `-LIVING; to be `-ENJOYED by US, `-all!!!~' `-CURRENTLY; what is `-LEFT to `-UNFOLD, in `-ALL of `-OUR `-LIVES `-AHEAD!!!~'

AUTHOR: DWAYNE W. ANDERSON

"The REAL PROPHET of DOOM"!!!~'

SENIOR ENGINEER/PROPHET/SINGER & SONGWRITER/ AUTHOR EXTRAORDINAIRE!!!~'

 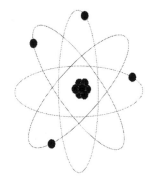 

/|\ -The Real Prophet Of Doom (Kismet)- /|
Dwayne W. Anderson

Printed in the United States
by Baker & Taylor Publisher Services